NATIONAL
GEOGRAPHIC
EXPEDITIONS
ATLAS

Bearers and pith-helmeted participants in the Citroën
Central African Expedition of 1924-25 pause at a waterfall
on the border of what was then the Belgian Congo and
French Equatorial Africa, now the Central African Repub-
lic and the Democratic Republic of Congo.
Previous page: Spiderlike mountain climber executes a
Tyrolean traverse between spires in the Italian Dolomites.

Flanked by an escort of bandits, explorer and self-taught botanist Joseph F. Rock exudes confidence here on the slopes of Mount Jamebeyan in China's remote Far West. Rock's objective, as reported in the July 1931 NATIONAL GEOGRAPHIC, was to visit mountains sacred to Tibetan Buddhists.

Machiguenga Indian boys gleefully flock to a plane as it arrives at their village near the headwaters of Peru's Urubamba River in 1972. Exposure to previous flights accustomed them and many other Amazonian Indians to such wonders of the modern world as canned food, clothing, and the cameras of GEOGRAPHIC freelance writer-photographer Loren McIntyre.

Scuba diver wrests a jar perhaps a thousand years old from the murk of a *cenote*, or ceremonial well, in the late 1950s. The site is Dzibilchaltún, one of Yucatán's earliest Maya cities.

NATIONAL
GEOGRAPHIC
EXPEDITIONS
ATLAS

NATIONAL
GEOGRAPHIC

WASHINGTON, D.C.

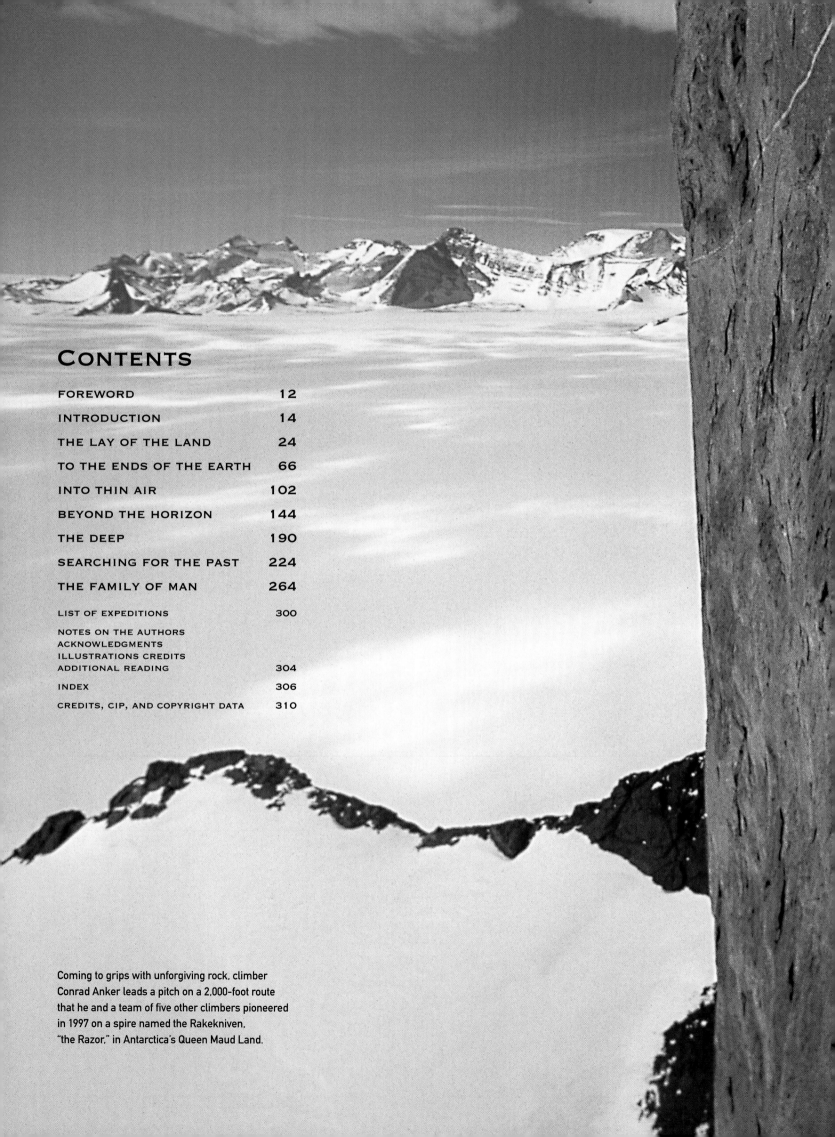

Contents

FOREWORD   12

INTRODUCTION   14

THE LAY OF THE LAND   24

TO THE ENDS OF THE EARTH   66

INTO THIN AIR   102

BEYOND THE HORIZON   144

THE DEEP   190

SEARCHING FOR THE PAST   224

THE FAMILY OF MAN   264

LIST OF EXPEDITIONS   300

NOTES ON THE AUTHORS
ACKNOWLEDGMENTS
ILLUSTRATIONS CREDITS
ADDITIONAL READING   304

INDEX   306

CREDITS, CIP, AND COPYRIGHT DATA   310

Coming to grips with unforgiving rock, climber
Conrad Anker leads a pitch on a 2,000-foot route
that he and a team of five other climbers pioneered
in 1997 on a spire named the Rakekniven,
"the Razor," in Antarctica's Queen Maud Land.

By Peter H. Raven

Chairman, Committee for Research and Exploration; Director, Missouri Botanical Garden, St. Louis

Foreword:

A Unique Blend of Exploration and Science

An early childhood spent among the physical and biological wonders of northern California soon led me to treasured copies of National Geographic—copies that led me well before I was ten years old to appreciate Roy Chapman Andrews's motorized expeditions of the Gobi, the variety of butterflies in the United States and the thrill of collecting and understanding them, animals on the plains of Africa, the awesome beauty of the world's polar regions, and even an introductory glimpse of the tropical rain forests that would occupy so much of my attention later in adult life. Those Geographic issues from the 1920s and 1930s featured diverse peoples and places as well as incredibly exciting frontiers where images, facts, and relationships were literally awaiting discovery. All this gave me a great sense of geography, a wonderment of the world—and led me to the personal realization that we are all citizens of a planet that nurtures us in ways we can only dimly perceive.

Eventually I came to understand that the National Geographic Society not only reports on faraway places and interesting peoples but also plays an important role in sponsoring expeditions and scientific investigations. From the depths of the seas to the tops of the highest mountains; from tropical forests, verdant and teeming with life, to the most severe deserts; from the history of ancient civilizations to the wonderful ways humans have adapted to diverse habitats; the National Geographic has sponsored many key scientists and explorers who have helped build our basic knowledge of the world today. Many of the most significant expeditions carried out by the Geographic's extended family through the years are brought to life in this spectacular volume featuring outstanding new prose partnered with previously published maps and evocative photographs.

For nearly 20 years I have served as a member of the Committee for Research and Exploration; currently I chair that committee. I delight in a tradition that stretches back more than a century to the founding of the Society in 1888. It has been a joy to participate in the unique blend of exploration and science that is the subject of this book and which has resulted in the accumulation and dissemination of so much knowledge about the world. I find it especially intriguing that, since 1900, the world population has nearly quadrupled to 6.1 billion people. Of that number, about 3.6 billion have been born since 1950. Within the next half-century, the population will grow to 9 billion. Currently, human beings are using almost half of the world's photosynthetic productivity on land and are consuming over half of the available renewable fresh water. About a quarter of us live in poverty. The prospects for the future are enormously challenging. For example, despite all the work of biologists and explorers, science has managed

to identify only an estimated one-sixth of the world's species of organisms—yet most of these may disappear forever during the coming century.

In today's rapidly changing world the Geographic still has a vital role to play, since the dimensions of the physical and biological realms, the wonders of the geological past, and the accomplishments of human civilization will continue to occupy our attention. By bringing such knowledge to a wide audience effectively and accurately, the National Geographic Society will continue to serve, to illuminate, and to instruct. I also expect that it will help determine and achieve conditions for a better world in the future, building—as the Society always has done—on the impressive foundations laid in the past.

The Morden-Clark Asiatic Expedition, shown here plodding through the Mintaka Pass in the Pamirs of Central Asia in 1927, was reported in NATIONAL GEOGRAPHIC.

BY BART MCDOWELL

INTRODUCTION:
THE ELEMENT OF SURPRISE

PERHAPS TODAY—PERHAPS NEXT YEAR—a one-passenger submarine named *DeepWorker* will slip into saltwater and head toward the ocean floor, a tool for new scientific discoveries. The Expeditions Council of the National Geographic Society is using this craft in a five-year research initiative called the Sustainable Seas Expeditions.

What will *DeepWorker* discover? You and I cannot possibly know, for each discovery made by an expedition has, by definition, its own element of surprise. And often danger. The book you hold in your hand contains facts that explorers have risked their lives to gather—the course of a river, the height of a mountain, the extent of a lava flow, the age of an ancient ruin. Why such risky questing?

Well, consider the world map as it looked back in 1888. Large areas were unexplored and blank. Many coastlines were delineated by dotted lines, a stuttering apology for mere guesswork. People knew they had unfinished business. Some wanted to fill in the blanks.

So, on a foggy January night that year, 33 men came together in Washington, D.C. They were a disparate group—teacher, geologist, lawyer, topographer, banker, military officer, naturalist—with one uncommon quality in common: curiosity about the world and everything in it. That night they organized the National Geographic Society and stated its purpose: "The increase and diffusion of geographic knowledge." The Society charter became a "hunting license" for adventure.

It has been my lucky fate during half a century to know a number of the scientists and explorers who have increased our knowledge of the world. As an editor of NATIONAL GEOGRAPHIC, I have sometimes looked over their shoulders as they worked. And what adventures they have had!

The Society's first expedition, in 1890, set out for an uncharted area in Alaska. Israel C. Russell and men from the U.S. Geological Survey wanted to explore a rough terrain of glaciers and forests in the vicinity of Mount St. Elias. They braved grizzly bears, clouds of mosquitoes, rockslides, crevassed ice, storms, and avalanches. And they mapped some 600 square miles of wilderness, discovering in the process the second-highest mountain in North America, Mount Logan, elevation 19,524 feet. They also established a tradition of support for scientific study through the Society's Committee for Research and Exploration, which has funded nearly 7,000 projects, as well as 40 Expedition Council grants as of 1999.

I have always had special respect for scientists who work in icy regions. On assignment in Siberia, I learned what I consider the only good thing about a temperature of 40° below zero F: the figure is the same for both Fahrenheit and Celsius, thus no math.

As a boy in the 1930s, I was thrilled by reports of Rear Admiral Richard E. Byrd from his Antarctic base, Little America. I actually shook the admiral's hand when he was on a lecture tour of the U.S. How I envied the Boy Scout—an Eagle Scout!—chosen to accompany Byrd to Antarctica. His name was Paul Siple. Later as a scientist himself, he returned many times to the most southern of continents.

In fact, Paul Siple eventually spent more time in Antarctica than any other living person. Yet, as he told me once in the Society's Washington, D.C., headquarters, he had an allergy to extreme cold.

On May 8, 1902, on the Caribbean island of Martinique, volcanic Mont Pelée exploded. In less than three minutes, steam, smoke, ash, and flaming gases engulfed the port of St. Pierre. Some 30,000 people were killed. The National Geographic Society promptly sent an expedition to collect data. And, therewith, another tradition began: the Society would continue to study and report on major disasters.

In 1980, when a blast from Mount St. Helens devastated 200

square miles of the U.S. West, the magazine's Rowe Findley was already on the scene, studying the tremors and small eruptions that preceded the main blow. "I am lucky to be alive," he told me afterwards. Less lucky was Reid Blackburn, a 27-year-old staff photographer for the Vancouver *Columbian*, on loan to NATIONAL GEOGRAPHIC for Mount Saint Helens coverage. He died under four feet of ash.

There is no safe way to study volcanoes. After the 1985 eruption of Nevado del Ruiz in Colombia, when 23,000 people died under a lahar, or mud slide, I joined the celebrated volcanologist Stanley Williams on the slopes of the mountain. Swarms of individual quakes suggested that the volcano might spit pumice or lava at any moment. "If there's an eruption," Stan told me, "find shelter—maybe an overhanging rock. Or if you can't, look up at the sky. When a flying rock seems to get bigger, *move*."

Stanley Williams followed his own good advice in 1993 while studying the crater of Galeras, an active volcano in Colombia. When it suddenly erupted in an inferno of lava, ash, and fire-hot stones, Williams dodged the rocks as best he could and dragged himself to the protection of a large boulder. He suffered a fractured skull, crushed ear, broken jaw, broken legs, and extensive burns. But he fared better than his six colleagues, who were killed.

Whether hot or cold, any mountain can have its dangers. When NATIONAL GEOGRAPHIC's Barry Bishop left our offices in 1963 for the National Geographic Society's American Mount Everest Expedition, I wished him luck. "I'm going to the top!" he said with the same determination that ultimately took him there. The cost of his victory would be severe frostbite and the amputation of his toes.

Mount Everest has always been stingy with its secrets. But veteran mountaineer and cartographer Bradford Washburn was determined to survey and map

On a visit to the Bahamian capital of Nassau in 1922, 75-year-old Alexander Graham Bell comes up smiling from a flexible submarine tube that a friend devised to observe coral reef life. Bell, an inventor of the telephone, was married to a daughter of Gardiner Greene Hubbard, one of the Society's founding members, and served as its President from 1898 to 1903.

the terrain surrounding the world's highest peak. Washburn and his wife, Barbara, began this project after he retired as director of Boston's Museum of Science, when he was already in his 70s. With consummate diplomacy, he enlisted the cooperation of people in nine countries and secured permissions from Nepal, India, and China to use state-of-the-art stereophotography. Aerial photos had to be taken in cloudless weather when sub-zero gales swept loose snow from the peaks. After Barbara was felled by a rare blood disease in the Himalaya, Washburn returned to the U.S.—but not before he had set the team effort in place. The results: the first truly accurate maps of 350 square miles of the Everest region.

The coterie of National Geographic explorers is close-knit. For example, Washburn got his first instruction in aerial mapping from Capt. Albert W. Stevens, whose balloon *Explorer II* set an altitude record in 1935. Stevens, in turn, learned from fellow balloonist Auguste Piccard, the 1931 veteran of man's first flight into the stratosphere. Piccard's son Jacques took off in a different direction: In a bathyscaph, he explored the Mariana Trench, 35,800 feet beneath the surface of the Pacific Ocean. Jacques' own son, Bertrand, returned to balloons and the sky. In 1999, with copilot Brian Jones, Bertrand Piccard flew around the Earth in 20 days, achieving the first nonstop orbit of the world in a piloted balloon. "Our family's destiny," he called it—"if there is such a destiny."

All three generations of Piccards were chronicled in the pages of NATIONAL GEOGRAPHIC magazine. So, too, was the pioneering undersea work of Capt. Jacques-Yves Cousteau and his Aqua-Lung. And in 1957, GEOGRAPHIC writer and photographer Luis Marden found the wreck of H.M.S. *Bounty* off Pitcairn Island. Much more recently, George F. Bass plumbed the eastern Mediterranean to find and recover objects from a Bronze Age vessel, while Robert Ballard discovered the sunken *Titanic* in the Atlantic. In each instance, National Geographic was there.

In 1903 Alexander Graham Bell wrote in the magazine, "I have the feeling that…a properly constructed kite should be capable of use as a flying-machine when driven by its own propellers." Six months later, Wilbur and Orville Wright triumphed at Kitty Hawk. And ever since, the Society has faithfully reported on progress in the Age of Flight. We look today at Charles Lindbergh's cramped *Spirit of St. Louis* and wonder how it could have crossed the Atlantic in 1927. No doubt future generations will have the same feeling about the rockets and space modules of our own time.

Of course, discovery itself is the greatest adventure. Imagine the high jungle of Peru in 1911, as Hiram Bingham told his story: "On all fours we pulled ourselves up through slippery grass, digging with fingers to keep from falling.… The heat was oppressive.… We rounded a knoll and suddenly faced tier upon tier of Inca terraces rising like giant stairs.… Stone steps led to a plaza where white granite temples stood against the sky." Bingham had rediscovered Machu Picchu, one of the world's most dramatic ruins.

Granted, archaeology seems less exciting when you dig with a camel hair brush. But the reward of discovery! I can think of no experience quite like the time I found a small metal figurine on an expedition in Yucatán—and realized I was the first person in recorded history to see this Maya deity. Hardships are worth such a moment.

Even those described by Robert F. Griggs in 1915, as he studied volcanic ash in Alaska: "Trying to bathe in creeks clouded with pumice was like scrubbing ourselves with sandpaper." He vainly tried to strain the drinking water, but one of his companions "refused to wash his face for three days because he 'did not want to dirty it with the water we had to drink.'" True grit.

Theodore Roosevelt complained of "the mosquitoes, the poisonous ants, the maribondo wasps," in his report given at Convention Hall just after completing a 1914 expedition to Brazil. In a voice weakened by jungle fevers, he observed that "the standard maps are so preposterously wrong."

Indeed, his expedition added a formerly uncharted river to the world's maps, the Rio da Dúvida, or River of Doubt, later renamed Theodore Roosevelt River.

In 1998 half a world away from the Dúvida, an eight-man team explored the wild Tsangpo River of Tibet. Since 1924, adventurers had searched for a fabled waterfall in the serpentine and largely unmapped Tsangpo Gorge. The 1998 group found an inner canyon where the river dropped an average of 65 feet per mile—eight times faster than the Colorado rushes through Grand Canyon. The Tsangpo River's voluminous rapids proved too much for prize-winning kayaker Doug Gordon. Recalled a teammate, "He was swept right into this huge crashing thing. I never saw him again."

So it was both a sad and triumphant moment when at last a second group found and photographed the Hidden Falls of Dorje Phagmo, as they named their discovery. Maps thus list one more name.

Every place-name has its special story. Whether accurate or preposterously wrong, maps incite us to think. Young Christopher Columbus was a seller of maps. His own wares made him restless to sail west. As a boy, Sebastian Cabot daydreamed over the sailing charts of his navigator father. As a man, he redrew the landfalls of a New World.

In a Spanish prison, Miguel de Cervantes let his mind break free. "Journey over all the universe in a map," he wrote, "without…suffering the inconveniences of heat, cold, hunger, and thirst." Those words became part of his masterpiece *Don Quixote*.

So journey the universe through the following pages. Experience the element of surprise. Good reading. Good thinking.

Theodore Roosevelt's "last chance to be a boy" came in 1914 with his exploration of Brazil's rumored Rio da Dúvida, or River of Doubt. Three men perished on the trip. The former U.S. President suffered injury and fever but survived the ordeal; the Brazilian government later renamed the river in his honor.

NATIONAL

GEOGRAPHIC

EXPEDITIONS

ATLAS

THE LAY OF THE LAND
(Physical geography: exploring mountains,
glaciers, volcanoes, and caves)

TO THE ENDS OF THE EARTH
(Polar expeditions)

INTO THIN AIR
(Flight and space expeditions)

BEYOND THE HORIZON
(Expeditions to remote and exotic places)

THE DEEP
(Undersea explorations)

SEARCHING FOR THE PAST
(Archaeological expeditions)

THE FAMILY OF MAN
(Physical anthropology and primate studies)

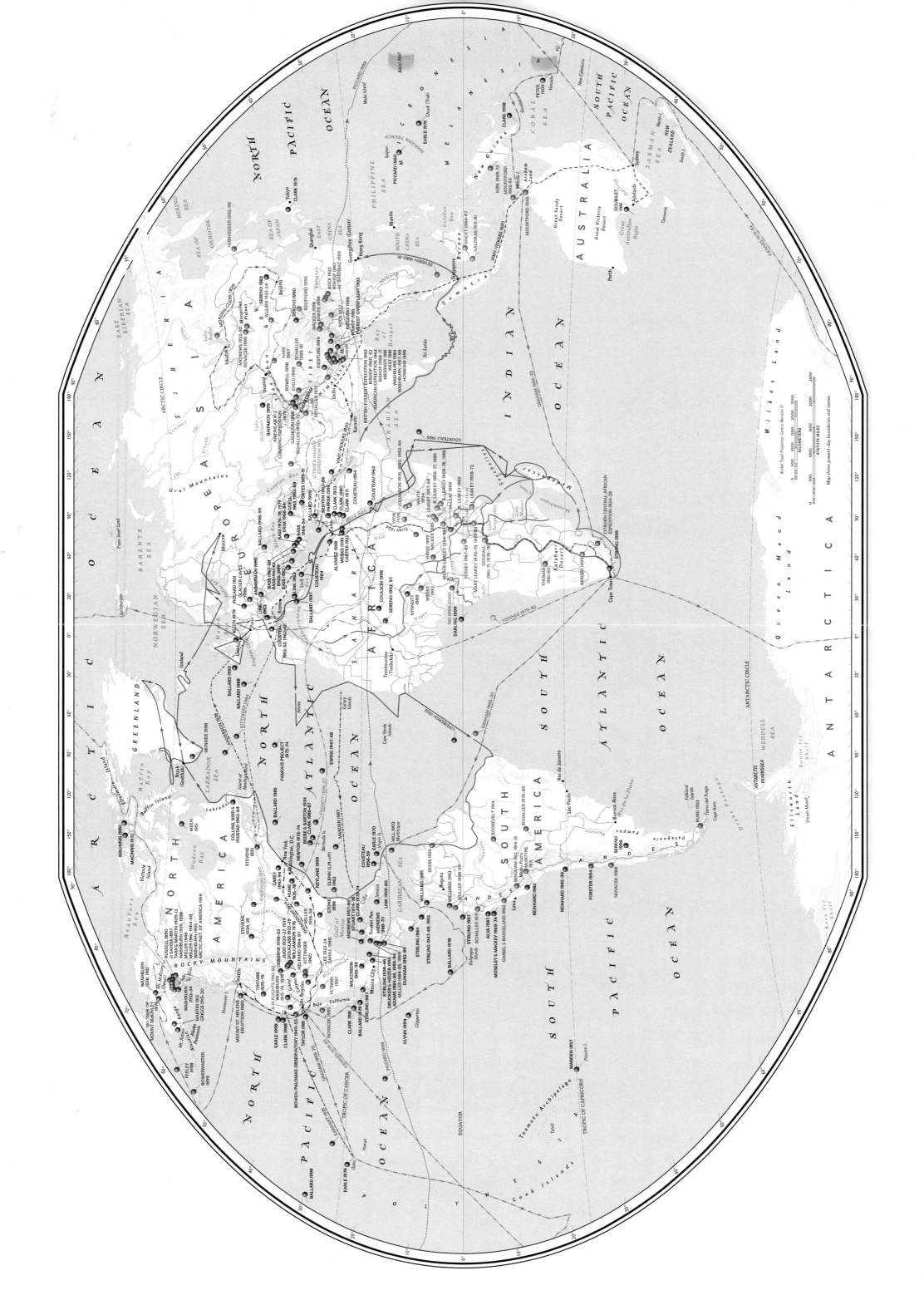

TIMELINE FOR NATIONAL GEOGRAPHIC EXPEDITIONS ATLAS

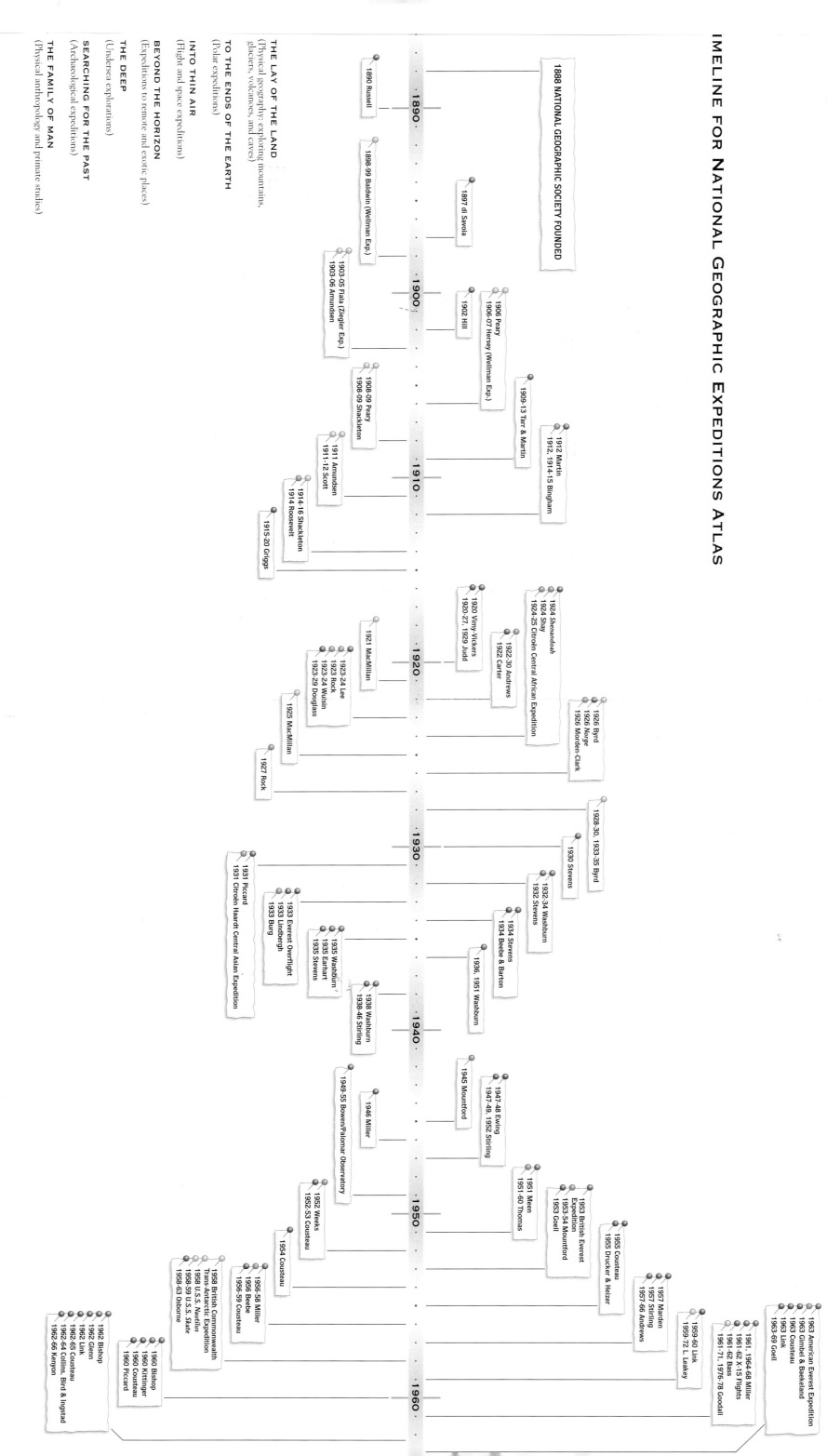

THE LAY OF THE LAND
(Physical geography: exploring mountains, glaciers, volcanoes, and caves)

TO THE ENDS OF THE EARTH
(Polar expeditions)

INTO THIN AIR
(Flight and space expeditions)

BEYOND THE HORIZON
(Expeditions to remote and exotic places)

THE DEEP
(Undersea explorations)

SEARCHING FOR THE PAST
(Archaeological expeditions)

THE FAMILY OF MAN
(Physical anthropology and primate studies)

1888 NATIONAL GEOGRAPHIC SOCIETY FOUNDED

1890 Russell

1897 di Savoia

1898-99 Baldwin (Wellman Exp.)

1903-05 Fiala (Ziegler Exp.)
1903-06 Amundsen

1902 Hill

1906 Peary
1906-07 Hersey (Wellman Exp.)

1908-09 Peary
1908-09 Shackleton

1909-13 Tarr & Martin

1911 Amundsen
1911-12 Scott

1912 Martin
1912, 1914-15 Bingham

1914-16 Shackleton
1914 Roosevelt

1915-20 Griggs

1920 Vimy-Vickers
1920-27, 1929 Judd

1921 MacMillan

1922-30 Andrews
1922 Carter

1923-24 Lee
1923 Rock
1923-24 Wulsin
1923-29 Douglass

1924 Shenandoah
1924 Shay
1924-25 Citroën Central African Expedition

1925 MacMillan

1926 Byrd
1926 Norge
1926 Morden-Clark

1927 Rock

1928-30, 1933-35 Byrd

1930 Stevens

1931 Piccard
1931 Citroën Haardt Central Asian Expedition

1932-34 Washburn
1932 Stevens

1933 Everest Overflight
1933 Lindbergh
1933 Burg

1934 Stevens
1934 Beebe & Barton

1935 Washburn
1935 Earhart
1935 Stevens

1936, 1951 Washburn

1938 Washburn
1938-46 Stirling

1945 Mountford

1946 Miller

1947-48 Ewing
1947-49, 1952 Stirling

1949-55 Bowen/Palomar Observatory

1951 Meen
1951-60 Thomas

1952 Weeks
1952-53 Cousteau

1953 British Everest Expedition
1953-54 Mountford
1953 Goell

1954 Cousteau

1955 Cousteau
1955 Drucker & Heizer

1956-58 Miller
1956 Beebe
1956-59 Cousteau

1957 Marden
1957 Stirling
1957-66 Andrews

1958 British Commonwealth Trans-Antarctic Expedition
1958 U.S.S. Nautilus
1958-59 U.S.S. Skate
1958-63 Osborne

1959-60 Link
1959-72 L. Leakey

1960 Bishop
1960 Kittinger
1960 Cousteau

1962 Bishop
1962 Glenn
1962 Link
1962-65 Cousteau
1962-64 Collins, Bird & Ingstad
1962-66 Kenyon

1960 Bishop
1960 Piccard

1961, 1964-68 Miller
1961-62 X-15 Flights
1961-71, 1976-78 Goodall

1963 Marden
1963 Gimbel & Baekeland
1963 Cousteau
1963 Link
1963-69 Goell

1963 American Everest Expedition

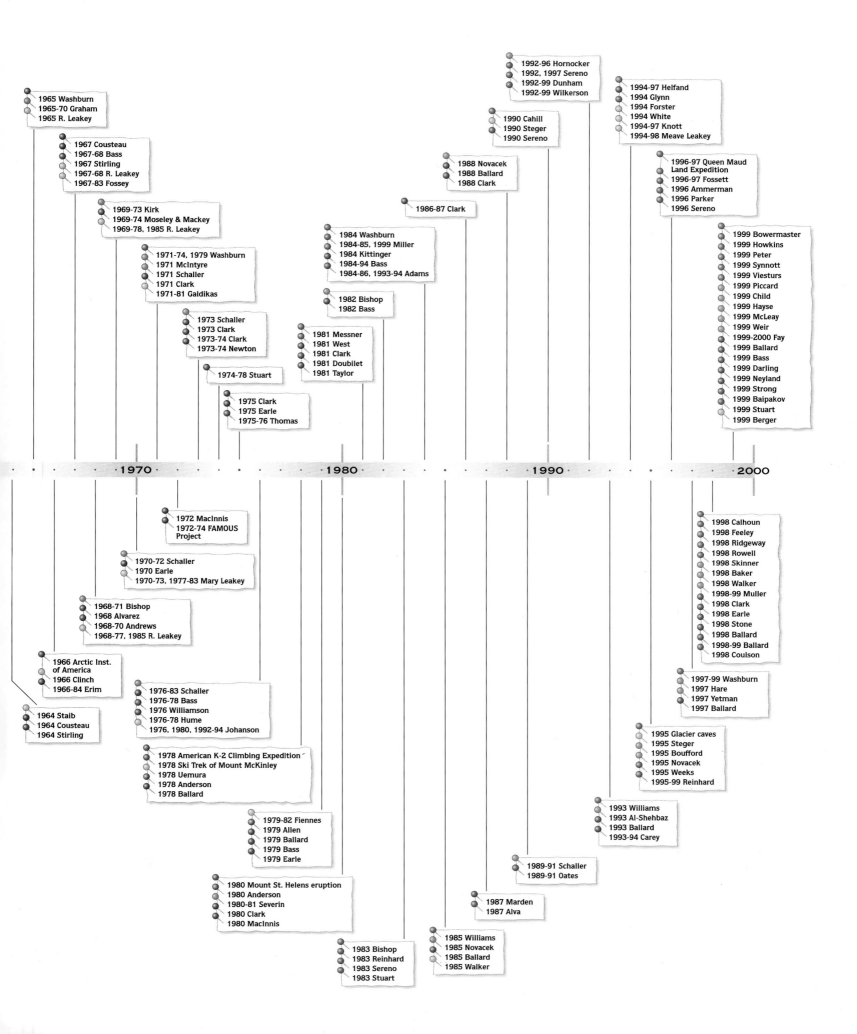

1965 Washburn
1965-70 Graham
1965 R. Leakey

1967 Cousteau
1967-68 Bass
1967 Stirling
1967-68 R. Leakey
1967-83 Fossey

1969-73 Kirk
1969-74 Moseley & Mackey
1969-78, 1985 R. Leakey

1971-74, 1979 Washburn
1971 McIntyre
1971 Schaller
1971 Clark
1971-81 Galdikas

1973 Schaller
1973 Clark
1973-74 Clark
1973-74 Newton

1974-78 Stuart

1975 Clark
1975 Earle
1975-76 Thomas

1992-96 Hornocker
1992, 1997 Sereno
1992-99 Dunham
1992-99 Wilkerson

1990 Cahill
1990 Steger
1990 Sereno

1988 Novacek
1988 Ballard
1988 Clark

1986-87 Clark

1984 Washburn
1984-85, 1999 Miller
1984 Kittinger
1984-94 Bass
1984-86, 1993-94 Adams

1982 Bishop
1982 Bass

1981 Messner
1981 West
1981 Clark
1981 Doublet
1981 Taylor

1994-97 Helfand
1994 Glynn
1994 Forster
1994 White
1994-97 Knott
1994-98 Meave Leakey

1996-97 Queen Maud
Land Expedition
1996-97 Fossett
1996 Ammerman
1996 Parker
1996 Sereno

1999 Bowermaster
1999 Howkins
1999 Peter
1999 Synnott
1999 Viesturs
1999 Piccard
1999 Child
1999 Hayse
1999 McLeay
1999 Weir
1999-2000 Fay
1999 Ballard
1999 Bass
1999 Darling
1999 Neyland
1999 Strong
1999 Baipakov
1999 Stuart
1999 Berger

·1970·   ·1980·   ·1990·   ·2000·

1972 MacInnis
1972-74 FAMOUS
Project

1970-72 Schaller
1970 Earle
1970-73, 1977-83 Mary Leakey

1968-71 Bishop
1968 Alvarez
1968-70 Andrews
1968-77, 1985 R. Leakey

1966 Arctic Inst.
of America
1966 Clinch
1966-84 Erim

1964 Staib
1964 Cousteau
1964 Stirling

1976-83 Schaller
1976-78 Bass
1976 Williamson
1976-78 Hume
1976, 1980, 1992-94 Johanson

1978 American K-2 Climbing Expedition
1978 Ski Trek of Mount McKinley
1978 Uemura
1978 Anderson
1978 Ballard

1979-82 Fiennes
1979 Allen
1979 Ballard
1979 Bass
1979 Earle

1980 Mount St. Helens eruption
1980 Anderson
1980-81 Severin
1980 Clark
1980 MacInnis

1983 Bishop
1983 Reinhard
1983 Sereno
1983 Stuart

1985 Williams
1985 Novacek
1985 Ballard
1985 Walker

1987 Marden
1987 Alva

1989-91 Schaller
1989-91 Oates

1993 Williams
1993 Al-Shehbaz
1993 Ballard
1993-94 Carey

1995 Glacier caves
1995 Steger
1995 Boufford
1995 Novacek
1995 Weeks
1995-99 Reinhard

1997-99 Washburn
1997 Hare
1997 Yetman
1997 Ballard

1998 Calhoun
1998 Feeley
1998 Ridgeway
1998 Rowell
1998 Skinner
1998 Baker
1998 Walker
1998-99 Muller
1998 Clark
1998 Earle
1998 Stone
1998 Ballard
1998-99 Ballard
1998 Coulson

THE LAY OF THE LAND

NOTHING CAN REPLACE COURAGE,
A RESOUNDING MOTIVATION
AND THAT LITTLE BIT OF LUCK.

—MOUNTAINEER SIR EDMUND HILLARY

BY
CYNTHIA RUSS RAMSAY

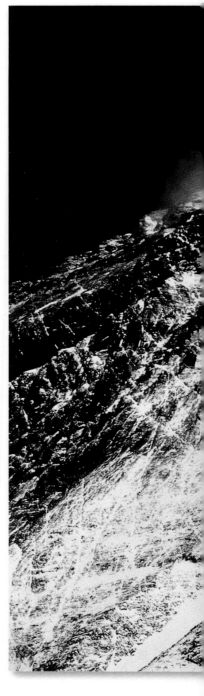

"Had there been wind, I would not be talking to you now," said Barry C. Bishop, one of six men who achieved the summit of Mount Everest in May 1963, as part of the first successful American expedition to the world's highest peak. But he and Lute Jerstad had left the top too late; now the sun had set, yet they continued down, roped together, with only one expiring flashlight for illumination. They were on the treacherous Southeast Ridge, where a single false step could plunge them thousands of feet down one side or the other. Clumsy with exhaustion and cold, they stumbled on, goading and cajoling each other to keep going toward the tents of Camp VI.

Around 9:30 p.m. Bishop and Jerstad were joined by teammates Willi Unsoeld and Tom Hornbein, descending from another ascent route. As their descent became more complicated and they grew fearful of losing the way, the four men decided to make an emergency bivouac at 28,000 feet—without sleeping bags or tents. They slumped down about midnight to await the dawn—huddling together to conserve body heat. They had no water, no food, no supplemental oxygen. Still, their oxygen masks helped protect their faces from the intense cold. It was minus 18°F, a deadly temperature in the savage winds that sweep across Everest most nights. But that night, the air was unusually calm. Otherwise they probably would have died, as have 144 climbers through 1998.

At dawn's light the four climbers began to move again—three of them shuffling awkwardly on frostbitten feet that had lost all feeling. Fortunately they were soon met by two ascending teammates from Camp VI, each carrying two bottles of oxygen. Restored by the oxygen and assisted down to that camp at 27,450 feet, the climbers drank cup after cup of lemonade, tea, hot chocolate, and soup as fast as snow could be melted. Liquid was all they wanted. Afterwards they resumed their descent, stamping along on feet frozen hard as wood. They kept moving all day long, continuing by flashlight into the night.

At the lower levels, a new torment added to their misery. Their feet began to thaw, and each step brought ever-increasing agony. But with amazing speed the men trudged into Base Camp, at 17,800 feet, at dusk on the second day. From there the two suffering the most serious frostbite—Bishop and Unsoeld—were carried piggyback for 20 miles to an evacuation helicopter—four Sherpas to each man, working in 20-minute relays.

In a hospital in Kathmandu, Nepal, Bishop ruminated on the challenges of Everest's "harsh and hostile immensity." He concluded, "There are no true victors, only survivors."

He paid a price for achieving the summit: All his toes had to be amputated, and he lost the tips of his little fingers. The other severe frostbite victim, Willi Unsoeld, forfeited nine toes. But the experience never diminished what Bishop referred to as his "passion for mountains and getting to high places."

Previous pages: Bounding across a rock-strewn glacier in the Pamirs of Central Asia, William Garner, left, and Randy Starrett— the first Americans to scale the U.S.S.R.'s four highest mountains—train for a joint U.S.-Soviet expedition in 1985. Garner reported their adventure in the August 1986 issue of the NATIONAL GEOGRAPHIC.

Bishop was on the staff of National Geographic. And, like nearly all 18 other participants in the American Mount Everest Expedition, he was a scientist as well as a man of the mountains. Dedicated to both mountain climbing and research, this team represented a combination of science and adventure. The Society's Committee for Research and Exploration had approved grants for studies in glaciology, weather, and solar radiation.

In 1888 the Society's first President, Gardiner Greene Hubbard, in his acceptance address set an agenda for the new organization with his desire "to promote special researches by others, and to diffuse the knowledge so gained among men, so that we may all know more of the world upon which we live." Since then, close to 7,000 grants have been made, many of them focusing on the lay of the land—from the highest mountains to the deepest caves, from scapes forged in volcanic fire to topographies sculpted by glacial ice. The Society's first expedition was to a remote, poorly known area on the Alaska-Yukon border, dominated by 18,008-foot-high Mount St. Elias.

Plumes of blowing snow stream from Everest's South Summit as climbers cross the steep face of Lhotse on the Society-sponsored American Mount Everest Expedition of 1963. In this view, the mountain's true summit lies hidden behind the final ridge.

1963 AMERICAN MOUNT EVEREST EXPEDITION

En route to Everest, porters carrying 65-pound loads cross a log bridge on the 185-mile trek from Banepa, Nepal, to base camp at the foot of the Khumbu Icefall. The procession—part of America's first Everest expedition—included 19 Americans, 32 Sherpas for high-altitude work, and 900 porters to shuttle the necessary gear and supplies. The expedition placed three two-man teams on top, pioneered the West Ridge route, and made the first successful traverse of the mountain.

Suffering the agony of frostbitten feet, climber Barry Bishop (opposite) rides a porter's back to the helicopter that evacuated him and team member Willi Unsoeld after Sherpa teams carried the men from base camp to Namche Bazar, traveling some 20 miles in two days, working in 20-minute relays. Unsoeld, who pioneered the West Ridge route, waves farewell as the chopper takes off for Kathmandu (below). Months later, President John F. Kennedy presented the Society's Hubbard Medal to the American climbers—and received a white *kata*, a token of respect, from Sherpa Nawang Gombu (bottom) who accompanied Jim Whittaker to Everest's summit.

ISRAEL C. RUSSELL AND MOUNT ST. ELIAS, STORMY REALM OF SNOW AND ICE

FUNDED BY THE SOCIETY, the U.S. Geological Survey, and the private subscription of 28 individuals, the Mount St. Elias Expedition set out to study and map the area and, if practicable, make an attempt on the summit, which at that time was believed to be the highest in North America.

Expedition leader Israel C. Russell was a professor of geology at the University of Michigan. But he also had an interest in glaciers and a determination to climb Saint Elias, the first major peak ever attempted in Alaska. He headed north from Seattle aboard a steamer traveling the Inside Passage to Yakutat Bay. Canoeing along the shore with his team of nine, he established camp on a narrow strip of shingled beach at the base of the Malaspina Glacier, an ice field sprawling across some 1,500 square miles.

After a month Russell chose "a line of march toward Mount St. Elias" up the nearby Marvine Glacier. Setting out with topographer Mark B. Kerr, he ran into trouble by early afternoon. A colossal icefall—a collection of huge blocks and crevasses—blocked their way. For a while they were able to make a zigzag course up through these hazards despite fog and occasional rain, but a monstrous crevasse finally halted them.

In the meantime the weather grew worse, so they pitched a cotton cloth tent nearby. But they had little chance to rest. Torrential rains loosened tons of ice and rock that came roaring down the glacier. Rocks clattered all around them. Then one struck the ridgepole, collapsing the tent and inundating them with mud and rain. Russell referred to the night as "pandemonium" on the mountain.

But by the time the storm abated, it had altered the ever shifting, jumbled chaos of the icefall, and they were able to push on to the head of the Marvine. Several more hours of

climbing brought them to a ridge where they became the first people of European ancestry to see massive Mount Logan, at 19,545 feet Canada's highest mountain.

Delayed and forced to retreat again and again by another two storms, Russell tried to advance on the summit once more while Kerr went down for supplies. Carrying a double load through deep snow, Russell trudged wearily on to a previous high camp. He pitched his tent and slept until awakened by snow drifting inside. Beset by a blizzard, he tried to clear the tent roof of snow to keep it from caving in. But the tent collapsed. Russell then dug a snow house and huddled there in darkness and silence for three days. To warm what little food he had, he set it over a rag wick dipped in a can of bacon grease.

On the fourth day he awakened to a glorious sight: "The broad unbroken snow-plain seemed to burn with light reflected from millions of shining crystals.... On the steep cliffs the snow hung in folds like drapery.... St. Elias was one vast pyramid of alabaster. The winds were still; no sound broke the solitude; not an object moved."

But the snow surrounding him refused to crust over, making further climbing impossible. Russell abandoned his camp on the sixth day and started down. The vast solitude seemed so strange that, when Kerr and others came up to search for him, he watched them for some time before shouting a greeting.

Russell returned the following year with the help of funds raised by voluntary subscriptions within the Society. Again he was frustrated by the mountain's notoriously bad weather and failed to reach the summit. But his maps and notes would pioneer the way for a successful ascent six years later, chronicled in the March 1898 NATIONAL GEOGRAPHIC.

One of the more colorful explorers of his day, His Royal Highness Prince Luigi Amadeo di Savoia, the Duke of the Abruzzi, led that expedition, arriving in Alaska's Yakutat Bay with 2,700 pounds of baggage in 1897. The duke believed the key to conquering Saint Elias was careful and meticulous planning. He assembled an expensive and well-organized endeavor with an entourage that included a scientist-writer, the Italian surgeon Filippo de

Leading the Society's first expedition, geologist Israel C. Russell, seated, and his party cross the moraines of Alaska's Malaspina Glacier. The project, sponsored jointly with the U.S. Geological Survey, surveyed the Saint Elias Mountains.

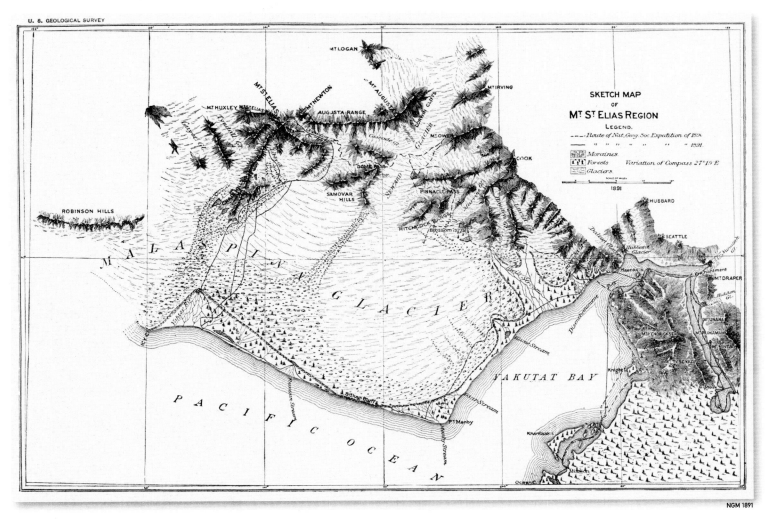

NGM 1891

Filippi, who would keep a record of the expedition and write an account of the trip; a photographer; and several Alpine guides. He brought foods that had been taste-tested to appeal to the failing appetites caused by high elevations and had iron bedsteads towed up the glacier on sledges.

Like Russell, the Italians had to contend with persistent snowfall. But on the day they stood atop Mount St. Elias, "Only the Malaspina Glacier and the sea were covered by a low-hanging curtain of fog; in every other direction the horizon was perfectly clear," Filippi noted. "The enormous extent of snowfields, glaciers, and mountains revealed to our sight surpassed all imagination."

Russell Expedition map published by the U.S.G.S. in 1892 reveals the extent of St. Elias's glaciers and mountains, as well as the team's route. The Russell group also discovered and named nearby Mount Logan, Canada's highest peak. Filling in such blank spaces on maps has long been a hallmark of Society expeditions.

MAYNARD M. MILLER: MOUNT ST. ELIAS AND BEYOND

GIVEN MOUNT ST. ELIAS'S GENERALLY nasty weather and its numerous glaciers, the Duke of the Abruzzi's ascent of this mountain was a significant climbing achievement. For the next 49 years no others would make the summit—not until Maynard M. Miller led friends, most of whom were former members of the Harvard Mountaineering Club, to the top on July 13, 1946, an adventure recalled in the February 1948 NATIONAL GEOGRAPHIC.

Miller and the Geographic would return again and again to Alaska's vast glaciers. He would become one of America's foremost glaciologists, spending some 54 years studying these rivers of ice and their impact on the land.

But back in 1946, the call of the ice was not science but adventure. Tall, athletic, and energetic, Miller was swinging his ice ax for the sheer fun of it—relishing the challenge of Mount St. Elias. As usual, the mountain's weather remained a major factor.

Most lethal were the avalanches. After one too many close calls, Miller and his companions realized that daytime travel on high slopes would be suicidal, and they restricted their climbing to the long twilight of the subarctic summer.

Their route took them through waist-

ISRAEL C. RUSSELL AND MOUNT ST. ELIAS

Imposing bulk of Mount St. Elias rears 18,008 feet into the sky, towering over Russell's team atop Libbey Glacier, part of the region's vast network of ice fields. Hampered for days by ferocious summer blizzards, Russell kept trying for the summit until faced with a serious avalanche threat. His lively first-person account of the scientific expedition, which appeared in the May 1891 NATIONAL GEOGRAPHIC, helped set the style for reporting future explorations.

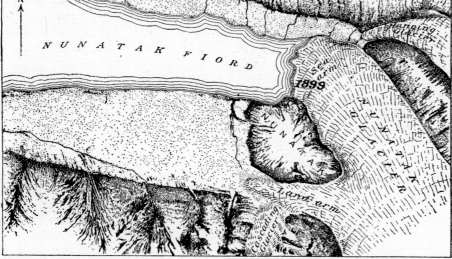

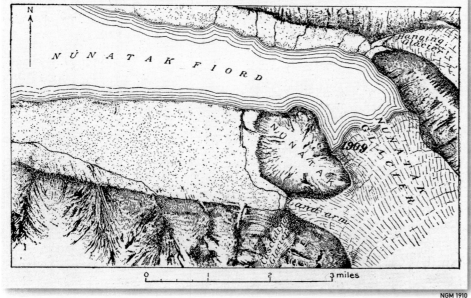

NGM 1910

deep snow, along a fog-bound ridge, and up pitches of blue glare ice, but the "fatigue, headaches, pounding hearts all were forgotten in the overwhelming feeling of exultation" of making it to the top.

In 1964, 18 years later, Maynard Miller returned to Alaska as director for the Society's Alaskan Glacier Commemorative Project, a five-year field study of the Juneau Ice Field and its many large glaciers scattered over about a thousand square miles. This project saluted the work, *Alaskan Glacier Studies,* of Professors Ralph S. Tarr and Lawrence Martin, who had conducted three Society expeditions in the early 1900s that had studied the glaciers in southeast Alaska. Their findings, published by the Society in 1914, still provide the best early descriptions of southern Alaska's ice fields.

In the February 1967 NATIONAL GEO-GRAPHIC, Miller reflected on the challenges of working on ice. Crevasses are a constant danger. The climate is harsh, comparable in places to the North Pole's. The weather is capricious, quickly turning from "80-degree sunshine to near-freezing murk." Winds can be violent, sweeping away roofs and doors. Simple routines of living become onerous—everything needed for life on the ice field has to be lifted, pushed, pulled, put up—and then taken down.

For Miller the rewards of glacier study—plotting the comings and goings of more than 200 glaciers in various phases of advance and retreat—have all been worth it. He is still studying glaciers today, having returned to the Juneau Ice Field as recently as 1999 with the University of Idaho's Summer Institute of Glaciological and Arctic Sciences.

"Glaciers are very delicate recorders of climatic change, and Alaska's coast-and-mountain landscape is one of Earth's most climatologically sensitive barometers," he said in October 1999.

His research has demonstrated that Alaska's ice masses wax and wane over long periods. In 1967, when Miller first presented these findings, competing models predicted a cooler cycle by the end of the 20th century.

"But contrary to normal climatic trends, we are in a period of global warming," he notes today. "…The surface area of the ice in these Alaskan glaciers has been reduced by 35 to 40 percent in the last 20 years. There's no question about it, we are warming the atmosphere of our planet."

ROBERT F. GRIGGS AND THE WILDS OF KATMAI

IN EARLY JUNE 1912, a colossal eruption took place in a rugged wilderness called Katmai, on the Alaskan Peninsula, some 300 air miles southwest of Anchorage.

One of the most violent cataclysms in recorded history, it began with a series of earthquakes lasting five days. On June 6 the Novarupta volcano blew its top, spewing incandescent ash and rock fragments into the sky. This was but a prelude to a succession of major explosions that included the collapse of the entire summit cone of Mount Katmai.

Despite the remoteness of the region, news of the blasts spread quickly, because clouds of ashfall and booming sounds of the eruption rolled across Alaska as far east as Juneau, 750 miles away. Winds dumped a 60-hour blizzard of volcanic ash on the settlement of Kodiak on Kodiak Island, a hundred miles from the eruption site, creating a blackness so dense that a lantern was barely visible at arm's length. Birds' wings became so weighted with ash that they fell helplessly from the sky.

Within a month of the eruption Society grantee George C. Martin was in Kodiak interviewing residents about those awful days of darkness. In August he went ashore at Katmai Bay, where he found the tiny abandoned village of Katmai entombed in ash 3 to 15 feet deep. Although the heavy accumulations of ash blocked further travel inland, Martin's report in the February 1913 NATIONAL GEOGRAPHIC triggered such widespread interest that the Society sponsored expeditions to Katmai every year from 1915 to 1920.

On the first of those expeditions, botanist Robert F. Griggs waded ashore at Katmai Bay with two companions. He described the scene in his book *The Valley of Ten Thousand Smokes*, published by the Society in 1922: "…A pall of fine volcanic dust which obscured everything above a thousand feet…heightening the unearthly aspect of the landscape."

The team's goal was Mount Katmai at the head of Katmai Valley, which was covered with soft, sticky mud. River channels had become choked with ash.

"One will go along easily ankle deep for a few steps and then suddenly drop down to his waist," wrote Griggs about crossing Soluka Creek. "The labor involved in such travel

Map shows present-day boundaries and names.

cannot be described, but must be experienced to be appreciated."

Where mountain slopes were too steep for the volcanic ash to stick, it had slid and spread out in gigantic fans. Climbing these slides was wretched; the men found themselves as if on a treadmill, sinking to their ankles and slipping back two paces for every one forward. They even tried going on all fours, but the sharp pumice soon ground away their fingertips.

Through it all, Griggs remained circumspect, noting that "the labor of climbing the ash slopes was somewhat compensated by the sport of sliding down."

At one point, a companion thrust his alpenstock into the ash—and found they were standing on hollow ground. Beneath the one-foot-thick ash layer was a cavernous space, created as snow had "glued" the ash in place and then melted. The gap could be 5 feet deep or 50, depending on how much snow had disappeared. And the thin ash arch on which they stood could cave in anytime!

Reluctantly but wisely, Griggs and his companions turned back, taking a different route. They passed through an oppressively gloomy region, where skeletal trees sprouted from ashfall in an eerily noiseless, spectral landscape. "One could travel all day without

The Society's early expeditions to Alaska (above) helped spur the growth of its membership, which took pride in supporting geographic research.

Opposite: Part of a landmark study of Alaskan glaciers led by Ralph S. Tarr and Lawrence Martin. a trio of maps document the retreat of glacial ice from southeast Alaska's Nunatak Fiord. The work, published in the NATIONAL GEOGRAPHIC in 1910. has helped guide glacier research ever since.

Wading through southwestern Alaska's ash-choked Katmai River in 1912, biologist Robert F. Griggs (above) explores a region recently despoiled by volcanic cataclysm. Countless fumaroles stud what Griggs called the Valley of Ten Thousand Smokes (right), which he discovered on one of eight Society-sponsored expeditions that surveyed the devastation. The volcanic forces that spawned the steam have long since cooled and the smokes have died, but Katmai's dramatic desert of congealed ash remains even today. Designated a national monument in 1918, Katmai gained national park and preserve status in 1980.

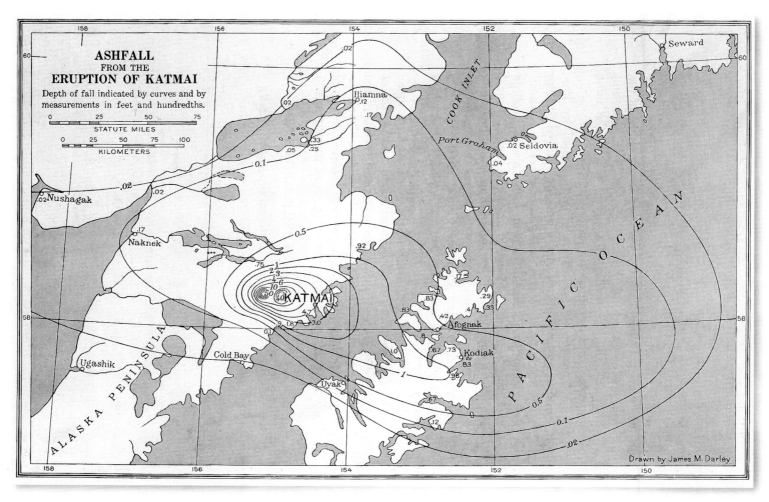

ASHFALL
FROM THE
ERUPTION OF KATMAI

Depth of fall indicated by curves and by
measurements in feet and hundredths.

STATUTE MILES

KILOMETERS

Drawn by James M. Darley

Eruption fallout:
Prevailing winds
carried Katmai's ash
more than 200 miles
eastward, into the
Gulf of Alaska. Near-
by fishing communi-
ties on Kodiak Island
experienced a chok-
ing "blizzard" that
brought darkness at
midday. Some areas
were blanketed in ash
as deep as ten feet.

hearing a sound but his own footfalls and the
plunge of rushing water," Griggs later recalled.

On the third day of his 1915 trip, the fog
lifted, finally revealing the volcanoes Griggs
and company had sought so persistently. Soaring high above thousand-foot cliffs at the head
of the valley were Martin, Mageik, Trident,
and, at last, Katmai, a dirty, ash-covered,
decapitated cone, a stub of its former self.

Studying its slopes through field glasses,
Griggs could see glaciers with yawning
crevasses. He was more determined than ever
to return with a rope to climb Katmai's
ravaged heights.

The following July, he did just that,
accompanied by photographer Donovan B.
Church and Lucius Folsom. The trio plodded
up the Katmai Valley to the volcano, encoun-
tering dry mud at the lower elevations, then
soft, slippery ooze. At about 3,500 feet, snow
alternated with mud. Higher still, fresh soft
snow made the going easier.

Suddenly the men reached the crater's
crumbling, knife-edge rim, arriving so
abruptly that they almost tumbled over into
the abyss. They peered down into the caldera,
where swirling clouds of steam all but
obscured "something blue, far, far below."

When the clouds parted, they were struck
speechless to see "a wonderful lake, of a weird
vitriolic robin's-egg blue" with a crescent-
shaped island near its center.

All around the lake, columns of steam
hissed from every crevice. Although reaching
the top of Katmai had met the 1916 expedition's major objective, Griggs was not yet
ready to go home.

The next day the explorers noticed
strange clouds hovering above the valley
beyond Katmai Pass, which lies below the
volcano, and were curious about their source.
As they neared the summit of the pass, they
saw more than a hundred fumaroles issuing
from fissures in the ground. A distant column
of rising steam, much larger than the others,
lured them up one more rise for a better
view—and the party was left awestruck.

"The whole valley as far as the eye could
reach was full of hundreds, no thousands—
literally, tens of thousands—of smokes curling
up from its fissured floor.... Some were
sending up columns of steam which rose a
thousand feet before dissolving."

The discovery of this mysterious smoking
valley in Alaska and Griggs's report in the
January 1917 issue of NATIONAL GEOGRAPHIC

generated tremendous public interest.

Prompted by the NATIONAL GEOGRAPHIC magazine article and the findings of two subsequent Society expeditions, President Woodrow Wilson designated more than a million acres as Katmai National Monument, in 1918. Since then the boundaries have been extended, and Katmai has been reclassified as a national park and preserve.

Today the heat from the fiery ash flows that buried this valley to depths of 700 feet has subsided, and the land no longer smolders. The smokes have died out. The desert of ash has congealed into soft crumbly stone colored in muted shades of pink, yellow, orange, and beige.

Demonstrating the lightness of pumice, Griggs balances a boulder blown full of bubbles by the gases of Katmai's Novarupta eruptions.

EXPEDITIONS TO OTHER VOLCANOES

AS SPECTACULAR AS WAS THE KATMAI exploration, it was not the Society's first foray into volcanic upheavals. In 1902 the National Geographic sent a team of experts, including Israel Russell, led by the geologist Robert T. Hill to investigate an eruption of Mont Pelée on the Caribbean island of Martinique.

By interviewing witnesses as soon as possible after the eruption, the team learned how the quaint French colonial city of 30,000, St. Pierre, had been annihilated in less than three minutes. Clouds of flaming gases and superheated steam had roared down the mountain; the whole city went up in flames. Incredible heat had melted tableware and glass. Only one person had survived—a convict who had been jailed in a thick-walled cell, with a door facing away from the blast.

Over the years and decades since that blast, the Society has continued to report on other major volcanic cataclysms, from the fiery birth of Surtsey off the coast of Iceland to Mexico's disastrous El Chichón. In January 1929 the GEOGRAPHIC chronicled the Pavlof Volcano Expedition, which employed an amphibious craft to explore a remote volcanic wilderness on the Alaskan Peninsula. Since 1960, Society magazine, book, and television productions have captured for members the fiery spectacle of Hawaii's lava eruptions.

The 1980 eruption of Mount St. Helens, in Washington State, may be the best-documented volcanic event ever. Numerous

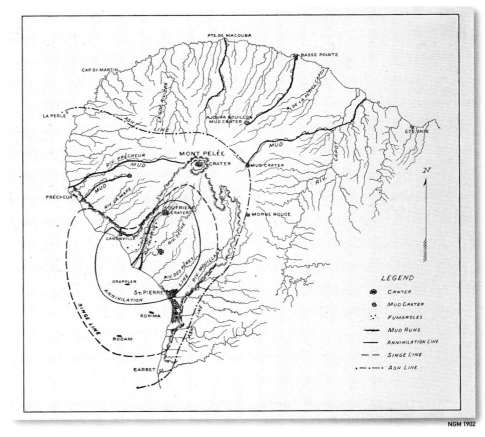

NGM 1902

photographers, including 21 featured in a dramatic report in the January 1981 NATIONAL GEOGRAPHIC, recorded the cataclysm on film.

MOUNT ST. HELENS did not blow without warning; the mountain had been sputtering

Mont Pelée's 1902 eruption produced a searing rain of steam and ash, obliterating the city of St. Pierre.

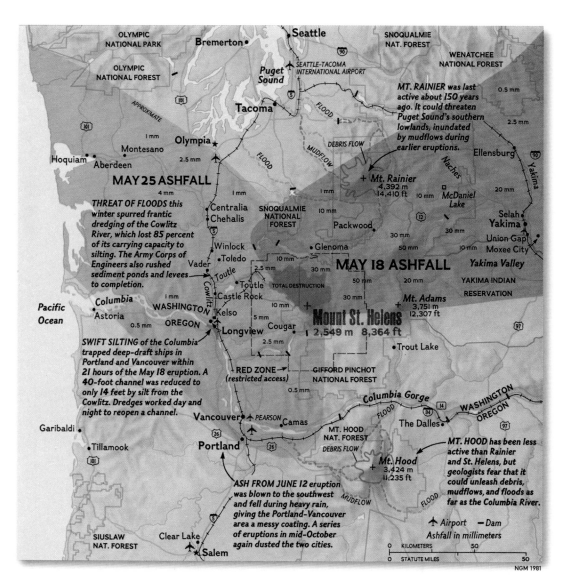

Timetable for destruction: After an initial earthquake and blast ripped away 1,300 feet of mountain from Mount St. Helens on May 18, 1980, massive landslides and mudflows left a zone of total devastation. Lesser blasts over succeeding weeks and months spread tons of ash to the east, west, and south.

for some time. The appearance of a 320-foot bulge on the volcano's north face was another menacing sign of what was to come.

Government geologist David Johnston was monitoring the mountain just six miles from the summit. NATIONAL GEOGRAPHIC assistant editor Rowe Findley had also arrived. Photographers were in place.

Then it happened. On the morning of May 18, 1980, Johnston radioed, "Vancouver! Vancouver! This is it...." An earthquake of 5.0 magnitude on the Richter scale shook the mountain and collapsed its north face, setting off a massive landslide. Pressures within the bowels of the volcano were suddenly released, and scalding, exploding gases shot hot debris out of the disintegrating flank of the mountain with a roar heard 200 miles away. Seconds later, as magma rose from the depths, the eruption turned upward, blasting glassy ash and pulverized rock 12 miles into the sky. From the gash in the mountainside, streams of superheated gas and fiery ash began flowing down to the valley below.

Johnston's alert would be his last words. He vanished in the initial blast of gases and debris. Nearby, photographer Robert Landsburg had his camera focused on the cloud of ash surging toward him. He frantically clicked the shutter, rewound the film, and crammed the camera into his pack—which was recovered when his lifeless body was found in the ash. Another photographer, Reid Blackburn, who set up radio-triggered cameras for the government and the GEOGRAPHIC at a post eight miles from the crater, lost his life as well.

More fortunate, photographer Gary Rosenquist, camped at Bear Meadow on the northwest side of the mountain, survived the blast. He also captured the sequence triggered by the collapsing north face in the first seconds of the eruption. In the days that followed, Rowe Findley and photographers surveyed the grim devastation by helicopter: the smothered valleys, twisted vehicles, mud-bloated and flooding rivers, flattened forests with trees toppled like jackstraws, and the calamity of 61 human beings dead or missing.

CARLSBAD: ADVENTURERS PLUMB THE DEPTHS

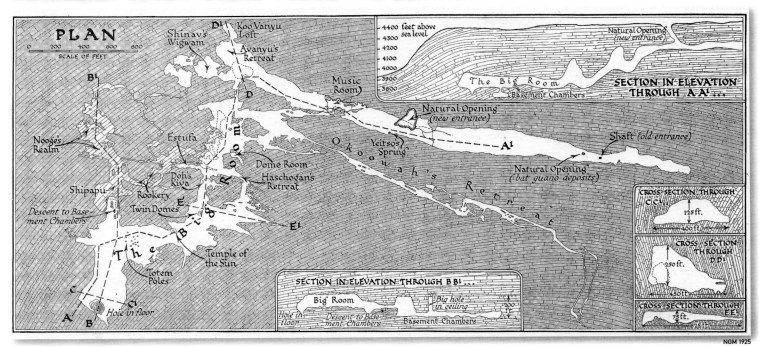

NGM 1925

LIKE KATMAI, THE VAST UNDERGROUND REALM of Carlsbad Caverns remained relatively unknown until the Society brought it to worldwide attention with two articles in the NATIONAL GEOGRAPHIC—in 1924 and in 1925.

The story began 250 million years ago, when what is now southeastern New Mexico lay beneath a shallow inland sea; the remains of its creatures formed a reef many hundreds of feet thick. In time the sea dried up, and the reef turned to limestone. Then, some 20 million years ago, the uplift that created the Rockies also heaved up this sea's basin. Hydrogen sulfide from nearby petroleum deposits combined with water to produce sulfuric acid, which dissolved huge amounts of the limestone, creating enormous chambers. Within the last 500,000 or 600,000 years, mineralized water seeping into those chambers slowly built the fantastic formations we see today, drop by drop, each leaving a tiny deposit of limestone as it evaporated. Stalagmites standing up and stalactites hanging down grew and grew, all hundreds of feet below the surface.

Locals had known of a cave from which free-tailed bats funneled out by the millions every summer evening, swirling across the sky like clouds of smoke to hunt insects. An area near the cave entrance had even been mined for guano, but no one explored the deeper

recesses until 1901, when miner James Larkin White worked his way down holding a kerosene lamp and first beheld Carlsbad's underground wonders. His tales were met initially with indifference or disbelief. Finally, he took photographer Ray V. Davis to document his stories. News reached the federal government, and in 1923 President Calvin Coolidge declared the area a national monument.

At this point the Society bought the Davis photographs and sponsored a visit in 1923 and an exploring and mapping expedition in 1924, both led by Willis T. Lee of the U.S. Geological Survey.

Like other early visitors, Lee entered Carlsbad through a guano-mining shaft. He rode down, he said, in "a steel bucket on the end of a line which seems like a mere thread over a black hole 170 feet deep."

While today thousands of visitors descend by elevator and stroll paved, well-lighted walkways, Lee and his companions picked their way through the pitch-black passageways using torches and lanterns. At one point Lee wryly observed that a limited view might be advantageous, for if the whole prospect were visible at once, it could be so daunting that only a hardy climber would ever undertake the journey.

Some passageways were low and narrow; some were wide and branched. Like Tom

Published in the NATIONAL GEOGRAPHIC in 1925, the first extensive map of New Mexico's Carlsbad Caverns depicts chambers and crannies explored and surveyed by Willis T. Lee with the help of a Society grant. Insets indicate vertical dimensions of the underground passageways as they appear along various transects.

Vintage photograph published in 1925 (below) reveals visitors admiring Carlsbad's Dome Room with its graceful pillars, draperies, and thousands of tiny stalactites. Created as mineral-rich water slowly evaporates and leaves its mineral burden behind, such decorations encrust nearly every surface of the complex. In nearby Lechuguilla Cave (opposite), spelunkers Bob Coney and Kathy Minter camp beside the squat stalagmites of Underground Atlanta, which they discovered and named. It is part of a labyrinth of tunnels and rooms whose far reaches are still unexplored. Lechuguilla abounds in a variety of rare and fantastic stone formations.

Wearing nothing but his helmet, caver Chris Stine squeezes through a cleft leading to Lake Castrovalva in Lechuguilla. Concern for this cave's many pristine lakes prompts spelunkers to go nude, rather than contaminate the waters with dirt from their clothing.

Sawyer, the explorers unrolled kite string as they progressed, to guide themselves back to the exit. Many passages were obstacle courses filled with huge jagged rocks and debris. One of Lee's companions compared their struggle to "a train of ants making its way through a brick pile."

The second expedition negotiated huge cavities with a precarious swinging wire ladder, a device Lee described as having "an erratic nature and an obstinate disposition."

Lee's enthusiasm, however, never faltered. And the fantastic subterranean world that had existed unseen for eons captured the world's imagination: The thousands of stalactites hanging from the ceilings—some massive icicles, some thin as soda straws; stone drapery "looped back in graceful folds"; great fluted pillars; lily pads; and an ornate fountain "worthy of the gods." Today, hundreds of thousands of people each year visit the Carlsbad

Caverns, a spectacle that obtained national park status in 1930.

Only experienced cavers, however, venture into the depths of Lechuguilla Cave, a cave system near Carlsbad that abounds in rare and fantastic stone formations and—at 1,565 feet—ranks as America's deepest. Place-names like Death Pit, Freakout Traverse, Fortress of Chaos, and The Void evoke the exhausting effort involved in exploring this convoluted cavern whose existence was confirmed in May 1986. And new passages are being found all the time.

Writer Tim Cahill and photographer Michael Nichols, veterans of numerous daring assignments, undertook the rigors of Lechuguilla for the March 1991 issue of NATIONAL GEOGRAPHIC. Lechuguilla, Cahill wrote, "is not demanding technically.... A typical move is like getting up onto a table, crawling across it, then climbing down. Easy, unless you have to do it 50 times in a row, in the dark, with a 50-foot drop-off beneath you." "Lechuguilla cavers," he adds, "like to joke that the labyrinth stretches 50 miles with only three flat spots. Hard-core cavers literally live for the challenge." They are "impelled by 'borehole lust,' 'virgin passage fever,' the passion for discovery."

OF MAPS AND MOUNTAINS: BRADFORD WASHBURN

CERTAINLY A PASSION AND FASCINATION FOR discovery has commanded Bradford Washburn's mind and energy for more than 70

Practically honeymooners at 10,000 feet on Alaska's 13,828-foot Mount Hayes, Barbara and Bradford Washburn pause during their 1941 climb. Together, the couple completed numerous expeditions, including the mapping of Arizona's Grand Canyon, an ongoing project for seven years.

years. Mountaineer, cartographer, aerial photographer, and museum administrator, Washburn stands in the great tradition of those who have been lured, inspired, and challenged by the unknown.

The quintessential scientific explorer, Washburn, director of Boston's Museum of Science from 1939 to 1980, has had a long and brilliant association with the Society. From 1935, when the GEOGRAPHIC published his article on the conquest of Alaska's Mount Crillon, to the publication of his large-scale maps of the Grand Canyon and Mount Everest in 1978 and 1988, respectively, Washburn shared with Society members his "love of high and distant places and wilderness vistas."

Although Mount Crillon is no giant by Himalayan or even Alaskan standards, the 12,723-foot peak, part of the Fairweather Range and now within the boundaries of

Glacier Bay National Park, has its own set of difficulties. During a 1930 reconnaissance expedition, Washburn's team had to unload supplies standing waist-deep in surf and then backpack for three weeks through dense forest, where no trails existed, before reaching the base of the mountain.

But Washburn was a trailblazer in more ways than one. In 1933 he relied on air support, a strategy that was a harbinger of a new style of mountaineering. A Lockheed Vega seaplane hauled supplies from the coast to his base camp at Crillon Lake, and in 1934 he had the plane drop additional provisions at even higher camps. In 1934 Washburn, funded by the Geological Society of America, used a second plane to ferry the team to base camp and to make reconnaissance flights over the unmapped heart of the mountain range.

It was also during his expeditions to Crillon that Washburn began his pioneering work in Alaskan aerial photography, documenting mountains from the sky and observing the "unbelievable" retreat of ice that had occurred since Tarr and Martin had made their glacier studies for the Society in the 1910s.

Washburn and his friends had attempted to climb Crillon in 1933 but were turned back by a storm. He made a second, and successful, attempt in 1934 with Adams Carter. After a grueling ascent, Washburn and Carter were just 200 feet from the top of Crillon—but a yawning crevasse blocked their way. The only option, apart from retreat, was to scale a steep ridge covered with bluish-green ice. They were not easily discouraged: "With the summit but a stone's throw away we were not going to give up without a last and desperate struggle."

By hacking steps in the ice, the two progressed "at a snail's pace" until a series of heavy drifts and a mound materialized amid the swirling snow. After ten-and-a-half hours of nonstop climbing, the duo trudged onto the summit of Crillon with exultant yells.

Then-President of the Society Gilbert H. Grosvenor rewarded the determination and energy of the 24-year-old Washburn by sponsoring his next expedition, to a vast unexplored region of mountains and glaciers in Canada's Yukon Territory and Alaska's Saint Elias Range. A six-man party of friends, including Ad Carter, Bob Bates, and Ome Daiber, flew into the heart of this 5,000-square-mile blank spot on maps. In the course

of three months of surveying and photography, the team discovered 19 peaks above 10,000 feet. For ground surveys they relied on sled dogs, mushing them across more than a thousand miles of snowy wilderness. Able to travel 18 miles a day, the huskies only faltered in the deepest and heaviest snows. On such occasions the expedition would wait a day or two, for the wind to settle and firm the snow. On especially steep grades the men unhitched their dogs and hauled their gear themselves.

A single-engine plane, fitted with retractable skis, landed on glaciers with needed supplies and performed aerial surveys. Washburn often climbed aboard with his bulky camera to record the "colossal scenery" and to scout a route across the awesome Saint Elias Mountains—another of the expedition's landmark achievements.

Immediately after his 1936 Yukon expedition, Washburn embarked on another mountain project for the National Geographic, this one to Alaska's Mount McKinley, also known by the Athapaskan Indian name, "Denali," "the Great One." At 20,320 feet McKinley is North America's tallest mountain.

As Washburn tells it, the Society was interested in a bit of geographical exploration that, according to Dr. Grosvenor, "could be pulled off at not-too-great expense." This posed no problem, Washburn recalls, because he was aching to fly around and over the great mountain of the north and put his skills in aerial photography to the test. Jointly sponsored by Pan American Airways, the mini-expedition produced for Grosvenor "…some two hundred 8x10 photographs and a check for $37—the unspent balance of his $1,000 grant."

Those photos were shot from an unpressurized twin-engine Lockheed Electra, with Washburn sitting on a gasoline can beside the cabin door with the door removed, sucking supplemental oxygen. A rope tether around his waist served as his "safety belt" as he leaned out

Terrain too rough to land an airplane on wore out this horse on Bradford Washburn's 1938 expedition to Mount Sanford, in the Wrangell-St. Elias Range. An innovator in the use of air support for exploration, Washburn began his lifelong relationship with National Geographic with the publication of his conquest of Alaska's Mount Crillon in 1935.

Backed by the U.S. Army, climbers on Mount McKinley's Karstens Ridge (opposite) test cold-weather gear for mountain troops in 1942. Boots like the one shown with a crampon (below, bottom) were used by Washburn's team on Mount McKinley during his 1953 expedition. Washburn eventually made the first large-scale map of Mount McKinley, North America's highest peak. His well-planned ascent of nearby Mount Hayes in 1941 (below) served as dress rehearsal for his later McKinley triumph by a route never before climbed: the rugged West Buttress.

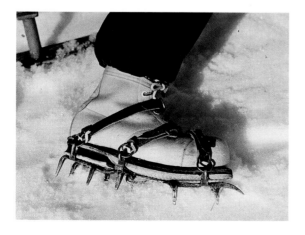

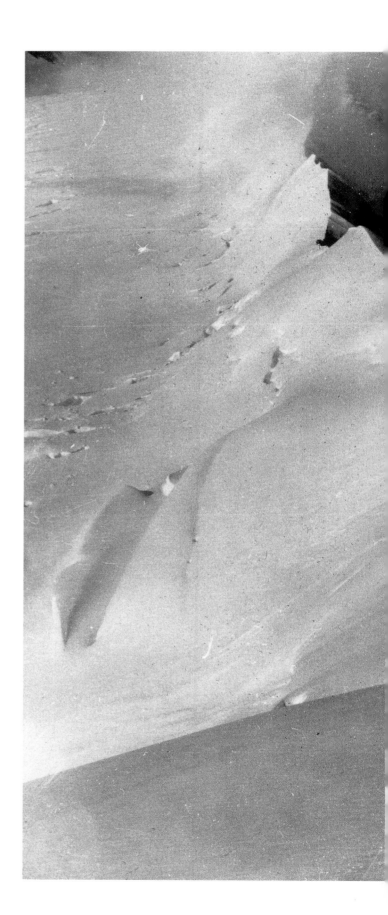

North and east of Mount St. Elias, a vast mountain-crowned wilderness of subarctic Canada remained a blank on the map until the Society's 1935 Yukon Expedition. By using aerial surveys and planes equipped with skis, Washburn and his team were able to penetrate and map the heart of this vast virgin territory.

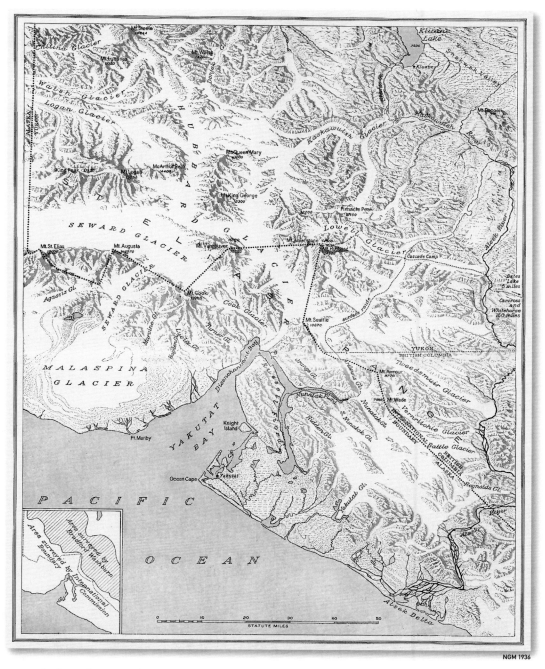

NGM 1936

to get the best photographs possible.

Fifty years later, Washburn would graduate to a Learjet, focusing on McKinley through an emergency door equipped with a three-quarter-inch-thick optical glass window, while his wife Barbara directed warm, dry air from a blower to the window to keep it clear of frost.

In addition to his aerial encounters with the Great One, Washburn has also climbed to its top three times, once with Barbara, the first woman to ever reach the summit. He has snowshoed, cramponed, and hacked his way up its slopes. In 1951, following a plan based on his NATIONAL GEOGRAPHIC aerial photographs, he pioneered the now popular West Buttress route, which uses ski-planes to land climbers on the Kahiltna Glacier, nearly

one-third of the way up the mountain.

He and three others spent about two weeks at their Kahiltna base camp at 10,300 feet, testing polar equipment, taking sightings on the surrounding peaks for his McKinley map, and hauling more than a ton of air-dropped supplies to caches higher up.

Experience had taught Washburn that igloos make ideal shelters for surviving the climatic extremes of a glacier—they are cool and shady on a sunny day, warm and quiet in the wildest storm. They don't flap in the wind, and they obviate the necessity of pitching tents.

Washburn's assault on the mountain began after a roaring blizzard that had blocked the entrance to their igloo solid with snow-drift. The men, he recalled, had "a real job digging themselves out for breakfast."

Setting out from Windy Corner, their advanced base camp, the climbers ran into snow conditions that Washburn called "wretched"—deep and loose, with layers of thin crust. They could walk only with snowshoes; without them they broke through to the waist. They tried shoveling a trail and wound up utterly exhausted after just two hours.

Then they came upon the West Buttress, so steep and icy it required using crampons and ropes, and chopping a 600-foot-long staircase painstakingly into the ice, one step at a time, each step requiring 20 to 30 whacks. They set fixed ropes alongside their trail to help future climbers. From there, after camping in an igloo at about 17,300 feet, it was relatively easy going to Denali Pass, where the West Buttress route intersects the earlier Harper Glacier route to the summit. At that point, the climbers had achieved their goal: They were on the saddle between the mountain's North and South Peaks. But the great cone of the main South Peak rose some 2,000 feet directly ahead—beckoning.

Washburn and his team members, all of whom had reached the summit of the mountain on previous trips, kept going. Four hours later they stood on the crest once more, taking in a panorama that stretched some 400 miles from horizon to horizon. To Robert Tatum, who had made his first ascent of the mountain in 1913, "It was like looking out the very windows of heaven."

Washburn, however, still had work to do. He wanted to make the world's first large-scale map of McKinley. "Except for the thrill of surveying from the top of McKinley," he has written, "the most exciting experience with the mountain came in July 1960, when I watched my map of Mount McKinley roll off the presses in Switzerland."

Another large-scale Washburn map—one of the Grand Canyon—earned him and Barbara the Society's Alexander Graham Bell Medal for "unique and notable contributions to geography and cartography." The 1988 map of Everest—a lifelong dream for Washburn—remains the most meticulously detailed and accurate large-scale map of a high Himalayan region ever produced. It is yet another legacy of a notable explorer and his long and successful association with National Geographic. As recently as 1999 Washburn's research led to an increase in the official elevation of Mount Everest: now 29,035 feet.

EVEREST, ARENA FOR HEROICS

FOR MOUNTAINEERS EVERYWHERE, Mount Everest is the crowning target, the ultimate goal. Before Edmund Hillary and Tenzing Norgay first reached its summit in May 1953, it had defeated seven major earlier expeditions. Since that time it has brought other victories and many defeats. As of 1998, there have been 916 ascents and 146 deaths.

John Hunt, leader of the triumphant British team in 1953, called climbing Mount Everest "the epitome of adventure and high endeavor." It remains so to this day, capturing the imagination of the entire world.

Hunt's words were given at the White House in 1954, during a presentation of the Society's Hubbard Medal to Everest's conquerors. The next day, the heroes delivered Everest lectures to record Society audiences. Millions of readers, traveling in the GEOGRAPHIC armchair, experienced the Everest saga in the magazine's July issue, which

Weary victors: Sherpa Tenzing Norgay and New Zealander Edmund Hillary relax at Camp VII (altitude 24,000 feet), after making their historic first ascent of Everest on May 29, 1953.

featured accounts by both Hillary and Hunt, as well as photographs by other members of the expedition.

The climb that transformed Hillary from an obscure beekeeper into one of the

Part of the most detailed map ever drawn of the Mount Everest area, this Bradford Washburn creation shows relief features with amazing accuracy. Supported by a Society grant, Washburn spearheaded the project, which converted and digitized stereo photographs from the space shuttle *Columbia* and aerials taken from a Learjet into conventional contour lines. The map appeared as a supplement to the November 1988 NATIONAL GEOGRAPHIC. As a result of these surveys, the great mountain's elevation was recalculated at 29,035 feet—7 feet higher than officially recognized for 45 years.

MOUNT EVEREST
8850 m
(29035 ft)

Bei Peak

South Col

Lhotse

Lhotse Shar

Peak 38

Conqueror of Everest, Edmund Hillary unwinds at Base Camp after his historic climb, chronicled by him in the July 1954 GEOGRAPHIC. He recalled that, on reaching the summit, he felt no great elation—"just relief and a sense of wonder."

archetypal heroes of the 20th century was a landmark in mountaineering.

Fifteen expedition members, a brigade of 450 porters, and 34 Sherpa climbers set out across the Himalaya on foot, trekking the 175 miles from Kathmandu to the staging area at the monastery of Thyangboche.

Once Base Camp was established at 17,900 feet, the really grueling work began—lugging supplies up the mountain and setting up a series of higher and higher camps.

On the big day, May 29, Tenzing and Hillary—each carrying 30 pounds of oxygen gear—made their way from Camp IX up the crest of the Southeast Ridge, a spine of snow and rock rising abruptly from the South Col to the summit. On a stretch of what Hillary called "appalling steepness" the snow was loose and unstable and would not pack into place. An ice ax merely sank in, affording no support. Only a thin crust of frozen snow held it all together.

Hillary was forcing his way up with deep steps, when suddenly large sections of crust all around him broke off and slid, as he did. He managed to stop—while the crust gathered speed and slid out of sight. Hillary forged on. Again and again the fragile crust gave way, and he sank through up to his knees, sometimes backsliding. At any moment the whole slope might have avalanched. But he said to himself, "Ed, my boy, this is Everest; you've got to push harder! On Everest you sometimes have to take the long odds."

His climbing partner Tenzing, who was

on his sixth Everest expedition, also considered the conditions, "very bad, very dangerous." But he also was prepared to go on.

From the dome of South Peak, 300 feet below the real pinnacle, the Southeast Ridge narrowed, and the climbers moved along a knife-edge of hard snow, flanked on either side by immense drops.

To the left, rock cliffs fell away 8,000 feet to the Western Cwm; on the right, wind-carved cornices overhung the precipitous east face, "only waiting," Hillary later wrote, "for the careless foot of the mountaineer to break them off and crash 10,000 feet to the Kangshung Glacier in Tibet."

But Everest's snows and crags are just a few of its hazards, for the air here is dangerously thin. At 28,000 feet, air has only a third as much oxygen as it does at sea level. The resulting oxygen deprivation causes insomnia, headache, sore throat, nausea, diarrhea, loss of appetite, and a debilitating shortness of breath. Above 25,000 feet lies the so-called Death Zone, where the human physiology becomes so oxygen-starved that it starts to deteriorate; both body and brain slow down.

Yet on they climbed, the soft crunch of ice axes and boots the only sound in the vast silence. Hillary began to wonder "rather dully" how long he could continue chipping steps into an endless series of hummocks.

Finally after more than five hours, the ridge ahead simply dropped away in a great cor-niced curve, and there was nothing above. Nothing on the whole planet.

EVEREST CONTINUES TO BECKON

IN YEARS TO COME, OTHERS WHO REACHED the summit would cry like babies; some would laugh and cry at the same time. Some would fall on their knees and pray.

Hillary's first sensation was one of relief and a vague sense of astonishment—that he and Tenzing should be the lucky ones to attain the ambition of so many brave and determined climbers.

Since that day in 1953, mountaineers of many nations have applied new equipment and new techniques and have pioneered other routes to the top of the world. One of the most dramatic accomplishments involved

Thomas Hornbein and Willi Unsoeld, of the 1963 American Expedition to Everest—the same one in which Barry Bishop participated. Hornbein and Unsoeld made history by completing a first ascent of the mountain's West Ridge, then traversing the mountain, and coming down the South Col route that Hillary and Tenzing had used.

The two paused only 15 minutes on the summit, for the sun was low. Heading down toward South Col in a slow, precarious descent, they came upon two blotches in the darkness—team members Barry Bishop and Lute Jerstad, who would bivouac with them during the long night ahead.

The October 1981 NATIONAL GEOGRAPHIC covered yet another dramatic chapter in the Everest story—Reinhold Messner's ascent in 1980. It was the first successful solo climb of the mountain, made without supplementary oxygen or any support team. Two years earlier, Messner and Peter Habeler had made the first ascent of Everest without bottled oxygen. In his solitary push for the summit, Messner was seeking to break still another physical and mental barrier.

Messner compares a solo climber to a snail carrying his home on his back, moving slowly and steadily upward. No relays. No ferrying up of supplies. No supplemental oxygen.

On only the second day of his Everest solo, he found himself wading through snow so deep and soft that he was becoming exhausted. He contemplated a faster, alternate route, one that recently had been swept clear of fresh snow by an avalanche.

Although he knew the slope was dangerous, he felt it was worth trying. As he recalls, "It was my only chance."

After another night, camping on relatively snowfree stretches, he began to have difficulty breathing. The intervals between rest pauses became shorter and shorter. "I climbed instinctively, not consciously.… I still do not know how I managed to achieve the summit. I only know that I couldn't have gone on any longer.… I was at my limit."

He paused on the summit only long enough to document his visit with photographs, then descended.

Messner is part of a generation of climbers who question the validity of using supplementary oxygen on climbs, contending that unaided ascents are a truer test of a climber's strength and endurance. By using supplemental oxygen, Messner believes, climbers are no longer climbing a mountain but are bringing its summit down to their level.

Messner has climbed all 14 of the world's 8,000-meter peaks (that is, taller than 26,240 feet) without the use of bottled oxygen. As of 1999, only five other mountaineers have achieved that goal.

Now 39-year-old Edmund Viesturs, of Seattle, seeks to add his name to that list. Currently considered by many to be America's strongest high-altitude climber, he has already completed ascents on 12 of the 14 mountains.

Multicolored tree of prayer flags rises above a traditional shrine at Everest Base Camp, as a pair of ravens—believed by Sherpas to bear omens—soar above. Summit-bound climbers of all faiths continue to perform ritual ceremonies at such sites, in hopes of propitiating the gods.

Two of those climbs were supported by the Society's recently established Exploration Council. Concentrating on adventure-oriented projects, the Council endorses expeditions that reflect America's enthusiasm for the outdoors and fascination with extreme sports.

"I'm climbing for enjoyment, but I also want to challenge myself," says Viesturs, who has no intention of getting in over his head. "I turned back 300 feet from the summit of Everest one time in '87 when I ran out of time—and rope. But climbing is also a very clear look inward. I want to show how the body and mind can be pushed to extreme physical and physiological limits at very high altitudes."

Ed Viesturs is living proof that interest in scaling Everest and other extreme peaks has not flagged, despite the fact that they are less mysterious today, since they have been climbed numerous times and have been mapped in great detail.

The lure of Everest remains as compelling and inspiring today as it was when the legendary British climber George Leigh Mallory, whose body was discovered on Everest in 1999, first developed his mystic attachment to the mountain nearly eight decades ago. Surely the thrill and satisfaction of meeting and overcoming such challenges will continue to entice adventurers to experience first-hand the lay of the land, whether in alpine peaks or the far reaches of an underground grotto.

They each seek out their own Everest to climb, as Mallory so poignantly said, "Because it is there."

THE TARR-MARTIN ALASKA EXPEDITIONS

Probing the icepack of Alaska's Disenchantment Bay by whaleboat, the 1910 expedition led by Ralph S. Tarr and Lawrence Martin monitored glacial fluctuations and mapped numerous glaciers. Under the auspices of the Society, the pioneering glaciologists mounted two other expeditions, in 1909 and 1911, which explored glaciers of the Lower Copper River and Prince William Sound areas. Their findings, published in 1914 by the Society as *Alaskan Glacier Studies*, helped pierce the mystery of North America's Ice Age and would guide glacial research for decades.

THE AMERICAN K2 EXPEDITION

Jim Whittaker, first American to stand atop Everest, led the milestone 1978 first American ascent of the world's second-tallest mountain: K2, on the Pakistan-China border. Payday finds Whittaker (below, in cap), Jim Wickwire, and Rick Ridgeway counting out wages for the expedition's 350 porters. Their route included a traverse of the knife-edged Northeast Ridge (opposite) to minimize avalanche danger. As with most mountains of size, the greatest hazard was not terrain but weather; storm after storm blasted the Americans on their way to the 28,250-foot summit. Ridgeway, returning from his ascent, earns a hug from teammate Diana Jagersky (bottom).

SKI TREK OF MOUNT MCKINLEY

On cross-country skis in the shadow of Mount McKinley, also known as Denali—"the Great One"—in 1978, a four-man team takes 19 days to trek completely around North America's highest peak. This historic adventure marked the first successful circuit of the mountain since Frederick A. Cook completed a wider orbit in 1903. In his July 1979 article, author-photographer Ned Gillette reported on the challenging spectrum of snow conditions the team faced as it traveled from sunlight to shadow—and went from deep powder to "mashed potatoes" to ice.

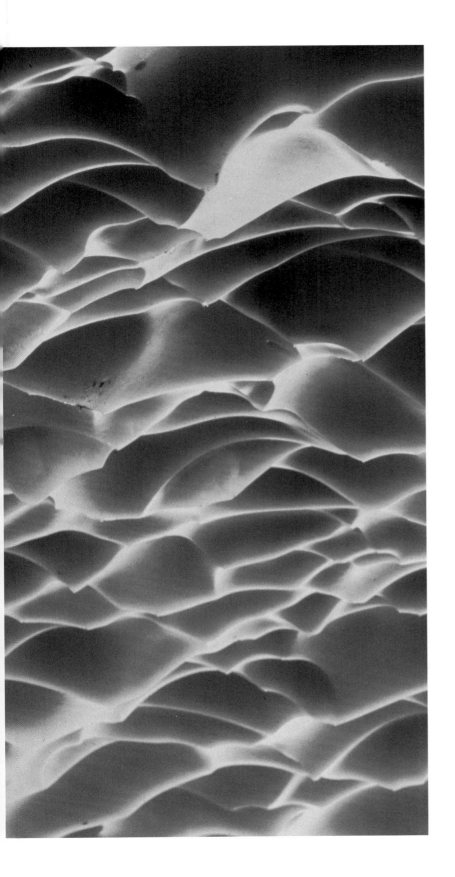

High on nature, Stefan Geissler (left) uses ice screws and other gear to negotiate the roof of a glacier cave in southern Germany. On another expedition into the same cave, Daniel Jehle (below) scales a massive icicle known as a frozen waterfall with ice tools, his carbide headlamp emitting a yellowish beam. Unlike terrestrial grottoes, ice caves often are suffused with natural light far from their entrances—the deep blue glow of sunlight refracted through ice. The two ice climbers appeared in the February 1996 NATIONAL GEOGRAPHIC.

EXPEDITION TO QUEEN MAUD LAND, ANTARCTICA

Driven to climb where no one ever climbed before, one member of a six-man mountaineering team hauls himself up the face of a rocky prong half again as high as the World Trade Center. Known as Rakekniven—"Razor" in Norwegian—this and other challenging peaks can be scaled by first securing climbing ropes to metal cams that have been inserted into natural cracks in the rock. The group's gravity-defying adventure explored landscapes "so alien we felt as if we should be wearing space suits," recalls author Jon Krakauer in the February 1998 GEOGRAPHIC.

TO THE ENDS OF THE EARTH

WHAT THE ICE TAKES, THE ICE KEEPS.

—POLAR EXPLORER ERNEST SHACKLETON

BY KIM HEACOX

"Polar exploration," wrote Apsley Cherry-Garrard, "is at once the cleanest and most isolated way of having a bad time which has been devised."

A member of Robert Falcon Scott's ill-fated final expedition to the South Pole, Cherry-Garrard was among those who found Scott and two other countrymen frozen to death in their tent on the Ross Ice Shelf in November 1912. For seven months and fourteen days, the three frozen men had lain in silent testimony to every mistake and piece of bad luck that had doomed them. Low on food and pinned down by a gale, Scott had presided over their slow suffering, writing these words, entitled "Message to the Public": "I do not think human beings ever came through such a month as we have come through.... I do not regret this journey, which has shown that Englishmen can endure hardships, help one another, and meet death with as great a fortitude as ever in the past."

The tough Norwegian, Roald Amundsen, had beaten Scott to the South Pole by nearly five weeks and had proved himself a more capable polar explorer, but Scott became the larger hero. He had failed with flair, while Amundsen had succeeded with silence. "The world largely saw the tale through Scott's eyes," wrote British biographer Roland Huntford. "His diaries were rapidly published and, quite simply, he was a better writer than Amundsen. Amundsen lacked the power of advocacy. He was too much the man of action; like so many of his kind, he squandered his talent on his deeds. Living the moment so intensely, he was denied the surplus energy to convey it to others."

Nearly seven decades before Scott's death, another Englishman, Sir John Franklin, had disappeared in the Arctic with two barque-rigged sailing ships and his entire crew—128 men—in search of the Northwest Passage, the fabled sea route over the top of North America. For a dozen years other expeditions had searched for Franklin and found only scant evidence of what happened. "It was not the British Navy that discovered the final truth about the lost ships," wrote Canadian historian Pierre Berton. "It was a private expedition, launched and paid for by the dead explorer's indomitable widow."

With Franklin's ships apparently crushed by ice, and Franklin himself already dead, his starving men had pulled heavy sledges over sea ice and tundra until they collapsed in their harnesses. Unable to go on, they shut their eyes and fell asleep, never to wake up. Franklin of the Arctic and Scott of the Antarctic—each would become a benchmark of disaster, a mantra in the ears of every polar explorer who followed: "It could happen to you."

The Poles offered neither hostile natives nor strange diseases but rather the raw elements of ice, wind, and bitter cold—a trackless, mapless icescape brilliant in summer's light, brooding in winter's dark.

By dogsled, foot, and ski, and later by snowmachine, airplane, and submarine, explorers sought to discover routes to the Poles. While early expeditions focused on national

Previous pages: With flags flying like laundry at the top of the world, Japanese explorer Naomi Uemura celebrates his solo arrival in 1978, at the North Pole, history's first. The four flags represent the countries that helped support his trek: Canada, Denmark, the United States, and Japan.

competition, later ones, such as the crossing of Antarctica by the American Will Steger and five other men from five other countries, focused on international cooperation, in keeping with what Steger called "the world's new awakening." As with so much of exploration, it wasn't geography they tested so much as themselves, the human condition, the reach that may exceed the grasp. Some went alone; others moderated the adversity with comradeship, forging friendships that 50 years later would be the most important in their lives.

"And I tell you," Cherry-Garrard wrote, "if you have the desire for knowledge and the power to give it physical expression, go out and explore. If you are a brave man you will do nothing: if you are fearful you may do much, for none but cowards have need to prove their bravery. Some will tell you that you are mad, and nearly all will say: 'What is the use?' For we are a nation of shopkeepers, and no shopkeeper will look at research which does not promise him a financial return within a year. And so you will sledge nearly alone, but those with whom you sledge will not be shopkeepers: that is worth a good deal."

Too late at the bottom of the world, Englishman Robert Falcon Scott's expedition attains the South Pole in January 1912. only to find Roald Amundsen's abandoned tent. The Norwegian had beaten them by 33 days. Scott's entire group froze to death on the return journey.

ROBERT FALCON SCOTT

Looking like fraternity brothers in a dormitory, members of Scott's *Terra Nova* Expedition (left) savor various creature comforts in their snug pre-fabricated winter quarters at Antarctica's Ross Island, as they await spring and their final assault on the South Pole. Expedition photographer Herbert Ponting clowns for his own camera (below), while a pair of spiked sealskin overboots (bottom) makes for a detached and pristine still-life.

AMUNDSEN ACROSS THE NORTHWEST PASSAGE

IT IS ODD THAT ROALD AMUNDSEN'S first hero was John Franklin, a former governor from Australia; for everything that Franklin did wrong, Amundsen did right. Franklin suffered and starved, while Amundsen—by his meticulous planning and methodical action—made polar travel look easy, so easy in fact that not until decades after he died would he achieve the stature he deserved. A professional among amateurs, Amundsen was called "the last of the Vikings."

As a teenager in Norway in the 1880s, he discovered Franklin's accounts of starvation in Arctic Canada and said they "thrilled me as nothing I had ever read before." For 300 years men had sought a sea route over the top of North America, and now young Amundsen, a boreal boy who disliked football but loved skiing, heard an inner voice that compelled him to find what the others could not: the Northwest Passage. Martin Frobisher, Henry Hudson, John Franklin, Edward Parry, and John Ross all had attempted and failed. All had set the stage. "The idealism of youth," Amundsen wrote, "which often takes a turn toward martyrdom, found its crusade in me in the form of Arctic exploration."

Though he admired Franklin, Amundsen had no intention to emulate him. Franklin had needlessly died in the high latitudes, ignorant of so much. Amundsen instead learned about Arctic ice dynamics from whalers and about Eskimos from the great Norwegian explorer, Fridtjof Nansen, who had skied across Greenland in 1888. He learned how to treat dogs, ration food, and respect a crew, and how to ski and sledge with efficiency.

In June 1903, at age 31, he departed Norway with seven men in a 70-foot-long square-sterned walrus sloop, the *Gjöa*, equipped with a small gas engine, five years of provisions, and sundry instruments for making geomagnetic and other scientific observations.

He stopped in Greenland to pick up huskies and by late August arrived at Beechey Island, John Franklin's last known wintering place. Onward down Peel Strait into Franklin Strait, he approached the north magnetic pole and found his compass utterly useless. Providence greeted him with open lanes through

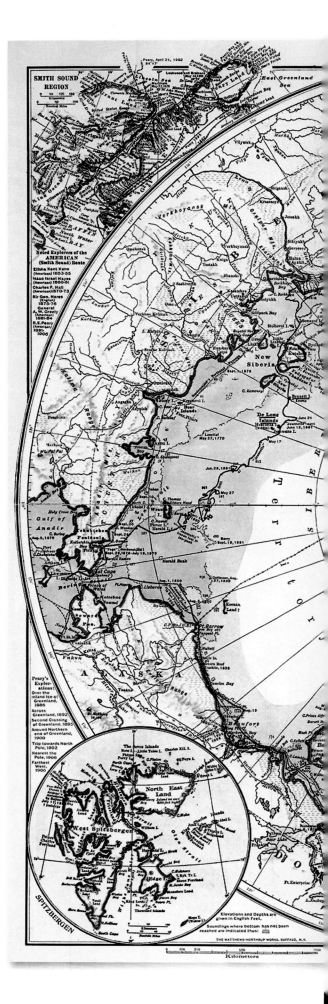

Supplement to the National Geographic Magazine, July 1907, Washington, D.C.

The National Geographic Magazine
Map of
THE NORTH POLE REGIONS
Prepared by
GILBERT H. GROSVENOR, Editor.

Goal of explorers for centuries, the legendary Northwest Passage lured the likes of Martin Frobisher, Henry Hudson, John Franklin, and many others with the promise of a commercial shortcut to the Orient. Franklin died. All others were forced by ice to turn back, until Roald Amundsen successfully sailed from the Atlantic to the Pacific through the Arctic Ocean in 1903-05. His triumph, however, established that the ice-choked "passage" would never become a commercially viable shipping lane.

NGM 1907

the pack ice, where in other years passage would have been impossible. The *Gjöa* made good progress.

On the last day of August 1903, with winter closing around the expedition, the engine room caught fire next to 2,200 gallons of oil. Working efficiently as a team, the crew doused the flames. The next day they fetched up hard on a reef and discarded 10,000 pounds of dog food to refloat the little boat. A gale slammed her into a rock and splintered her false keel, and the crew made ready the lifeboats. But a wave picked them up and carried them over the reef to deep water. Thereafter, Amundsen always stationed one man in the crow's nest and another on the prow.

For two winters and a summer they stayed in a snug embayment on King William Island—a spot Amundsen called Gjöa Haven—and met a band of Eskimos. Amundsen found them a delight and described them as among the cheeriest people in the world. They taught Amundsen and his crew how to build snow houses and treat frostbite and make animal-skin clothing, perfect for Arctic travel—skills that would one day enable him to reach the South Pole before any other man.

That interim summer, Amundsen resumed his explorations and discovered that the north magnetic pole had moved 30 miles from where James Clark Ross had located it some 60 years before, proving what many had suspected: that the magnetic poles migrate.

In August 1905 the coast was ice free and Amundsen zigzagged the *Gjöa* westward through Queen Maud Gulf and Coronation Gulf, rock-infested stretches of uncharted water. Two weeks later his crew sighted whaling ships that had come from the Pacific, and

Amundsen, a stolid man, felt an uncharacteristic lump in his throat. He had crossed the Northwest Passage, proving that it did indeed exist and that it was not a practical commercial route for large ships. Only by going small and slow, only by learning from those who called the region home, had he accomplished what larger, impatient expeditions had not.

In November he traveled 500 to 700 miles by ski and snowshoe to Eagle, Alaska, to telegraph the news of his success. NATIONAL GEOGRAPHIC reported that the people of Eagle were startled to learn that a man "who came in on snowshoes" said he had "come from Europe via the Arctic Ocean. Not until the outside world identified him by telegraph would they believe it was Amundsen."

Two years later, on December 14, 1907, Amundsen received the National Geographic's highest honor, the Hubbard Medal. The Norwegian offered his gratitude and acknowledged among the members "many brilliant gentlemen, famous for achievement in scientific research. I see here tonight one who I think I can say is the most excellent of the scientific explorers in the United States—in fact the most experienced scientific Arctic traveler of the day—Commander Robert E. Peary."

The applause was no doubt enthusiastic, as Amundsen's comments showed careful diplomacy. He and Peary burned with equal desire but were, in fact, very different kinds of explorers. Each knew the other by reputation only. And each knew another explorer, Ernest Shackleton, who on that very evening was in New Zealand, en route to Antarctica, hoping that he, not Amundsen or Peary, would be the first man to claim one of the Earth's great geographic Poles.

SHACKLETON'S FARTHEST SOUTH

"THE END IS IN SIGHT," a tired Ernest Shackleton wrote in his diary on January 4, 1909. "We can only go for three more days at the most, for we are weakening rapidly. Short food and a blizzard wind from the south, with driving drift, at a temperature of 47° of frost, have plainly told us today that we are reaching our limit, for we were so done up at noon with cold that the clinical thermometer failed to register the temperature of three of us at 94°."

More than a hundred miles from his prize, the South Pole, Shackleton knew he wouldn't make it. Not at this rate, not if he rationed food for the long march back for himself and his three companions. They could eat it all now, of course, and reach the Pole and die there, for death itself is not so bad as dying, and when dying in the Antarctic…you just close your eyes against the cold, slip into sleep, and never awaken. Perfect heroes, frozen

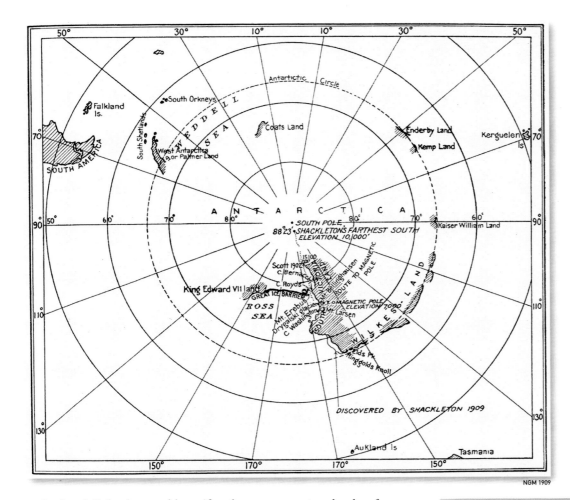

"Better a live donkey than a dead lion," muttered heroic polar explorer Ernest Shackleton (below, second from left) after aborting his 1908-09 *Nimrod* Expedition to reach the South Pole. He returned, barely alive, with (from left) Frank Wild, Dr. Eric Marshall, and Lt. Jameson Boyd Adams. The trip established a new "farthest south" of 88° 23' (left), eclipsed three years later when Roald Amundsen successfully pioneered a route to the Pole itself.

at the South Pole, they could sacrifice themselves and plant the Union Jack where no flag had ever flown.

But Shackleton was a husband and a father, an uncommon leader, and this would be a defining moment in a career of brilliant failures. His companions, like himself, had their whole lives before them. They were his men, his responsibility—their pathetic scarecrow faces, with eyes like bruises, watching him, trying to read his decisions. He could tell that Eric Marshall, the physician, was already upset with him that he had got them into this absurd position. They should have turned back days ago, on the Beardmore Glacier when they lost Socks, their last Manchurian pony. Since then, the four of them had done all the pulling, incarcerated in their harnesses, and it was killing them.

A storm whipped up and pinned them down for three days. When it cleared, they could go only a few more miles.

"We have shot our bolt," wrote Shackleton on January 9, his farthest south, less than a hundred miles from the bottom of the world. "While the Union Jack blew out stiffly in the icy gale that cut us to the bone, we looked south with our powerful glasses, but could see nothing but the dead white snow plain…. We

stayed only a few minutes, and then, taking the Queen's flag and eating our scanty meal as we went, we hurried back.…"

They had to cover 700 miles on a long torturous march back to the coast at Cape Royds, on Ross Island, where their little ship, the *Nimrod*,

waited. Shackleton had told his crew that if he didn't return by March 1, they should presume him dead and leave without him and the others, leave before winter's ice entrapped everyone for nine long months.

"I do not know how [Shackleton] stands it," wrote Frank Wild, a companion, "both his heels are split in four or five places, his legs are bruised and chafed, and today he has had a violent headache…and yet he gets along.…"

Down the Beardmore Glacier and across the Ross Ice Shelf they staggered and stumbled. When Wild grew weak with dysentery, Shackleton offered him his only breakfast

Colossal challenges beset Shackleton's legendary *Endurance* Expedition of 1914-16. Towering icebergs slowed the ship (left), while freezing leads trapped and eventually destroyed it. Shackleton and five others boldly set out from Antarctica's Elephant Island (below) crossing some 800 miles of stormy sea by dinghy and dead reckoning as they navigated to South Georgia Island and then mounted a rescue mission for team members who had remained in Antarctica. Frank Hurley's sketch of the "snuggery" (bottom) on Elephant Island reveals sleeping arrangements for the marooned explorers, improvised from two overturned boats. Amazingly, all survived the ordeal.

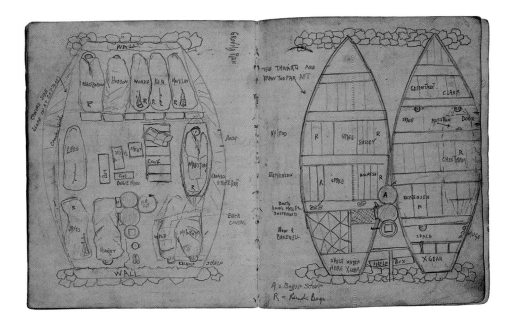

biscuit; Wild wrote in his diary, "I do not suppose that anyone else in the world can thoroughly realise how much generosity and sympathy was shown by this...."

They reached the *Nimrod* with no time to spare, and the elated crew was taken aback by Shackleton's haggard appearance. He and the others looked like the living dead. They hadn't reached the Pole, but others from the *Nimrod*—Douglas Mawson, Edgeworth David, and Alistair Mackay—had reached the south magnetic pole.

Upon arriving back in England, Shackleton told his wife, Emily, that he thought she'd prefer a live donkey rather than a dead lion.

In a few short years he'd be ready to return, but by that time both Poles would have been claimed and Shackleton would propose something even more outrageous, a crossing of the Antarctic continent by sled dog, foot, and ski. Then as before, in his own incomparable style, he would both fail and succeed, and not until the late 1950s would men actually cross the white continent.

ROBERT PEARY TO THE NORTH POLE

IN 1891 GARDINER GREENE HUBBARD, first President of the young National Geographic Society, strode across a stage in front of Society members and presented the Stars and Stripes to Robert E. Peary, and said to the ambitious man, "Now take this flag and place it as far north on this planet as you possibly can!"

Peary did just that. Over the next four years he made two major expeditions to northern Greenland, naming that region Peary Land. He had attempted to cross the Greenland ice cap at its widest point in 1886 and made little more than a hundred miles—what he later called a "reconnaissance." "But it was not in his nature to countenance failure," wrote historian Pierre Berton. "In all of Peary's Arctic adventures, he always managed to emerge with some trophy, real or imagined, that would carry with it the aura of success."

Greenland was merely a prelude, as Peary wanted to possess the North Pole, the prize that had always possessed him. "Remember, Mother," he wrote home after that first journey north, "I *must* have fame." In 1898, back in

As if daring the camera to stand between himself and fame, Robert Peary strikes a pose prior to making his final assault on the North Pole.

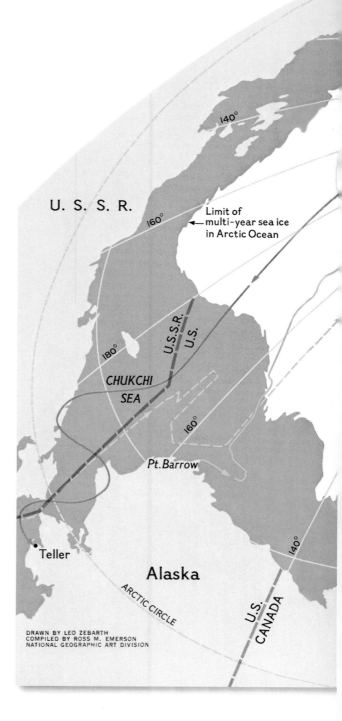

Murmansk
Vadsø
70°
Novaya
Zemlya
BARENTS
SEA
Svalbard
(NORWAY)
Franz Josef Land
(U.S.S.R.)
Spitsbergen
U.S.S.R.
80°
Kongsfjorden
0°
GREENLAND SEA

ARKTIKA
1977
BYRD
1926
SKATE
1959
North Pole
NORGE
1926
UEMURA
1978
HERBERT
1969
PEARY
1909
GREENLAND
(DENMARK)
PLAISTED
1968
Alert
Cape Columbia
Ward Hunt I.
766 air kilometers
to the North Pole
NAUTILUS
1958
Ellesmere
Island
Thule

80°
BAFFIN
BAY
Islands
Queen Elizabeth
Devon Island
Limit of
multi-year sea ice
in Arctic Ocean
Melville Island
Resolute
Baffin Island
A
BEAUFORT SEA
Banks
Island
C   A   N   A   D
Air supply base
for Uemura
Victoria Island
100°
120°
70°
ARCTIC CIRCLE

NGM 1978

Who really was first at the North Pole? The debate continues even today, as scholars question the credibility of Peary's claim to have made an incredibly rapid "sprint to the Pole" in 1909. Byrd's farthest north, reported in 1926, also has been criticized. As early as the 1820s, England began setting its sights on achieving the nearly mythical Pole. "The race to succeed," writes historian Pierre Berton, "took on some of the aspects of an international sporting event. How humiliating it would be for England if a mariner from another nation—a Russian, perhaps, or an upstart American—should get there first and seize the prize!" British Admiralty bureaucrat John Barrow, Jr., encouraged early polar interest by mistakenly advising that the high Arctic consisted of an ice-free "Open Polar Sea." It would take many expeditions and sacrifices to prove Barrow wrong.

Constantly shifting winds and currents cause
Arctic pack ice to part and collide, creating
tortuous pressure ridges such as the one Peary's
team negotiated in 1909 (right). Like the Norwegians Nansen and Amundsen, Peary and Matthew
Henson (below) benefited from contact with the
Inuit, who instructed them in the use of animal
skins and furs and how to prevent frostbite and
snow blindness. In Greenland, Peary's wife,
Josephine, swaddles daughter Marie in an
American flag (bottom).

Contributing to high spirits on the way to the Pole, Eskimo girls dance across the main deck of Peary's expeditionary ship, the *Roosevelt*, as it steams north to Canada's Ellesmere Island in 1908.

Greenland yet again, pushing north, always north, he lost eight toes to frostbite. Then in 1906, on his fourth try, he reached to within 175 miles of the Pole, the farthest north for any man. Back in Washington that December, President Theodore Roosevelt presented him with the Society's first Hubbard Medal. "The true explorer," Peary told the large audience, "does his work not for any hope of rewards or honor, but because the thing he has set himself to do is a part of his very being, and must be accomplished for the sake of accomplishment.…"

Little more than two years later, in early 1909 while Shackleton retreated from his attempt on the South Pole, Peary was northbound again. He established a base camp at Cape Columbia, at the northern tip of Ellesmere Island, and pushed on. He exhausted his support parties, letting them carry the greatest loads so the final polar team could be fresh and strong. On April 1 the last support party turned back, leaving Peary, his sledger Matthew Henson, 4 Eskimos, and 40 dogs to cover 133 miles, allegedly reaching the Pole on April 6, 1909. "The Pole at last!!!" Peary exulted. "The prize of 3 centuries, my dream and ambition for 23 years. *Mine* at last.…" After taking photographs and observations for 30 hours, the team retreated south and arrived at Cape Columbia in 16 days.

On September 8, Peary wired President William Howard Taft: "Have honor to place North Pole at your disposal." "Thanks for your generous offer," responded the President. "I do not know exactly what I could do with it. I congratulate you sincerely on having achieved, after the greatest effort, the object of your trip.…" The Pennsylvania farm boy who had grown up fatherless and attended Bowdoin College but lived off campus with his doting mother, who preferred hiking in the woods to organized sports, and who married the daughter of a Smithsonian scholar—now a man in his early 50s, had gained a place in a pantheon with Magellan and Columbus. "I am not entirely selfish, mother," he once wrote. "I want my fame *now* while you too can enjoy it."

Such fierce ambition can sometimes blind a man, and as the decades passed and discrepancies and inconsistencies appeared in Peary's story, people began to ask, quietly at first, then openly, if he had indeed really reached the North Pole. The Society enlisted Wally Herbert, a veteran of 13 years of polar exploration, to investigate Peary's claim. In the National Archives Herbert found blank pages in Peary's diary. "Mine at last," was not written in the diary, but on a separate sheet of paper, as if added later. In fact, Herbert noted, in the September 1988 GEOGRAPHIC, that the notebooks Peary used for his diary entries "offered absolutely no record of his activities during the 30 hours he and his companions spent in the vicinity of the North Pole.… The central issue—did Peary reach the North Pole or not; did he, in fact, tell the truth—seems straight enough. But I would find no simple yes or no, for the story of Peary's last expedition exposes a far more human conflict and a far more human hero than previously realized."

The Society also asked the Navigation Foundation, a group devoted to preserving the art of navigation, to study all the evidence of Peary's claim and draw its independent conclusion. That foundation spent a year examining the data, employing various analytical methods, including close-range photogrammetric analysis of Peary's photographs and digital mapping of his ocean depth soundings. The results led the foundation board members to unanimously agree that Peary had "reached the near vicinity of the North Pole." The January 1990 issue of the GEOGRAPHIC ran a description of the study and a final report.

Nevertheless, for Robert E. Peary, the tragedy is—and always will be—the uncertainty of his achievement. Regardless of the questions that still hover around Peary's alleged achievement, Herbert for one still found Peary admirable in his determination and fortitude and concluded that "he extended the bounds of human endeavor."

ADMIRAL OF THE ENDS OF THE EARTH

"WHAT THE ROUND EARTH WAS to Columbus, what circumnavigation of the globe was to Magellan, polar exploration was to Richard Evelyn Byrd," wrote Melville Bell Grosvenor, Editor of the NATIONAL GEOGRAPHIC and President of the Society. "If Columbus was Admiral of the Ocean Sea, Byrd, first man to fly over both Poles, was Admiral of the Ends of the Earth." Grosvenor wrote those words in 1957, more than 30 years after Byrd began his polar career. How absurd it seemed back in the mid-1920s that a man could fly to the North Pole.

But in 1926, a year before the name Charles Lindbergh was on the lips of everyone in America and Europe, Richard Byrd did just that: he and copilot Floyd Bennett made the first successful flight over the North Pole.

"What are you going to do next?" Roald Amundsen asked him on his triumphant return to New York. "Fly over the South Pole," Byrd replied. Amundsen nodded. "Take a good plane, take plenty of dogs and take only the best men."

Byrd did—and wasted no time. In 1928, the year he turned 40, he organized and led a 14-month expedition to Antarctica, taking with him 95 dogs, more than 50 men, and 3 planes specially outfitted for polar conditions. He established his base camp, Little America, on the Ross Ice Shelf, not far from the Bay of Whales, where Amundsen had made his base in 1911-12.

While reconnoitering in the Rockefeller Mountains, one of Byrd's teams, under the command of Laurence Gould, became pinned down by a gale. A 100-mph wind lifted their plane from its tethered mooring—screwed into the ice—and sent it flying backwards for 900 yards, smashing it. Gould and his men were about to attempt a walk back to Little America when they heard Byrd flying in to rescue them.

Winter found everyone safe in chambers beneath the snow and the planes in deep pits covered with tarpaulins. Byrd wrote, "Blizzards…pounded the surface, and the darkness above us was a never ending cyclone of sound and drift, [but] we were snug below. Time didn't drag; for we never lacked plenty to do."

They planned their assault on the Pole. The following austral spring, in November 1929, while Wall Street began its long steep spiral into economic depression, four men—Bernt Balchen, pilot; Richard Byrd, navigator; Harold June, radio operator; and Ashley McKinley, photographer, lifted off the ice, southbound in the Ford trimotor *Floyd Bennett.*

Visibility was poor at first, like flying inside a bottle of milk. Over the Ross Ice Shelf and up the Liv Glacier through the Transantarctic Mountains, the plane rocked and bounced against the wind. The wings rattled; the engine screamed. At the top of the glacier, more than 10,000 feet above sea level, the controls went slack, and Balchen shouted to Byrd that they were too heavy; they'd have to drop cargo or turn around.

Out went a bag of food, then another, as the plane nosed over the top with what seemed like only inches to spare. They reached the Pole, flew around it for just 11 minutes, and returned home safely. In just under 16 hours Byrd had covered the same distance that had taken Roald Amundsen three months, turned back Ernest Shackleton, and killed Robert Falcon Scott.

Byrd's article, "The Conquest of Antarctica by Air," appeared in the August 1930 issue of NATIONAL GEOGRAPHIC, two months after President Hoover presented him with the Society's Special Gold Medal of Honor.

"To an ordinary man," reflected Melville Bell Grosvenor, "successful first flights over both Poles might have been enough. Byrd could easily have basked in glory. The Congress of the United States honored him by promoting him to Rear Admiral on the Retired List; book publishers, magazines, and lecture agencies sought him out…. But to Byrd the vast unknown Antarctic Continent was irresistible, and in 1933 the second Byrd Antarctic Expedition got under way."

It nearly killed him. In the winter of 1934 he imprisoned himself in a weather station 123 miles south of Little America, an experiment in solitary winter confinement to test the effects of extreme isolation on the human

Visual relief from the monotonous landscape for Richard Byrd's ice party— bound for the South Pole soon after his North Pole flight— arrives off Antarctica in the form of a fin whale spy-hopping between floes.

Getting ashore: Richard Byrd's Arctic team off-loads his Fokker trimotor from a steamer and rafts it through ice-choked waters off the Norwegian island of Spitsbergen (left), from which the U.S. Navy lieutenant commander mounted his 1926 flight over the North Pole. Since magnetic compasses are useless at the Poles, Byrd and copilot Floyd Bennett navigated with the aid of a "sun compass" invented by Albert H. Bumstead, chief cartographer of the National Geographic Society. First Native American air guide in the Far North, the Eskimo known as In-you-gee-to (below) served with Peary in 1909 and helped assemble and maintain planes for polar aviator Byrd.

In 1929, only three years after his North Pole expedition, Richard Byrd flew over the South Pole. Expedition photographer Capt. Ashley McKinley captured a particularly haunting view of the polar continent during the perilous flight (right). When winds threatened to stall the plane, Byrd jettisoned food—but not fuel. The team reached the Pole, spent just 11 minutes circling it and charting their position, then headed back north to the comforts of Little America (below), the commander's base camp set up on the edge of the continent.

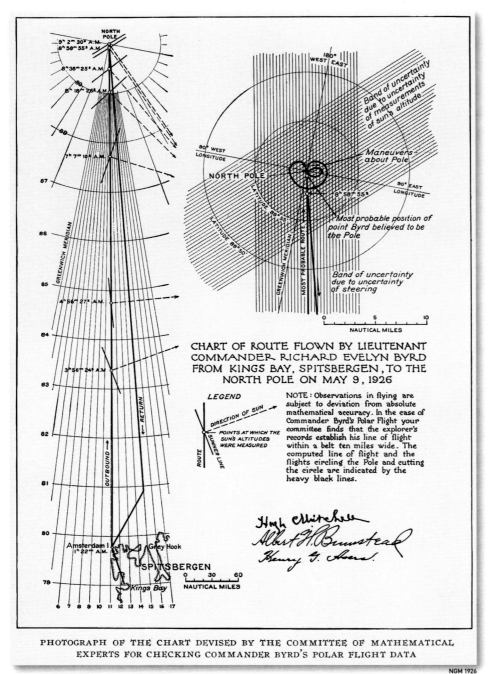

PHOTOGRAPH OF THE CHART DEVISED BY THE COMMITTEE OF MATHEMATICAL
EXPERTS FOR CHECKING COMMANDER BYRD'S POLAR FLIGHT DATA

NGM 1926

mind and body. The shack was too small for three men, and although two would have fit, Byrd believed that would be a mistake.

"In the woods it would be another story," he elaborated. "Even the trees are alive. There is noise in their rustling and from birds on their branches, and the call of the wild. The sun rises and sets. But two men living alone…jammed together in a silent, dark, dead, bitter cold environment, staring at each other for six months… Someone had to go… It seemed to be up to me." He went alone and posted a notice on the wall of the shack: "There will be no gossiping."

All went well until carbon monoxide, leaking from his stove, began to poison him. He didn't radio this to his men at Little America, concerned that they would attempt a dangerous rescue through the polar night. But his garbled words and weak voice betrayed him, and three men came in a Citroën tractor, arriving on August 10.

Seeing the eerie lights advance over the stygian blackness, Byrd stepped outside and said, "Hello, fellows. Come on below. I have a bowl of hot soup waiting for you."

Not for two months was he well enough to board a plane back to Little America, and from there back to big America. "I climbed the hatch and never looked back," he recalled. "Part of me remained forever at Latitude 80° 08' South: what survived of my youth, my vanity, perhaps, and certainly my skepticism. On the other hand, I did take away something that I had not fully possessed before: appreciation of the sheer beauty and miracle of being alive, and a humble set of values."

Flying straight as a line of longitude, Richard Byrd and Floyd Bennett wasted neither time nor geography making their aerial round-trip from Spitsbergen to the North Pole on May 9, 1926. This chart, published in the September 1926 NATIONAL GEOGRAPHIC, reflects the chart of their route.

ACROSS THE POLES BY SUBMARINE AND SNO-CAT

RICHARD BYRD LIVED ANOTHER 23 years after his 1934 expedition, dying in 1957, but polar exploration hardly died with him.

The so-called heroic age—the time of Amundsen, Shackleton, and Scott—surrendered to the mechanical age, when diesel dogs replaced sled dogs, and the throb of engines broke the eternal white silence; when polar regions served as cold labs to test not just human fortitude but also the latest inventions in transportation and communications.

In January 1959, NATIONAL GEOGRAPHIC

magazine reported: "Two of the greatest achievements in the annals of exploration marked the year 1958. They came within six months of each other, at opposite Poles of our planet. First a British Commonwealth expedition led by Dr. (now Sir) Vivian Fuchs succeeded in crossing the great white 2,000-mile-wide continent of Antarctica.

"Then the United States Navy's atomic submarine *Nautilus,* captained by Comdr. William R. Anderson, blazed a sea route from Pacific to Atlantic under the ice of the Arctic

Ocean. For the first time by land or sea, the ends of the earth had been crossed by way of the North and South Poles, a feat heretofore accomplished only by air."

The world's first atomic submarine, *Nautilus* cruised 1,839 nautical miles beneath the ice pack to transit the Arctic Ocean from Alaska to Greenland in only four days. As the crew approached the Pole on August 3, 1958, they turned the jukebox off and Commander Anderson announced that *Nautilus* was about to "accomplish two goals long sought by those who sail the seas. First, the opening of a route for rapid voyages between the great Pacific and Atlantic Oceans. Second, the attainment of the North Pole by ship."

"As we watched in awe," reported Lt. William G. Lalor, Jr., in NATIONAL GEOGRAPHIC, "our gyrocompasses swung, finally to point back to where we had been.... I asked how close we had come to the exact Pole."

"We pierced it," navigator Tom Curtis responded.

John Franklin would have been amazed. A northern passage by ship was indeed possible from Atlantic to Pacific, via the Pole no less, but by ships under the sea, not upon it, at a sounding of 13,410 feet. Lalor noted that *Nautilus* "carried 116 men in comfort that would have astounded the oak-tough individualists of past Arctic exploration."

More than 40 years earlier, in May 1916, a bedraggled Ernest Shackleton and two other men had walked into a whaling station on the remote island of South Georgia, stunning the Norwegians working there. Shackleton's wooden barkentine, *Endurance,* last seen in December 1914, was presumed lost at sea with all hands drowned, or dead on the Antarctic ice.

But here he was, alive, a miracle, and saying that all of his 25 castaways were alive and in need of rescue.

"When was the war over?" Shackleton asked, referring to the conflict in Europe that had begun in the unsettling summer of 1914; he assumed it had lasted only months.

"The war is not over," he was told. "Europe is mad. The world is mad."

Shackleton listened to reports of poison gas and Zeppelins and submarines, mankind's newest tools of mass destruction. Then he told his own story.

He had not crossed Antarctica from one end to the other as he'd planned; he hadn't even reached the mainland. *Endurance* had been crushed in the Weddell Sea pack ice, leaving him and his crew marooned, and only by a series of fantastic adventures—an epic story of leadership and survival—had he reached South Georgia.

Forty-two years later, he too would have been astounded by submarines beneath Arctic ice. While some of his crew lived long enough to hear of it, Shackleton did not.

He died of a heart attack in 1922 and was buried on South Georgia, according to his wife's wishes, for she knew the Antarctic

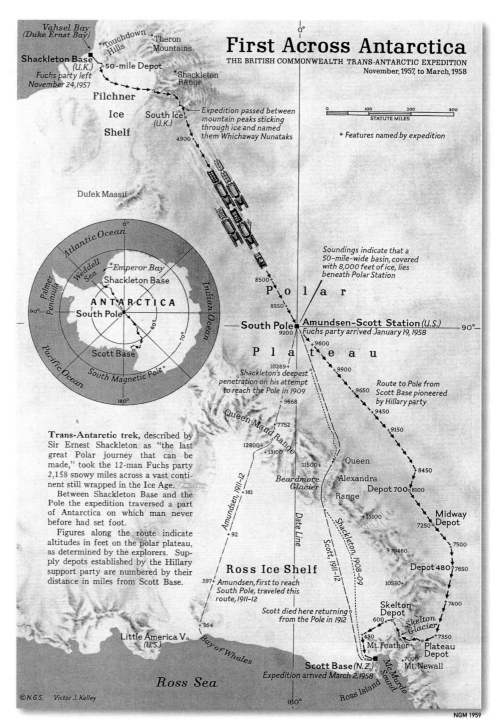

First Across Antarctica
THE BRITISH COMMONWEALTH TRANS-ANTARCTIC EXPEDITION
November, 1957, to March, 1958

* Features named by expedition

Modified tractors and Sno-Cats enabled Vivian Fuchs' Trans-Antarctic Expedition to traverse the continent in only 98 days (99 days due to crossing the date line) in 1957-58, 45 years after Shackleton's aborted attempt.

Arctic solitaire: Nuclear
submarine U.S.S. *Skate*
erupts through polar ice
pack 300 miles from the
North Pole in March 1959.
It surfaced at ten different
locations during its historic
voyage through the Arctic
Ocean, including at the Pole
itself on March 17, 1959.
The NATIONAL GEOGRAPHIC
published its story in July
of that year.

Comdr. William R. Anderson triumphantly strides the deck of the U.S.S. *Nautilus* after his ship became the first to reach the North Pole by navigating beneath the Arctic Ocean's icy surface. The 1958 feat earned Anderson the Legion of Merit, while his ship received the first Presidential Unit Citation ever awarded in peacetime.

tors, Vivian Fuchs, with assistance from Edmund Hillary, of Everest fame, crossed the white continent in 98 days (99 due to their having crossed the International Date Line).

It was a struggle the entire way, and at one point a Sno-Cat nearly disappeared into a crevasse. Fuchs reported that "the weather even at the height of summer was atrocious.... If these factors had affected Shackleton's party, his chances of success would have been small indeed. It may therefore be permissible to comment that the loss of *Endurance* may have saved a worse disaster."

It may have.

Shackleton never attained any of his geographical goals, but he never lost a man, he never lost hope, and these facts would inspire a whole new generation of explorers—Naomi Uemura, Reinhold Messner, Will Steger, and others—who found purity on dog sled and ski, muscling over the ice with nothing but stamina, determination, and wits.

had always been his first love.

While *Nautilus* planned its assault on the North Pole, another expedition, one perhaps closer to Shackleton's heart, crossed Antarctica, but not in the manner he had envisioned.

Using Sno-Cats and modified farm trac-

NAOMI UEMURA: SOLO NORTH

"THE SWEAT POURS FROM ME," wrote Naomi Uemura while tentbound on the Arctic ice, his sled dogs scattered and barking in the distance. "Outside I can hear the bear slashing through the food supplies—pemmican, frozen seal meat, a bucket of...whale oil. 'May he be satisfied with that!' I pray silently...."

But the polar bear isn't satisfied.

"Turning to the tent, he begins ripping at the flimsy nylon with his great claws and grunting loudly as I literally hold my breath. A new terror seizes me as the tent wall bulges inward and I feel the bear's nose thrust against my back. 'Now it's surely over,' I think. 'Live human meat is tastier than pemmican or frozen seal. He's found my scent. I'm finished.' And suddenly, unaccountably, the bear leaves. With a final sniff at the tent he pads off, the sound of his heavy footsteps slowly receding. Silence at last."

Uemura stepped from his tent, alone in a sea of ice, four days north of Cape Columbia, the same place from where Robert Peary embarked for the North Pole in 1909. But unlike Peary, Uemura was alone, the Japanese man with the broad face, now savaged by frostbite, his thousand-kilowatt smile dimmed

by conditions that would break most men.

It was March 1978, 20 years since *Nautilus,* and Uemura's bold solo attempt on the North Pole was, in a way, a repudiation of modern technology. He had begun this journey, as he said, "to challenge the limits of human endurance."

The thermometer steadied at minus 40°F, that frozen intersection where Celsius and Fahrenheit meet. His sled weighed 1,000 pounds, and the ice he traversed was hardly smooth. Sea currents and winds had buckled it into a maze of pressure ridges and shards, some 30 feet high. "I feel surrounded by giant thorns," Uemura wrote. "Often I must hack a passage through solid ice with an iron bar so that the dogs can scramble through....

"The great pressure ridges of ice remind me of the stone fences built by Sherpa tribesmen along the slopes of the Himalayas, where I have climbed. The fences were works of art; the ridges are nightmares."

Little surprise that his expedition fell behind schedule.

A support team maintained radio contact and dropped provisions by airplane. Other than that, the only voices Uemura heard were those of the wind, ice, and dogs. "No two have the same nature," he wrote of the dogs. He described "the dog that always pulls to the right side, another that pulls dead center, and still another that pulls to the left. There is the dog that cries 'Yap!' even when the whip does not touch it, and another that never cries, no matter how much it is whipped. Then there is the dog that begins pulling with all its might if I so much as raise my whip hand. And finally there is the dog that casts a sidelong glance at me while running, as if to say, 'Can't you see I'm doing my best?'"

When one dog delivered nine pups, two were eaten by the other dogs before Uemura could intervene.

The following day, with the mother and her surviving pups wrapped in a caribou skin inside the sled, he pushed on. A supply plane landed, off-loaded new dogs and picked up some of the original dog team, including the mother and her puppies. Taking off, it left

Uemura once again in the great alone.

Through shifting ice and open leads, past one danger after another, past one disappointment after another, he trudged north until, on April 29, 1978, his 55th day out from Cape Columbia, he reached the Pole. All that day and part of the next he confirmed his position by sextant, and then, giddy from his own success, he wrote: "For the first time man has reached the North Pole alone."

The pickup plane arrived and flew him back to base camp.

He knew his wife, Kimiko, worried about him, but he seemed hardly to finish one adventure before embarking on another.

In February 1984, Uemura died on Mount McKinley, North America's highest peak. He had reached the top, solo in winter, another first, but disappeared on the way down. A pilot saw him and dipped a wing in salute. Uemura waved back just before a storm engulfed him. His body has never been found.

AROUND THE WORLD—THE HARD WAY

"THE IDEA WAS PREPOSTEROUS," wrote Ranulph Fiennes, "but my wife, Ginnie, insisted: 'Why not go around the world the *hard* way—through both Poles?'"

"There were any number of reasons why not," Fiennes argued, as if reason somehow applied to polar exploration, "and I began to list them, but Ginnie is stubborn. 'It's the last great journey left,' she interrupted, 'and it can be done.'"

A former British Army officer with experience on the Nile River and the glaciers of Norway, Fiennes could barely pay his mortgage that summer of 1972. But the idea developed a life of its own, ineluctable, like a tide, and when Prince Charles—later a patron of Fiennes's expedition—heard of it, he called it "splendidly mad."

Perhaps so, thought Fiennes, "But then so were all the great pioneers of British polar exploration—splendidly mad in their challenge of the unknown. Though Sir John Franklin and Robert F. Scott paid...with their lives, both contributed much to man's knowledge of the polar regions. Another countryman, Vivian Fuchs, achieved the first traverse of Antarctica in 1957-58, and British explorer

Wally Herbert first crossed the frozen Arctic Ocean a decade later."

By September 1979 Fiennes was ready, thanks in no small measure to 1,800 organizations, firms, and individuals in 19 countries. The 29-member Transglobe Expedition, which included Ginnie, sailed down the Thames and quickly put the English Channel behind it. The expedition crossed Europe by Land-Rover, then Africa, through the blistering hot Sahara. From Côte d'Ivoire travel was by ship to Cape Town, and beyond to the Fimbul Ice Shelf, Antarctica.

On October 28, 1980, Fiennes and two other men departed "by snowmobile for a 2,200-mile traverse of Antarctica, the first ever made in open vehicles...the temperature stood at a relatively balmy minus 60°F, though the danger of frostbite was constant. Our route was uncharted, so we took regular barometric readings for topographical mapping."

They reached the bottom of the world on December 15, where the research staff at the U.S. Amundsen-Scott South Pole Station treated them to hot showers and ice cream. Pushing on, they reached the other side of Antarctica at New Zealand's Scott Base,

beneath the steaming volcano Mount Erebus on January 10, 1981.

Six months later found them in the far north, at the mouth of the Yukon River. In rubber rafts pushed by outboard motors they traveled 1,200 miles upstream to the gold rush town of Dawson City, in Canada's Yukon Territory. Then overland to the Mackenzie River. Fiennes reported in October 1983 NATIONAL GEOGRAPHIC magazine that from the mouth of the Mackenzie, "in a Boston Whaler equipped with twin 60-horsepower engines, we navigated the Northwest Passage, going 4,000 miles in less than a month, the only such voyage made in a single season."

It had taken Roald Amundsen more than two years.

"After a grueling, 200-mile overland snowshoe trek to Alert on Ellesmere Island's north coast," Fiennes reported that he and his companion set up winter camp to wait for their spring assault on the North Pole. When it came, they were back on snowmobiles, which broke down "in the great welter of pack ice. We continued on foot, each man dragging 160 pounds of supplies and dehydrated food on a single sledge behind him. After a hundred memorable miles of hauling, the ice improved, and our faithful Twin Otter delivered two more snowmobiles for the remaining 400 zigzag miles to the Pole. We arrived there on Easter Sunday, the only people ever to reach both Poles by surface routes."

Perhaps the miles were "grueling" and "memorable" for Fiennes, as they were among the few he covered by snowshoe and foot, not on the back of an iron dog or in a motorboat.

Southbound, a drifting ice floe trapped them for 99 days until they could paddle canoes to a relief ship 12 miles distant. They returned to a warm homecoming in August 1982, almost ten years after the expedition had been conceived. Fiennes reflected, as polar explorers often do: "Perhaps our greatest accomplishment lay in human rather than geographic terms. Our team lived cheek by jowl for three years under extraordinary pressure and occasional danger. We emerged as friends with a deeper understanding of human tolerance and capability—both in greater measure than we could have believed."

Comfortable back home and knighted for his deeds, Fiennes added, "I live in constant apprehension of Ginnie's next idea."

Bundled in furs, Ranulph Fiennes and other members of the British Transglobe Expedition prepare to traverse Antarctica by snowmobile, part of their historic circumnavigation of Earth "the *hard* way"—via both its Poles. Their achievement was reported in the October 1983 GEOGRAPHIC.

THE MACMILLAN EXPEDITION

First to make extensive use of airplanes in Arctic exploration, the 1925 MacMillan Expedition (reported in the November 1925 GEOGRAPHIC) included a U.S. Navy unit led by Richard Byrd. It obtained valuable data and specimens for the National Geographic Society and recorded Native Americans of the Far North on film. This portrait of an Eskimo hunter and his bull walrus trophy (below) followed an exciting hunt that witnessed one kayak overturned and two bladder floats punctured, all by a herd of more than 100 walrus. A young Smith Sound Eskimo (right) finds a ten-cent harmonica at least as fascinating as the movie camera being focused on him by a Navy Aërographer.

WILL STEGER AND THE 1995 TRANS-ARCTIC EXPEDITION

No hot water for a shower? Try "bathing" with snow every morning, as did Victor Boyarsky (below), a Russian member of Will Steger's 1995 Trans-Arctic Expedition via the North Pole. The group used dogsleds until the ice grew too soft. Then air support delivered canoe-sleds and flew the dogs off. After slogging across pack ice for 116 days, the party came ashore (right) at Canada's Ward Hunt Island, near Ellesmere Island. The Arctic Ocean, recalled Steger, "continually astonished us, from pressure ridges of ice piling up before our eyes to delicate snowflakes parachuting through icy fog."

THE 1989-1990 ANTARCTIC EXPEDITION

Making use of a natural ice bridge, Will Steger's dogsleds and company skirt the awesome maw of a major crevasse in Antarctica's Weyerhauser Glacier in 1990. Such openings can yawn more than a hundred feet deep, providing constant danger for any Antarctic adventurer who trusts too much to surface appearances. Steger's team was part of a multinational group on a seven-month trip. They left from Seal Nunataks on the Antarctic Peninsula on July 27, 1989, and completed the crossing on March 19, 1990. The November NATIONAL GEOGRAPHIC published an account of the expedition.

INTO THIN AIR

WE HAVE ACHIEVED THE CRAZIEST
OF OUR CRAZY DREAMS.

–BALLOONIST BERTRAND PICCARD

BY WILLIAM R. NEWCOTT

On a second-floor balcony in the Smithsonian Institution's National Air and Space Museum, I seek out a seven-foot metal sphere. I find it, tucked into a corner a few feet from the Wright brothers' plane, beneath an X-15, and right near a backup interplanetary space probe. White on top, black on the bottom, it looks more like a bathysphere than an aircraft. But early one morning in 1935, the largest balloon yet made gently lifted this pressurized ball, and the two men inside, 72,395 feet above the Badlands of South Dakota.

For 21 years, no human would fly higher than Albert W. Stevens and Orvil A. Anderson did that day, as part of a balloon expedition sponsored by the National Geographic Society and the U.S. Army Air Corps.

Throughout the 1930s, as other Society-sponsored adventurers explored the Yukon, searched for vanished civilizations in the Yucatán, and plumbed the ocean's depths by bathysphere, another breed of National Geographic explorer dangled perilously above them, approaching the near edge of outer space at the bottom of a big bag containing 3.7 million cubic feet of helium.

Alexander Graham Bell, an early Society President, experimented with kites. Aviators from Charles Lindbergh to John Glenn brought their stories to the pages of NATIONAL GEOGRAPHIC magazine. But it was in ballooning that the Society invested its considerable assets and reputation.

In 1906 National Geographic sponsored the winning balloon in the first Gordon Bennett Cup International Balloon Race, to this day the world's premier balloon distance competition. Less than 30 years later, the Swiss physicist Auguste Piccard gave readers a description of his balloon ride more than ten miles aloft, into the stratosphere. Of the view through two windows in his aluminum gondola—pressurized thanks to revolutionary welding techniques borrowed from the European beer vat industry—the wild-haired, mustachioed Piccard wrote: "You will probably want to know what the earth looks like from ten miles up.

"The sky is beautiful up there—almost black. It is a bluish purple—a deep violet shade—ten times darker than on earth, but it is still not quite dark enough to see the stars.... Forests, rivers, and fields are visible.... The towering summits of the Alps from ten miles up assume the aspect of miniature reproductions."

Piccard's descriptions tantalized readers worldwide. Although the exploits of early aviators and of World War I pilots were already the stuff of legend, the world was, for the overwhelming majority of people, still two-dimensional, measured in longitude and latitude. Statistically speaking, virtually no one had flown in an open cockpit, much less a pressurized cabin. So all this talk about forests and fields and little toy Alps in a very real way made GEOGRAPHIC readers party to a type of adventure and exploration never before heard of in human history.

High-tech in a pre-plastics era, balloonists Paul Kipfer (left) and Auguste Piccard wore wicker helmets for their first flight into the stratosphere. Here, Piccard's wife and two children join them in front of their pressurized cabin.

Ballooning with Stevens, Kepner, and Anderson

NOT CONTENT to cover other adventurers' high altitude exploits, the Society in the fall of 1933 announced plans for its own balloon expeditions into the stratosphere. *Explorer,* as the spherical gondola was christened, was made of Dowmetal, a material lighter than aluminum. It contained room for three passengers and the scientific equipment to measure barometric pressure, cosmic rays, and altitude. Also on board were a radio donated by the fledgling NBC network and— since this was a Geographic expedition— several cameras.

As a base of ballooning operations, the Society chose a large natural bowl in South Dakota, about halfway between Rapid City and Mount Rushmore, where at the time work was being done on the now well-known colossal sculpture of four presidential heads.

"Three considerations determined this choice," wrote Capt. Albert W. Stevens, one of the original *Explorer* crew members, in 1934. "The point was far enough west to permit the balloon to drift even 700 or 800 miles to the eastward and still come to earth in relatively level, unforested country; the record of the region was promising for good summer flying weather; and the site was sheltered from surface winds." The site quickly became known as Stratocamp and eventually as the Stratobowl.

Driving along U.S. Route 16 south from Rapid City toward Mount Rushmore, I found it. The turnoff is right there, designated only by a standard corner street sign: "Stratobowl Road." A winding pine-lined roadway leads to

the steep-sided bowl, and at its rim is a plaque commemorating what happened here.

Along this road, caravans of trucks carried tons of steel canisters containing compressed hydrogen for the balloon. On a flatbed railroad car came the spherical gondola from Midland, Michigan, where it had been built by the Dow Chemical Company. And finally, in a huge box, came the balloon, shipped from the Goodyear-Zeppelin Corporation plant in Akron, Ohio, where it had been cemented together in a sealed room with filtered air.

Finally, around 5 a.m. on July 28, came the order, "Cast off!" The several busloads of troopers from nearby Fort Meade who'd been holding the inflated gas bag to Earth let go. *Explorer,* with Stevens, pilot Maj. William W. Kepner, and Capt. Orvil A. Anderson on board, cleared the Stratobowl rim for the long ascent into the stratosphere.

Or so the men thought. At around 60,000 feet, Stevens recalled, "A small rope fell from the bag and clattered on top of the gondola. Through the port I looked up, startled, to see the large rip in the balloon's lower surface...."

Enthusiastic well-wishers salute the launch of the first *Explorer* in 1934. Troopers from nearby Fort Meade, South Dakota, were bused in to help. Though lacking previous balloon experience, they quickly mastered the techniques of inflating and launching the 35,000-cubic-foot envelope. *Explorer II*'s successful 1935 route (left) took it from its Black Hills launching pad to the vicinity of White Lake, South Dakota, 225 miles to the east.

Previous pages: Piloted by Bertrand Piccard and Brian Jones, *Breitling Orbiter 3* skims the Alps soon after its March 1999 liftoff and continues toward Africa and beyond, becoming the first balloon to circle the globe nonstop.

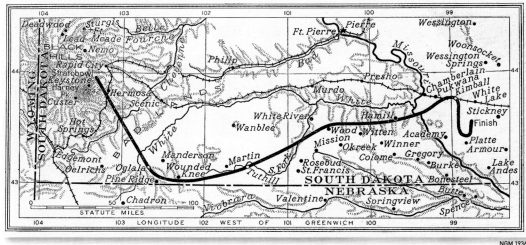

NGM 1936

Straining at its leashes (opposite), *Explorer II*'s helium-filled envelope seemed eager to escape the confines of South Dakota's Stratobowl on November 11, 1935. Minutes later, the balloon carried the National Geographic-U.S. Army Air Corps-sponsored expedition 72,395 feet into the stratosphere. Ringing the balloon's equator, the so-called lower catenary band had been assembled by workers in Akron, Ohio (left). Ropes suspended from each tab supported the gondola. So strong was the design that a similar band survived the explosion that sent the first *Explorer* plummeting into a Nebraska field (bottom).

Nov 11, 1935
"Explorer II"
Stevens &
Anderson
13·71 miles
72,395 feet
22,066 meters

July 28, 1934, "Explorer I"
Kepner, Stevens, Anderson,
60 613 feet
11·48 miles
18 475 meters

Nov 20, 1933
Settle & Fordney
61,237 feet
11·59 miles
18 665 meters

Oct. 23, 1934
Mr. & Mrs. J. Piccard
57,579 feet
10·9 miles, 17550 meters

August 18, 1932
A. Piccard
53,152 feet
10·07 miles
16 201 meters

May 27, 1931
A. Piccard
51,775 feet
9·81 miles
15 781 meters

52,900 feet

April 12, 1934
Donati,
47,572 feet
9·01 miles
14,500 meters

Nov. 4, 1927
Gray, 42,470 feet
8·04 miles

June 4, 1930
Soucek
43 166 feet
8·17 miles

Sept. 16, 1932
Uwins, 43,976 feet
8·33 miles

Approximate Base of
The Stratosphere
33,700 feet

Cirrus

Cirro Stratus

Mt. Everest
29,141 ft.

Cirro Cumulus

Mt. McKinley
20,300 ft.

17,960 feet

Alto Stratus

Mont Blanc
15,781 ft.

Alto Cumulus

Cumulo Nimbus

Cumulus

Mt. Washington
6288

Nimbo Stratus

Stratus

Sea Level

NGM 1936

After ascending for about 20 minutes, Stevens reported, "We started to descend. The rent grew larger. There was little talking as we strained to hear the swishing noises that signaled a new or longer rip. Outside, it was 80° below zero F; inside, it was 42 above. Ice formed on the gondola."

The *Explorer* began dropping; slowly at first, as hydrogen gas trapped in the damaged balloon continued to provide lift. *Explorer* dropped some 40,000 feet in an hour and a half—much too fast for a safe landing. But the crew remained almost alarmingly calm. They continued a routine of scientific readings. Also, as Stevens reported, "We all climbed out on top and took a good look at the balloon. It was pretty badly torn…. Suddenly the entire bottom of the bag dropped out.

"The bottomless bag was acting largely as a parachute. It was a pretty sight, quite round and tight and symmetrical."

Finally, just 6,000 feet above Nebraska, they decided it would be best to leave. Anderson and Kepner stood atop the descending gondola while Stevens waited inside.

Anderson's parachute pack had come open. "There was only one thing to do—that was to gather the folds of silk under one arm preparatory to leaping. While getting the fabric together, Anderson stepped down until both his feet were in the hatch from which I planned to leap. Andy is a big man, but never before had I noticed that his feet were large.

"I shouted, 'Hey, get your big feet out of the way! I want to jump!'… The feet disappeared. As he jumped, the balloon exploded…. The fabric burst at once in hundreds of pieces. The gondola dropped like a stone. Twice I tried to push myself through the hatch of the gondola, but wind pressure around the rapidly falling sphere forced me back."

He managed to get halfway out the hatch. But only a good push from the foot of Kepner, still atop the gondola, got him out completely.

The three men floated safely to the ground. *Explorer,* in Stevens' words, "hit with a tremendous thud."

Much scientific information was salvaged from the twisted wreckage, but the goal of setting a new altitude record was unmet.

And so, in early 1935, Society President Gilbert H. Grosvenor announced another try. And lest members think their $3.50 annual dues were being heedlessly frittered away, he added, "The financial loss resulting from the explosion of the balloon and the crash of the gondola was much reduced by insurance."

Kepner couldn't make the second attempt, but Stevens and Anderson were on board at around 7 a.m. on November 11, 1935, when *Explorer II* rose from the Stratobowl.

"At 11:40 the balloon stopped," wrote Stevens. "We were at the top. From our altimeter we made a rough estimate of our ceiling—73,000 feet!

"From nearly 14 miles above sea level, we saw the earth as a vast expanse of brown. Highways and houses were invisible, larger farms appeared as tiny rectangles. Streaks of green vegetation traced streams. Sunlight sparkled from rivers and lakes, but we saw no sign of life. It seemed a foreign and lifeless world."

The description is familiar to the billions of us who have flown in airliners. To Stevens and his companion, the sight was as unfamiliar as a Mars scape.

This time, the pair made an "eggshell landing" 225 miles to the east, near White Lake, South Dakota. The trip was an international event and a scientific success, but World War II and two decades would intervene before anyone else tried to duplicate or better the *Explorer II* feat.

MORE BALLOONS: KITTINGER, FOSSETT, AND PICCARD

SINCE THE EARLY 1940S, the U.S. Navy had been releasing high-altitude scientific balloons and recovering them in a program called Skyhook. So in the '60s, when the Navy decided to attempt a manned balloon mission called *Strato-Lab,* it turned to the 21-year-old *Explorer* data for clues of what to expect.

Like *Explorer* and *Explorer II, Strato-Lab*—consisting of a spherical ten-year-old surplus balloon gondola and a new super-thin balloon made by General Mills—rose from the familiar confines of the Stratobowl. In recognition of the Society's pioneering research, the crew carried the Geographic flag to a new altitude record of 76,000 feet.

It takes a special kind of courage to ride a balloon round trip into the stratosphere; it requires another kind altogether to take the balloon one way…and then jump out.

By those standards, Joe Kittinger may well be the bravest man who ever lived. On August 16, 1960, as part of a high-altitude parachute study, the U.S. Air Force captain rode a balloon gondola 18 1/2 miles above the New Mexico desert. As a special camera designed and built by National Geographic photographer Volkmar Wentzel clicked away, Kittinger took the longest, loneliest leap in history.

"Just before jumping, I had said a prayer, 'Lord, take care of me now,'" Kittinger wrote in the December 1960 GEOGRAPHIC. According to the Society's book *Great Adventures,* published in 1963, Kittinger continued, "Then I step into space. No wind whistles or billows my clothing. I have absolutely no sensation of the increasing speed with which I fall."

Years later, Kittinger would become one of the world's leading balloon adventurers, the first to fly solo, in 1984, across the Atlantic.

As ballooning became increasingly high-tech—and a century-long quest to fly around the world by balloon nonstop became an elusive possibility—lighter-than-air adventurers continued to share their experiences through NATIONAL GEOGRAPHIC. During the first transatlantic flight, in 1978, balloonists Maxie Anderson, Ben Abruzzo, and Larry Newman found their craft dropping a dizzying 19,500 feet.

"I was really upset," Newman, who had ballooned only once before, recalled in the magazine. "I said to Ben and Maxie, 'You know, guys, I don't think we're going back up'" and bet them a hundred dollars. He lost.

Chicago businessman Steve Fossett's repeated attempts to span the globe by balloon were covered by NATIONAL GEOGRAPHIC. In 1998 Fossett set a new distance record of 14,236 miles but nearly died in the attempt as his balloon *Solo Spirit 3* plunged nearly 29,000 feet into the Coral Sea during a thunderstorm.

"I am going to die," he said as flames from the burners melted the fabric of his deflating

Making one long and lonely leap, Air Force Capt. Joseph W. Kittinger steps out from a balloon gondola at 18 1/2 miles altitude to test space survival systems. Nearly 14 minutes later, he safely reached the ground.

Adrift in a tranquil sky, helium-filled *Kitty Hawk* (right) soars above
Wyoming at 18,000 feet en route to making the first nonstop balloon transit
of North America. Maxie Anderson wrote in the August 1980 GEOGRAPHIC that,
within hours of this photograph, he and his son Kristian—seen here standing on a helium tank—found themselves "encircled by violent thunder-
storms that threaten[ed] to slam *Kitty Hawk* into the ground or loft us to
our death at 50,000 feet." Fortunately the storms subsided, and *Kitty Hawk*
continued cross-country. Following the first transatlantic crossing by balloon
in 1978, crew members of the *Double Eagle II* (above), left to right—Maxie
Anderson, Ben Abruzzo, and Larry Newman—celebrate in a French barley
field. Sighed farmer's wife Rachel Coquerel, whose crop was ruined by
the balloon and well-wishers, "They had to land somewhere." The crew
compensated the Coquerels for their loss.

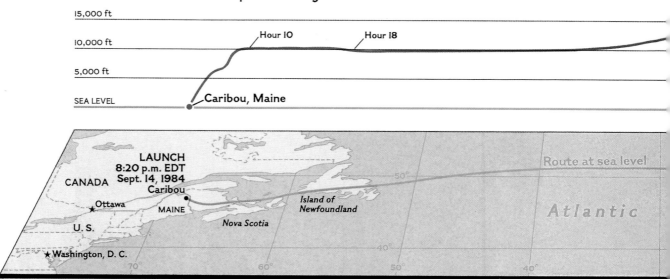

Altitude profile of flight

15,000 ft

10,000 ft — Hour 10 — Hour 18

5,000 ft

SEA LEVEL — Caribou, Maine

LAUNCH
8:20 p.m. EDT
Sept. 14, 1984
Caribou

CANADA

Ottawa

MAINE

U.S.

Washington, D.C.

Nova Scotia

Island of
Newfoundland

Route at sea level

Atlantic

Staying on board this time, Joe Kittinger—the man who jumped from a high-altitude balloon and lived—navigates from Maine to Italy in 80 hours, making the first solo crossing of the Atlantic by balloon, in September 1984.

balloon. Knocked unconscious by impact with the ocean, Fossett came to in an upside-down capsule partly filled with water and partly on fire. As he pulled his life raft away from the capsule, the propane fuel tanks exploded.

The next day, he was found by rescuers, thanks to an emergency beacon.

On March 21, 1999, Bertrand Piccard—grandson of Auguste Piccard, whose ballooning had inspired GEOGRAPHIC readers nearly 70 years earlier—and copilot Brian Jones completed their flight around the world. "We have," Piccard wrote in the GEOGRAPHIC, "achieved the craziest of our crazy dreams."

EXPLORING VIA THE DIRIGIBLE *SHENANDOAH*

WHEN IT CAME TO BLIMPS AND DIRIGIBLES, the skies were ruled by Europeans—and particularly Germans—in the 1920s and '30s. So it was with a flourish of national pride that the dirigible *Shenandoah*, designed and built by the U.S., was launched in 1923. And to prove the craft's durability even above the Rocky Mountains, on October 7, 1924, *Shenandoah* set out on a record-making 9,000-mile round trip across North America.

Along with the handful of crewmen on board was NATIONAL GEOGRAPHIC magazine writer Junius B. Wood, who penned the official chronicle of the trip.

"As the *Shenandoah* was led out of the big hangar [in Lakehurst, N.J.]," he wrote, "every man on the station…came running into the drear, misty morn like little ants pulling an immense gray worm out of its nest."

"Personal luggage was limited to six pounds," he wrote. "A pair of socks, a suit of underwear, two handkerchiefs, a towel and a cake of soap, and an…assortment of toilet articles had replaced a wardrobe trunk…. The clothing problem was solved by wearing two lightweight instead of one heavy suit."

From the vantage point of a supersonic

age, the droning, leisurely pace of dirigible travel seems almost as incomprehensible today as jet travel would have been to author Wood.

After pushing across Delaware and Maryland at 55 miles per hour, "The ship passed between the [Washington] Monument and the White House, and…the District of Columbia was crossed in 10 minutes. We paused beyond the Potomac to drop flowers on the Tomb of the Unknown Soldier at Arlington, Virginia."

After passing over El Paso, Texas (which gave "a welcome of whistles, flashing flares, and a searchlight"), *Shenandoah* headed for its major hurdle: Dos Cabezas [Arizona] canyon, flanked by towering mountains.

"A 25-miles-an-hour wind was whistling out of the mountain pass. The moon had slipped behind a cloud, and the dim line of railroad which we had been following was no longer visible. The headlight of a locomotive flashed into view far ahead in the pass and the *Shenandoah* drove toward it into the wind. The current caught her broadside. She drifted for a breathless second. The rudders held and she slowly slid forward between the towering peaks.…

"Cochise was passed…even narrower Dragoon Pass was ahead.… In the dim starlight it

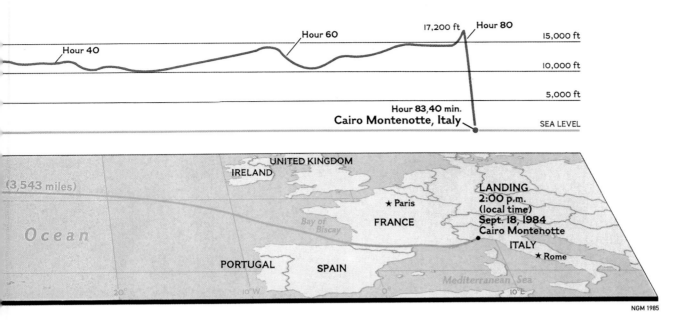

Hour 40

Hour 60

Hour 80   17,200 ft   15,000 ft

10,000 ft

5,000 ft

Hour 83, 40 min.
Cairo Montenotte, Italy   SEA LEVEL

(3,543 miles)

UNITED KINGDOM
IRELAND

★ Paris

LANDING
2:00 p.m.
(local time)
Sept. 18, 1984
Cairo Montenotte

Ocean

FRANCE

PORTUGAL   SPAIN

ITALY
★ Rome

Bay of
Biscay

Mediterranean Sea

20°   10° W   10° E

NGM 1985

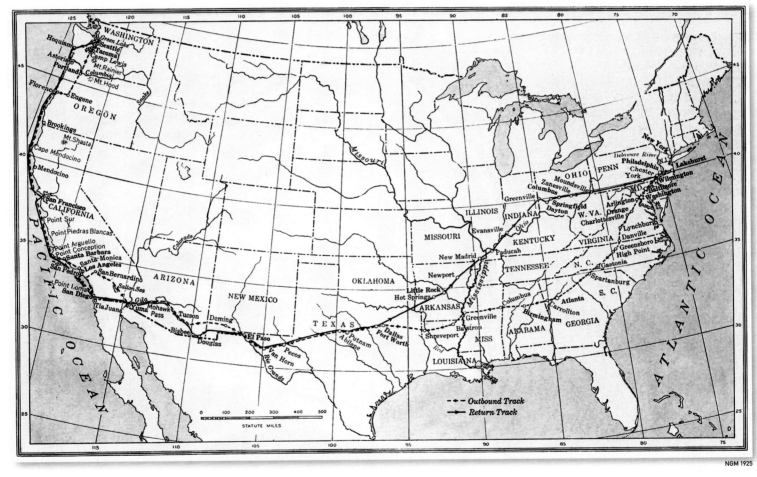

- ∙ - Outbound Track
→ Return Track

NGM 1925

seemed…the mountain walls were within…
feet…. A freight train showed the way into
the inky tunnel and the ship worked slowly
through…the worst of the Rockies had been
crossed. Commander Lansdowne climbed the
ladder and threw himself on his bunk."

The voyage of the *Shenandoah* proved that
the Rockies were no barrier to airship travel. It
also proved that helium, the lifting medium of
choice for U.S. airships, was as practical as
hydrogen, widely used but highly flammable.

German airmen continued to opt for
hydrogen. They would pay a tragic price 13
years later as the *Hindenburg* exploded in
flames…mere yards from the hangar where
the *Shenandoah* was built.

Dirigible *Shenandoah*
crossed the nation in
1924, proving the
reliability of lighter-
than-air craft. But the
mighty ships soon
became dinosaurs
of the skies.

Full house: Back in Lakehurst, New Jersey, from a cross-country cruise in 1925, the American dirigible *Shenandoah* berths next to the commercial ship *Los Angeles,* or *ZR-3.* A dozen years later at Lakehurst, the age of airships would go up in flames with the fiery end of the *Hindenburg.*

HEAVIER-THAN-AIR FLIGHT: THE VICKERS-VIMY TESTS ITS WINGS

ALEXANDER GRAHAM BELL had pretty much conquered the world by 1907. But the man who had linked the globe electronically with his telephone was obsessed with conquering distance another way: through high-speed powered flight.

Beginning in the late 19th century, the President of the National Geographic Society experimented with seemingly endless variations of a basic kite fashioned of tetrahedrons. In 1903 one such contraption, dubbed by Bell the *Cygnet,* was so formidable with its more

Nearly to their goal, Australia-bound members of the Vickers-Vimy crew toast their imminent success with coconut milk in Timor, Dutch East Indies, now Indonesia, a short hop from Darwin and home.

than 40-foot span that a young Army officer named Thomas Selfridge volunteered to climb aboard. He subsequently soared 168 feet into the air on Bell's kite. Bell had published earlier that year: "...A properly constructed kite should be capable of use as a flying machine, when driven by its own propellers." Such a craft Bell called an aërodrome.

Selfridge agreed and went to work with a pair of bicycle repairmen from Ohio. He and the Wright brothers flew into history together.

The dashing image of World War I flying aces and the devil-may-care bombast of 1920s barnstormers enhanced the romance of flying. But for most people, the thought of taking a long voyage in an aëroplane, as the NATIONAL GEOGRAPHIC spelled it well into the 1920s, was simply a fantasy.

That idea changed with a single flight. In late 1919, four Australians flew in an open-

cockpit airplane from London all the way to Port Darwin, Australia. As often happens, it was the promise of money that sparked a spirit of adventure: Eager to open access to the world following the armistice of 1918, the government of Australia pledged £10,000 for the first flight by an Australian crew from London to Australia in 30 days or less.

Ross Smith, veteran of the Australian Flying Squadron; his brother Keith Smith, a Royal Air Force veteran; J.M. Bennett; and W.H. Shiers convinced the Vickers aircraft company to donate a plane—a standard, two-engine Vimy bomber—and began the competition flight from London on November 12.

"The forecast was Class V, or totally unfit for flying," wrote Ross Smith in his 109-page story for the March 1921 NATIONAL GEOGRAPHIC, still one of the longest single pieces ever run in the magazine. "But our minds were made up and, come fair, come foul, we were determined to start.

"A few friends had gathered to bid us God-speed.... We climbed into our seats and took off from the snow-covered aërodrome."

Almost immediately, the weather turned awful. "The machine speedily became deluged by sleet and snow. It clotted up our goggles and the wind screen and covered our faces with a mushy, semi-frozen mask.... the clouds were so densely compacted as to appear like mighty snow cliffs, towering miles into the air. There was no gap or pass anywhere, so I shut off the engines and glided down, hoping to fly under them.... Once more we became frozen up.... I determined to climb above the cloud-mass and, once above it, set a compass course for Lyons [France]."

The flight was strictly a seat-of-the-pants affair. "It [the plane] could cruise at 80 miles per hour for 13 hours. We would fly by maps and direct observation of the ground. When clouds intervened we would rely on Keith's navigation. We had an Admiralty compass, a ground speed and drift indicator, and our own experience to fall back on.

"Below, the shadow of our machine pursued us, skipping from crest to crest, jumping gulfs and ridges like a bewitched phantom. Around the shadow circled a gorgeous halo,

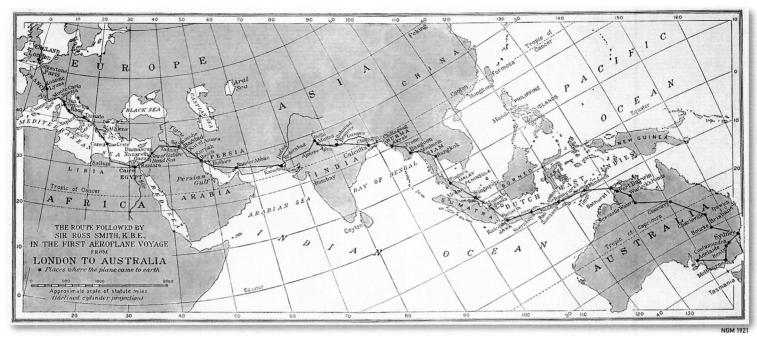

NGM 1921

a complete flat rainbow. I have never seen any-thing in all my life so unreal as the solitudes of this upper world.... For three hours we had no glimpse of the earth."

On the third day, when they attempted a takeoff from the sodden airfield in Pisa, Italy, "the wheels had become embedded in the mud; on the other hand, the tail lifted off the ground and there was the danger of the machine standing up on its nose.

"To hold the tail down, Sergeant Bennett crawled out and added his weight to it. This time we started to roll. Though Bennett was not secure, to stop once more would be to bog down for good. I was sure he would clamber back to his cockpit somehow.... After leaving the ground, I was delighted to see Sergeant Bennett on board."

On they pushed, taking short skips to Rome, Taranto, Crete, and Cairo. Their jour-ney gave the magazine the opportunity to publish aerial photographs of the landmarks they passed over—and for the first time, in full-page glory, readers experienced some of the world's most familiar monuments from the air.

On page 249, Bernini's great colonnade at St. Peter's in Rome reached out to embrace all of Christendom. A glimpse down the throat of Vesuvius on page 254 revealed a column of ominous smoke. The Taj Mahal, on page 290, gleaming like a pearl on a muddy riverbank, seemed oddly diminished in the context of its clamorous surroundings.

Wherever the aviators went, they met enthusiasm. And not just from humans, as Smith recalled of a stop in Allahabad, India.

"While we were taxi-ing to the far end,

preparatory to taking off, a fine bull broke on to the ground, and as we swung round to take off he charged head-on toward the machine. The position, though ridiculous, was extremely hazardous....

"I frightened him for the moment by a roar from the engines. Evidently he took the roar for a challenge, and stood in front of the Vimy, pawing the ground and bellowing defiantly. At this point a boy scout rushed out from the crowd to move the monster, and, much to the amusement of ourselves and the crowd, the bull changed his intention and turned on the hero. Our brave toreador retreated to the fence, pursued by the bull....

"What became of the scout I do not know, but as we circled above I noticed that the bull was still in sole possession of the aërodrome."

After a landing in a soggy field in what was then known as Singora, on the Malay Peninsula, now present-day Songkhla, Thai-land, "The whole population assembled. None had ever seen an aëroplane, and at first they would not venture near. But when they watched four ordinary humans climb out, they surged around. Some of them walked in front of the machine, flapping their arms to show how it flew. My brother, unobserved, climbed into the cockpit and moved the con-trol column, causing the ailerons and elevators to flap back. There was a wild scamper."

Only nine days remained before the 30-day prize-money deadline. After Singapore, they skipped along the island chain of what was then the Dutch East Indies, now Indone-sia. They then began their final leg.

Shortly after two p.m. on their 28th day, a

By 1919, intrepid fliers had visited many of the cities between London and Mel-bourne. But no one had ever strung them all together in a single itinerary and made the trip shown on this map, published in the March 1921 issue of NATIONAL GEOGRAPHIC. A sense of adven-ture—and the offer of a £10,000 prize—made all the differ-ence for a successful accomplishment of this goal by four Australians, led by Ross Smith.

Vickers-Vimy fliers sit down to a civilized cup of tea during a tour of Australia following their victorious flight from England to Australia. Seventy-five years later, pilots Peter McMillan and Lang Kidby would recreate the feat in a replica Vickers-Vimy and report on their flight in the May 1995 NATIONAL GEOGRAPHIC. The original crew's success helped popularize the concept of air travel to the world.

In the rosy hues of dawn's early light, the 1994 Vickers Vimy replica biplane circles Egypt's Pyramids of Giza (left). At times, parallels between the original flight and this one became downright eerie: The 1919 crew nearly lost their plane during a savage downpour in Pisa, Italy, and the 1994 version also endured slashing rains in the same city (above). Frantic crew members had to pit their muscles against gale-force winds. A nearby hangar offered refuge for the Vimy, saving it from almost certain ruin.

diary entry prosaically notes, "observed Australia." By three they landed in Darwin—27 days and 20 hours after leaving Hounslow.

"Two zealous customs and health officials were anxious to examine us, but so were about 2,000 just ordinary citizens.... The assemblage, brimming with enthusiasm, lifted us shoulder high and conveyed us to the *jail!* .... [We were]

dumped on a tree-stump [to] raucous howls of 'Speech! Speech!' ...After the exchange of much hot air...we returned to the Vimy, ...and lashed her down for the night."

The four did not forget to collect their £10,000 check (its canceled face was duplicated in NATIONAL GEOGRAPHIC). They split it four ways.

LEGACIES OF LINDBERGH AND EARHART

In a 1928 GEOGRAPHIC article, Charles Lindbergh documented his first-ever flight from the United States to Bogotá, Colombia, and back. In St. Thomas, U.S. Virgin Islands, dignitaries watched as he inspected the engine of his beloved *Spirit of St. Louis*.

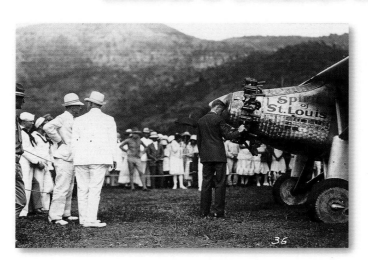

THE FACE OF AVIATION changed forever in 1927 when Charles Lindbergh flew solo across the Atlantic. His long, lonely flight proved the technical feasibility of air traffic between Europe and North America. Perhaps more important were his gentle personality and boyish looks, which somehow made the notion of air travel more accessible to the masses.

Lindbergh's landmark crossing was not in affiliation with the NATIONAL GEOGRAPHIC—in fact, the Society's in-house adventurer and aviator, Comdr. Richard E. Byrd, was at a ceremony christening his own transatlantic craft when word came of Lindy's hop. Robbed of his own thunder, Byrd reported to readers, "I was the first man to make a speech about his remarkable achievement."

After his most famous flight, Lindbergh charged ahead with more trips, determined to prove to a skeptical yet entranced populace that the future lay in scheduled air transportation. And NATIONAL GEOGRAPHIC played a large role in getting his message out.

The engine on Lindbergh's plane, *Spirit of St. Louis,* had barely cooled before he took her

up again, this time on a 22,000-mile tour of all 48 states. An important part of the achievement was that Lindbergh announced long beforehand where and when he would be landing, providing evidence that despite unpredictable weather conditions, scheduled airline routes were feasible.

An epic January 1928 NATIONAL GEOGRAPHIC article by Lindbergh's companion, Donald E. Keyhoe, along with photographs by Lindbergh himself, detailed the entire trip.

NATIONAL GEOGRAPHIC's September 1934 issue chronicled Lindbergh's continuing efforts to map efficient commercial air routes around the North Atlantic. Looking back, perhaps even more noteworthy was the author: the aviator's wife, Anne Morrow Lindbergh. The lovingly crafted article would become the basis for her 1938 best-selling book *Listen! The Wind.* It marked the beginning of a writing career that would span six decades.

On an early stop in Maine, she recalled "an old lady who climbed up the steps to the porch.... My husband was out on the plane, but she came up to me cordially. 'I would like to shake hands with Mrs. Lindbergh—though I'd much ruther shake hands with her husband!'"

As they landed their seaplane in Greenland, she wrote, "Kayaks on all sides kept up with us easily, cutting knifelike through the water with hardly a splash or mark, the narrow two-sided oar going deftly into the water like a needle.

"The town as we first came upon it looked like a toy village, with its bright-colored houses just set down by a child playing—a red church with white trims, a green house with yellow shutters, a yellow house with green shutters, and...a small bright-red house with a green door, just like an apple."

Realizing air travel's worldwide potential, Lindbergh and his wife, Anne, made a grand tour of the North Atlantic in 1933. It included four continents, the Arctic Circle, and the Equator.

Long before comic-book writers envisioned fictional superheroes soaring through the sky, the world was enamored of the real thing. Charles Lindbergh, the Lone Eagle, drew such a crush of admirers in France following his 1927 solo transatlantic flight that he feared for the safety of *Spirit of St. Louis* (right).

Amelia Earhart enjoyed a quieter arrival upon reaching Northern Ireland solo in 1932, sipping tea at the home of the farmer on whose pasture she landed (below). Both fliers helped change the world, and both told their stories in the pages of NATIONAL GEOGRAPHIC.

In 1934, Anne Morrow Lindbergh became the first woman to receive the Society's Hubbard Medal for distinction in exploration, discovery, and research. Two years earlier, the Society's Special Gold Medal had been presented to another pioneering woman aviator, Amelia Earhart, in recognition of the first solo Atlantic flight by a woman.

Earhart wrote one article for NATIONAL GEOGRAPHIC before her career of exploration was tragically cut short. In 1934 she became the first woman to fly solo from Hawaii to the U.S. mainland and shared her adventure with readers the following year.

"The night I found over the Pacific was a night of stars," Earhart wrote. "They seemed to rise from the sea and hang outside my cockpit window, near enough to touch, until hours later they slipped away into the dawn.

"But shortly before midnight I spied a star that differed from the others. It was too pink and it flashed as no star could. I realized I was seeing a ship, with its searchlights turned into the heavens as a lamppost to guide me on my way. I snapped on my landing lights, which are on the leading edge of the wings midway to their tips, and had them bravely blink a greeting to whoever might be watching."

Ready to make history, Amelia Earhart posed for her international pilot's license at age 24. Her exploits and early death, in 1937, somewhere in the Pacific would make her a legend.

A NEW TWIST: HUMAN-POWERED FLIGHT

Pedaling into the record books, Bryan Allen took just under three hours to pilot the human-powered *Gossamer Albatross* 22.5 miles from England to France in 1979.

BY THE LATE 1970S it seemed difficult to imagine any new frontiers in aviation. The Concorde was flying passengers across Lindbergh's Atlantic faster than the speed of sound; Boeing's 747 flew more passengers than ever before—with a second deck, even; military planes regularly spanned the globe nonstop.

But there was at least one unrealized dream, one that had dogged humankind since the days of Icarus: human powered flight.

Enter environmentalist and aeronautical engineer Paul MacCready. In 1977 he collected a £50,000 prize for engineering a lightweight plane which, powered only by a human pedaler, traced a designated figure-eight course. But the big test came on June 12, 1979, when 26-year-old California biologist Bryan Allen powered MacCready's 75-pound aircraft, the *Gossamer Albatross*, across the English Channel. The feat was documented by two photographers for NATIONAL GEOGRAPHIC.

Barely 15 minutes into his flight, Allen wrote in a diary for the magazine, "The first warning of trouble. Wind and swells make for constant air turbulence. Flying at an altitude of eight or ten feet, I must make frequent adjustments to stay on course. As I begin to sweat from exertion, moisture forms on the transparent cockpit walls, obscuring my view...."

An hour and a half in: "It's no use...I'll have to ditch...I'm near exhaustion. I raise my right hand, the signal for scrubbing the flight, and two Zodiacs zoom close alongside. Bill Watson stands ready with a fishing rod and grappling hook to engage a loop on *Albatross*'s underside. For Bill to hook up, I must gain altitude, and with a burst of energy I climb to 15 feet. I've gone too high for Bill to make contact, but I've made a big discovery: Above ten feet the turbulence is greatly reduced. In the smoother air I think I can continue...."

Thirty minutes later: "At last word comes over the radio.... 'We have France in sight—four miles to go....' Four miles or four hundred. I'm fading now and know it...I talk to myself.... Don't give up now, you *can* do it!"...the radio crackles again: 'Altitude six inches, six inches; get it up, you've got to get it up!' Somehow I do, then feel a stab of pain—a growing cramp in my right leg....

Long experience has taught me that cramps don't go away with exertion. I'm stuck with them now, along with thirst and head winds."

Two hours and 48 minutes: "Suddenly I am flying in smooth air, banking into a light head wind that runs parallel to the beach. People cheer and dash back and forth, trying to predict my landing point…. I think at last; time to land. I stop pedaling and am suddenly furious: After nearly three hours of desperate pedaling to stay aloft, *Gossamer Albatross…* perversely…hovers for seconds in the air. Are they going to have to *pull* me down?

"Finally my craft, having played its little joke, deposits me gently on the sand."

Clutching a victory bouquet moments after touching down in France, *Albatross* pilot Allen describes his epic flight to local reporters. The achievement won his team £100,000 in prize money.

FASTER THAN THE SUN

ROARING OVER THE MOJAVE DESERT in California, the Bell X-1 rocket pilots, in the words of author Frederick G. Vosburgh in a 1950 NATIONAL GEOGRAPHIC report, "have flown so fast…that if they were headed west the sun above them would appear not to move—in fact, it might go backward. In their two-and-a-half minutes of full power they can reach or even exceed the rate the world goes round at that latitude—852 miles an hour."

In the five short years since World War II had ended, the Air Force had been born, the jet fighter had been declared the plane of the future, and Chuck Yeager had become the first human to break the sound barrier, in an experimental jet called the X-1. Twelve years later, a descendant of that craft, the X-15, was very close to becoming an actual space plane.

NATIONAL GEOGRAPHIC photographer Dean Conger was asked by the National Aeronautics and Space Administration to chronicle the X-15 program. That meant accompanying the plane's intrepid pilots through training, enduring tests in an altitude chamber, and flying alongside the X-15 in supersonic F-104 chase planes. He even rigged an automatic camera in the cockpit of the X-15 itself.

Launched from beneath the wing of a B-52 bomber at 45,000 feet, the X-15 dropped like a stone until its single rear jet engine kicked in. Then the craft sprinted ahead and upward to altitudes as high as 60 miles.

"The X-15 has enough power to climb …142 miles," wrote X-15 pilot Joseph Walker,

whose record-setting 4,105-miles-per-hour flight was photographed by Conger, "but safe recovery from that height is very doubtful.

"X-15 pilots complain that there isn't any time for sightseeing, but we always take a quick look around from the top of the hill [in his case, above 99.996 percent of the earth's atmosphere]. On my left I saw the Gulf of California and looked down the peninsula of Baja California…. I was weightless immediately, and it felt pleasant, a welcome relief. The ends of checklist pages in my clipboard rose eerily, and a little cloud of dirt particles drifted up from the floor…. As we coasted over the hump and the nose tipped down, I could see the white glare of Rogers Lake, with its 12-mile length of sun-baked clay…. I felt regret at leaving space and returning to that old cumbersome gravity."

Just before landing, the X-15 pilot jettisons the lower stabilizer, which projects so far below the X-15 that you can't land with it. Once Walker was asked what he would do if it failed to jettison. "Well," he replied, "I guess I'd dig the fastest furrow ever plowed."

The X-15 program provided valuable data about re-entry temperatures, weightlessness, spacecraft maneuverability, and pilot efficiency at high speeds. On its own, the X-15 would most likely have evolved into a true space plane that took off from a runway, achieved orbit, and reentered.

But by the early 1960s the U.S. was in a space race with the Soviet Union. There was no time for research and development on a

THE GOSSAMER ALBATROSS

Driven by a 140-pound, 0.3-horsepower engine named Bryan Allen, the 75-pound *Gossamer Albatross* wings toward France. The first human-powered flight to successfully cross the English Channel was accompanied by a convoy of official observers, reporters, and potential rescue boats, as well as design, construction, and logistics experts.

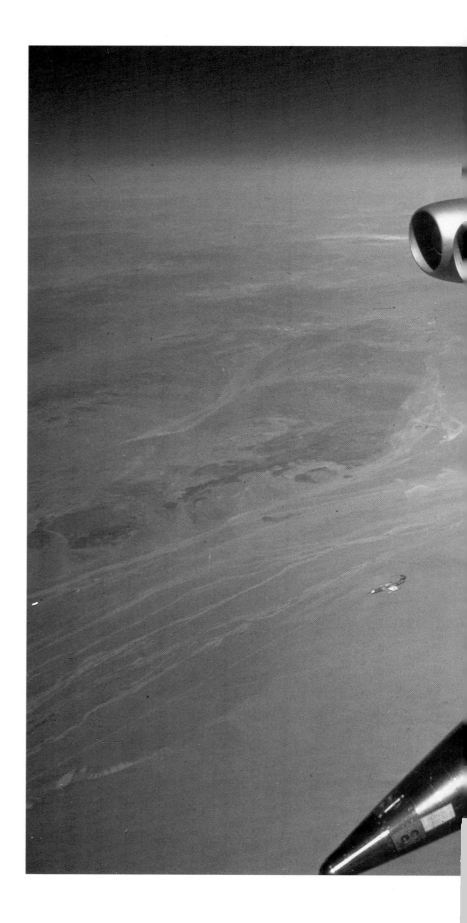

Freed of its shackles, the X-15 drops away from a modified B-52 bomber (right). For his 1962 coverage of the X-15 program, GEOGRAPHIC photographer Dean Conger set up a motor-driven camera in a window of the B-52; a crewman pressed the button. Riding in an F-104 chase plane thousands of feet below, Conger aimed upward and caught the mother ship's wispy condensation trails, while the X-15 headed for the stratosphere—a region that the most adventurous balloonists had only dreamed of reaching a mere 30 years earlier.

The Space Age accelerated in the clear skies over California and Nevada, as nervy test pilots put the rocket-powered X-planes through their paces. A 1962 GEOGRAPHIC illustration shows the paths of two historic X-15 flights: pilot Joseph Walker's record altitude achievement and Maj. Robert White's air speed record.

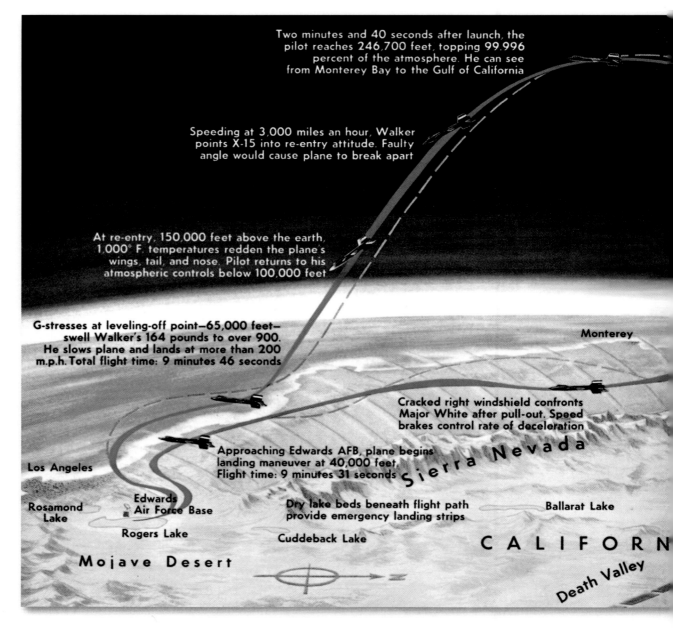

Two minutes and 40 seconds after launch, the pilot reaches 246,700 feet, topping 99.996 percent of the atmosphere. He can see from Monterey Bay to the Gulf of California

Speeding at 3,000 miles an hour, Walker points X-15 into re-entry attitude. Faulty angle would cause plane to break apart

At re-entry, 150,000 feet above the earth, 1,000° F. temperatures redden the plane's wings, tail, and nose. Pilot returns to his atmospheric controls below 100,000 feet

G-stresses at leveling-off point—65,000 feet— swell Walker's 164 pounds to over 900. He slows plane and lands at more than 200 m.p.h. Total flight time: 9 minutes 46 seconds

Monterey

Cracked right windshield confronts Major White after pull-out. Speed brakes control rate of deceleration

Approaching Edwards AFB, plane begins landing maneuver at 40,000 feet. Flight time: 9 minutes 31 seconds

Sierra Nevada

Los Angeles

Rosamond Lake

Edwards Air Force Base

Dry lake beds beneath flight path provide emergency landing strips

Ballarat Lake

Rogers Lake

Cuddeback Lake

CALIFORN

Mojave Desert

Death Valley

space plane when, using older technology, an astronaut could simply be shot into orbit at the top of a rocket. And so, as the jet jockeys continued to nudge closer to space over the California desert, a continent away their astro-naut colleagues prepared to be hurled, shot-put-like, into orbit.

One X-15 pilot did make the transition from flyboy to astronaut: A hotshot from Ohio named Neil Armstrong.

CHRONICLING NASA'S FORAYS INTO SPACE

EVEN BEFORE THERE WAS A SPACE PROGRAM, the Society was exploring space. In 1949, the Society began sponsoring the National Geographic-Palomar Observatory Sky Survey, an unprecedented photographic record of every star visible in the Northern Hemisphere. Through the Palomar Observatory's 48-inch "Big Schmidt" camera and telescope, 879 segments of the sky were photographed in 1,758 images over a seven-year period.

For nearly 40 years, the National Geographic-Palomar survey was the definitive sky map reference, only recently surpassed with digital technology. Among its discoveries was a tiny asteroid that is among a handful that actually pass inside Earth's orbit. The space rock was named Geographos, in honor of the Society's participation in the sky survey.

As the age of piloted spacecraft dawned, astronauts became America's newest form of

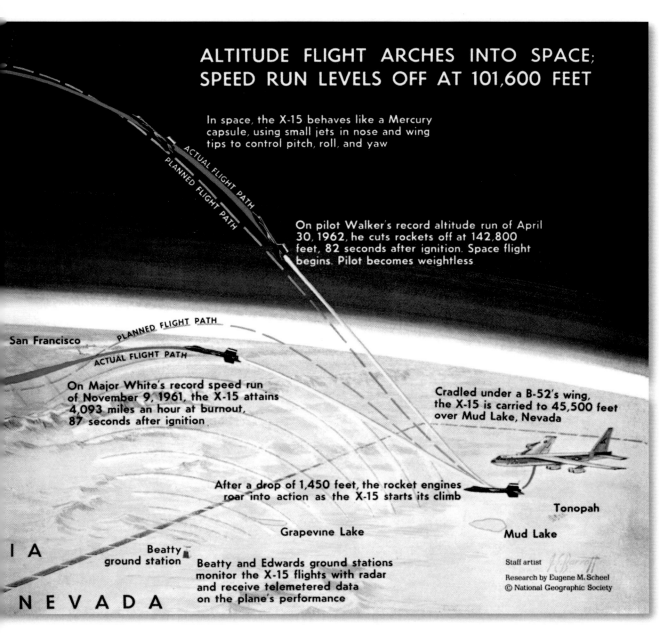

ALTITUDE FLIGHT ARCHES INTO SPACE; SPEED RUN LEVELS OFF AT 101,600 FEET

In space, the X-15 behaves like a Mercury capsule, using small jets in nose and wing tips to control pitch, roll, and yaw

On pilot Walker's record altitude run of April 30, 1962, he cuts rockets off at 142,800 feet, 82 seconds after ignition. Space flight begins. Pilot becomes weightless

San Francisco

PLANNED FLIGHT PATH

ACTUAL FLIGHT PATH

On Major White's record speed run of November 9, 1961, the X-15 attains 4,093 miles an hour at burnout, 87 seconds after ignition

Cradled under a B-52's wing, the X-15 is carried to 45,500 feet over Mud Lake, Nevada

After a drop of 1,450 feet, the rocket engines roar into action as the X-15 starts its climb

Tonopah

Grapevine Lake

Mud Lake

IA

NEVADA

Beatty ground station

Beatty and Edwards ground stations monitor the X-15 flights with radar and receive telemetered data on the plane's performance

Staff artist

Research by Eugene M. Scheel
© National Geographic Society

folk hero. Their smiling faces graced the cover of virtually every magazine. But NASA and the astronauts counted on the GEOGRAPHIC to present not just the sizzle of space travel but the steak of scientific discovery as well.

In recognition of the National Geographic's vital place in America's space-faring heritage, numerous NASA flights carried the Society's flag on board.

"At lift-off I started the clock-timer." With those prosaic words, Alan B. Shepard told the story of the flight that made him America's first man in space. Once again, NGS photographer Dean Conger provided the official NASA photographs of the mission.

Shepard's words were so matter-of-fact, the casual reader might have thought he was describing a drive in his new 1961 Corvette.

"Some roughness was expected during the period of transonic flight and of maxi-

mum dynamic pressure," he wrote, "…and there was general vibration associated with them.…"

Years later, as I sat with Sen. John Glenn in his Washington, D.C., office discussing his upcoming space shuttle flight in 1998, he mentioned Shepard, who had died a month earlier.

"He was once asked what he was thinking as he sat on top of that rocket," Glenn recalled with a smile. "And he answered, 'Well, I was mostly thinking that this thing was built by the lowest bidder.'"

After two more suborbital flights like Shepard's, on February 20, 1962, it was Glenn's turn to become America's leading space hero—as the pilot of America's first orbital flight, it was he who sat in that capsule atop a rocket.

"It was a novel experience to sit on top of the 70-foot Atlas vehicle after the gantry had been pulled back," Glenn told a 1962 National

"An incomparable experience," Col. Frank Borman dubbed the launch of Apollo 8, on May 5, 1961, the first piloted mission to ride the massive Saturn V rocket (below). GEOGRAPHIC photographer John E. Fletcher added, "From more than three miles away we saw flames shoot out hundreds of feet. But we heard no sound. The silence was eerie. Then, 15 seconds after ignition, the earth-shaking roar assaulted us." NATIONAL GEOGRAPHIC's Apollo articles capped a decade of manned space coverage beginning with Alan Shepard's 1961 suborbital flight and recovery of his capsule at sea (opposite).

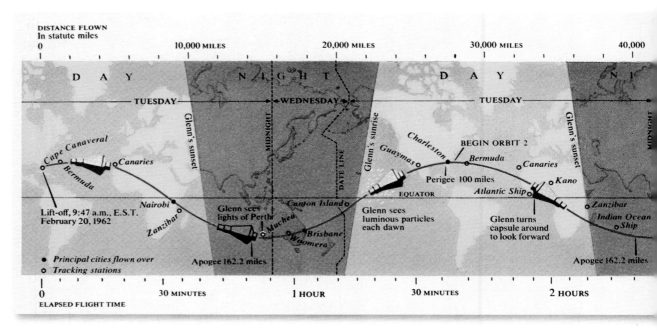

DISTANCE FLOWN
In statute miles

Tension mounts at Cape Canaveral's Mercury Control Center as flight physician Dr. William K. Douglas waits to hear from John Glenn, who is experiencing a 4½-minute communication blackout during reentry.

Geographic audience the night he was honored with the Society's Hubbard Medal. "If I moved back and forth in my seat, I could feel the whole vehicle move slightly under me."

As Glenn coasted through his three orbits, worries began to mount on the ground. Spacecraft data indicated his retropackage with the landing bag and heat shield might have come loose. Without an intact shield, Glenn and his spacecraft would incinerate in the 50,000°F heat of reentry. It was decided to leave the pack strapped to the bottom of the craft, rather than expel it with explosive bolts. A ground communicator told Glenn to leave the retropackage in place, but offered no explanation as to why. The flight transcript, published in NATIONAL GEOGRAPHIC, clearly shows that Glenn suspected something.

Glenn: "What is the reason for this? Do you have any reason?"

Texas cap com: "Not at this time. This is the judgment of Cape Flight...."

Glenn: "Roger. Understand."

Alan Shepard at Cape Canaveral cut in: "We are not sure whether your landing bag has deployed. We feel that it is possible to reenter with the retropackage on...."

What Glenn understood was that nobody could say with any certainty that he would come back alive.

Thirty-six years later, I asked Glenn about the inherent dangers of space travel, even in the space shuttle era.

"Nothing is 100 percent risk free—nothing," he said matter-of-factly.

History has revealed that John Glenn's reentry was a near-disaster. But in the 1963 National Geographic book *Great Adventures,* he downplayed the conditions that made his

Mercury capsule a searing sweatbox.

"Large flaming pieces of the retropackage broke off and flew past the window," he said. "This was of some concern, to put it mildly, because I wasn't real sure what they were. I had assumed that the retropack had gone when I saw the strap in front of the window. So I thought these flaming chunks could be parts of the heat shield breaking off.

"There was no doubt when the heat of re-entry occurred—at the same time as the fireball. But the heat didn't reach me for some time. I didn't feel particularly hot until I was getting down to about 80,000 feet.... By the time I reached the water I was sweating profusely."

For most Americans, the U.S. space program of the 1960s unfolded like a continuing, unpredictable saga. From the outset, however, members of the Society were kept way ahead of the curve with inside stories about not only what was happening at NASA but also what lay ahead a decade or so. Much of the Society's special access to such information came from Hugh L. Dryden, NASA's then-deputy administrator and a Society trustee since 1951.

A remarkable article published in July 1960, before the first American broke the barrier of space—before President John F. Kennedy's bold challenge to place a man on the moon by decade's end—detailed the NASA plan for a lunar landing. A lineup of model rockets shows not only the Atlas and Agena boosters that would power the Mercury and Gemini programs, but also a fully-rendered Saturn moon booster, nearly a decade prior to its history-making lunar flights. An even larger rocket in the lineup, the Nova, was never built.

Humans broke the bonds of Earth's

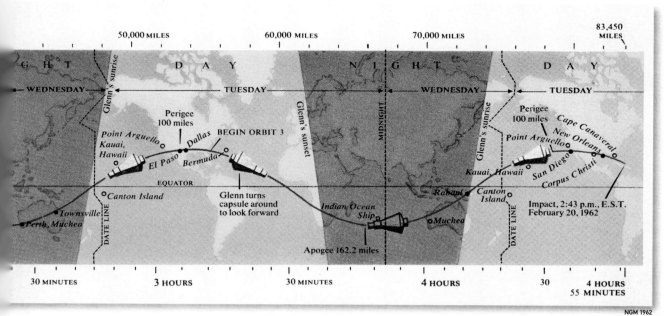

50,000 MILES 60,000 MILES 70,000 MILES 83,450 MILES

First American to experience sunset three times in a single day. John Glenn was more than a mere passenger in his *Friendship 7* space craft: He actually piloted it, changing its attitude to position himself for reentry.

NGM 1962

gravity on December 21, 1968, when the three men aboard the Apollo 8 spacecraft fired their outboard rocket and headed for lunar orbit. Air Force Lt. Gen. Sam C. Phillips, director of the Apollo Program, gave an account for May 1969 GEOGRAPHIC readers. His words reflect the by-then common space-flight status of calm routine amid high adventure:

"While some of us in Mission Control have cold coffee and baloney sandwiches for Christmas, the crew aloft enjoy their best meal of the trip—real chunks of turkey with… gravy that can be eaten with a spoon instead of squeezed from a plastic bag.

"They catch up on sleep, make pleasant jokes about flying saucers and Santa Claus and the fact that Isaac Newton is driving the spacecraft. At one point [Frank] Borman sums up the flight as 'a most fantastic voyage.'

"They enjoy news of congratulatory messages pouring in from all over the world, even from Russia and other Communist lands. Everyone seems impressed, in fact, except the few members of London's International Flat Earth Society, who say it is all a hoax."

When humans finally walked on the moon in July 1969, the National Geographic Society was along for the ride. The night that moon walker Neil Armstrong and his crewmates were presented the Hubbard Medal, he told the Society audience, "One other memento which we were privileged to take along with us on our trip was the flag that has accompanied every major recent expedition, the flag of the National Geographic Society.

"The National Geographic Society has been the sponsor, participant, contributor, documenter, enthusiastic recorder of every explorative expedition for…decades."

Sadly, by exploration standards, the United States abandoned the moon within three years of attaining it. Those who dreamed of following in the Apollo astronauts' dusty footprints would have to make do with descriptions from those who had walked there, among them David R. Scott, commander of Apollo 15, who wrote in the September 1973 NATIONAL GEOGRAPHIC, "To fall on the moon—and I did several times—is to rediscover childhood. You go down in slow motion, the impact is slight, the risk of injury virtually nil. Forsaking the adult attitude that regards a fall not only as a loss of dignity but also a source of broken bones, the moon walker—like a child—accepts it as yet another diversion. Only the clinging moon dust, the untoward demand on the oxygen supply occasioned by the exertion of getting up, pall the pleasure of a tumble.…

"Clutching the ladder, I raise my eyes from the now-familiar moonscape to earth, glowing in the black heavens—that incredibly vivid sphere, so blue, so beautiful, so beloved.… In eons to come, should astronauts from the deeps of space—from other solar systems in other galaxies—pass this way, they may find our spoor, our abandoned gear. We leave a piece of fauna—a falcon feather—and of flora—a four-leaf clover.

"In a little hollow in the moon dust we place a stylized figurine of a man in a space suit and beside it another metal plaque bearing the names of the 14 spacemen—Russians and Americans—who have given their lives so that man may range the cosmos. Finally we deposit a single book: the Bible.…

"Occasionally…I look up at the moon riding bright and proud above the clouds.…

THE FIRST FLIGHT OVER EVEREST

For years the often cloud-shrouded roof of the world had defied climbers and aviators who dreamed of seeing Everest's summit up close. But for the Houston-Mount Everest Expedition in April 1933, a team of British Army biplane fliers donned electrically-heated flight suits (bottom) and successfully maneuvered through the rarified air, high winds, and violent downdrafts to accomplish, in the words of a NATIONAL GEOGRAPHIC article, "the aerial conquest of Everest" (opposite). Before making that final assault, they received a bevy of Indian potentates on slate-gray elephants, eager to inspect the aircraft and the crew (below).

THE *NORGE*: FROM ROME TO THE NORTH POLE

Dirigible's-eye view of the Eternal City (below) comes from the Italian dirigible *Norge*—"Norway"—which set out in April 1926 with Roald Amundsen and a largely Norwegian crew to reach, improbably, the North Pole. The craft's designer and navigator, Gen. Umberto Nobile of the Italian Air Force, considered dirigibles superior to airplanes, due to their ability to slow and even hover, without having to land on fog-shrouded polar ice. Nobile chronicled the epic flight in the August 1927 issue of the GEOGRAPHIC. After stopping in

France and England, the ship proceeded to the Norwegian island of Spitsbergen, where it was moored in a roofless hangar some 800 miles from the Pole (below). On May 12, 1926, *Norge* became the first lighter-than-air craft to reach the top of the world, arriving just 48 hours after Richard Byrd and Floyd Bennett made their flight in a Fokker trimotor airplane. The dirigible then continued on to within 60 miles of Nome, Alaska, where high winds forced the crew to deflate and dismantle it, ending its 8,500-mile-long adventure.

BEYOND THE HORIZON

ALWAYS THERE HAS BEEN AN ADVENTURE
JUST AROUND THE CORNER—AND THE WORLD
IS STILL FULL OF CORNERS!
—NATURALIST ROY CHAPMAN ANDREWS

BY TONI EUGENE

From a ridge of South America's continental divide 18,300 feet above sea level in the Peruvian Andes, Loren McIntyre squinted through his camera's viewfinder. A sparkle of light gleamed in the lens. He gasped in the dry, thin air and blinked deliberately to make sure. Yes, the gleam was still there—a small mountain lake. Lightheaded from lack of oxygen, McIntyre cleared his throat and willed control into his voice. "I think we've found what we've been looking for," he told his two companions almost casually. The trio had fought hunger and altitude for days, struggling upward, step by painful step. Now—October 15, 1971—they were staring at what others had sought in vain for centuries—the ultimate source of South America's mighty Amazon, largest and longest river in the world.

Loren McIntyre, then 54, had been exploring South America for decades. By the age of 12 he had devoured everything in his local Seattle library about the continent and dreamed of exploring it himself. Finding the birthplace of the Amazon was one supremely satisfying payback for all the years he'd stubbornly pursued his dreams.

Of all the expeditions the Society has sponsored since its first foray in 1890, the most universally appealing are those made to remote and exotic realms beyond the horizon. Many of these are possible only with the resources and support of a major organization like the Geographic.

Some Society grantees have searched for the ruins of ancient civilizations, some have sought "lost" peoples, some have redrawn maps, while others have pursued their lifelong ambitions. But all these treks share something with even the most recent expeditions reported in NATIONAL GEOGRAPHIC: They spark the interest and imagination of the magazine's millions of readers and inspire images of dashing daredevils tramping through jungle-strewn slopes in the farthest reaches of the globe.

Geologist Israel C. Russell, one of the 33 founders of the National Geographic, led the Society's first expedition—to Alaska's Mount St. Elias, in 1890. Twelve years later Russell traveled to the Caribbean to report on the effect of volcanic eruptions there. A shipboard photograph shows a distinguished, bearded, almost somber gentleman standing ramrod straight against a rail. Russell's first-person prose, which captured the immediacy of the Caribbean tragedies, became the standard style of GEOGRAPHIC expedition narratives and helped inspire the public image of tough, yet touchable, explorers.

Midwesterner Eliza Ruhamah Scidmore must have been pretty tough, opting as she did for the life of a roving reporter rather than the traditional Victorian role of housewife. She became a geographer and an associate editor of NATIONAL GEOGRAPHIC, pursuing adventures that included a royal elephant hunt with the King of Siam and travels in what is now Sri Lanka, where "butterflies danced in clouds." Her "Young Japan" article, published in 1914, contains some of the GEOGRAPHIC's first color photographs—all hand tinted by the reporter herself.

Unlike Scidmore, most GEOGRAPHIC explorers to the back of beyond have not been on staff but were members of the wider National Geographic family, individuals who cherished an idea, won a grant or a field assignment, and followed through.

First female on the National Geographic Society's Board of Managers, globe-trotting geographer Eliza Ruhamah Scidmore (above) wrote and illustrated the magazine's July 1914 "Young Japan" article. Scidmore's signature hand-tinted photographs (right) still captivate.

Previous pages: Argo, replica of a Bronze Age galley, retraces the fabled route of Odysseus, Greek hero of the Trojan War.

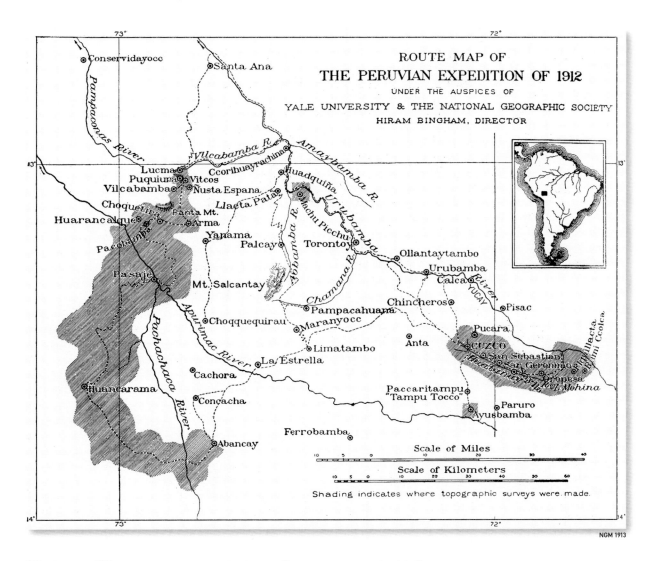

ROUTE MAP OF
THE PERUVIAN EXPEDITION OF 1912
UNDER THE AUSPICES OF
YALE UNIVERSITY & THE NATIONAL GEOGRAPHIC SOCIETY
HIRAM BINGHAM, DIRECTOR

Scale of Miles

Scale of Kilometers

Shading indicates where topographic surveys were made.

NGM 1913

Dotted lines mark the many paths explored by Hiram Bingham and his expedition to Machu Picchu in 1912, sponsored by Yale University and the National Geographic Society. This map accompanied his April 1913 magazine story, "In the Wonderland of Peru."

HIRAM BINGHAM AND THE LAND OF THE INCA

GEOGRAPHIC BACKING came late to Hiram Bingham, who led one of the Society's most famous expeditions. In 1908, three years before he would discover jungle-covered Machu Picchu that came to be known as the lost city of the Incas, this assistant Latin American history professor from Yale University sent articles and photographs of his earlier South American travels to NATIONAL GEOGRAPHIC Editor Gilbert H. Grosvenor, who summarily rejected the submission. The following year, Bingham published a book that contained many of those returned words and pictures; Grosvenor asked him for an article— and Bingham refused.

After stumbling on the city in the clouds, Bingham applied to the Society to help finance a trip to excavate Machu Picchu. Grosvenor advised him: "There is considerable feeling that the work is archaeological and not sufficiently geographic." Personally, however, the Editor favored the trip and urged Geographic support. A month later, in 1912, the Society awarded

Bingham its first archaeological grant.

Gangly nearly to the point of gauntness, the 36-year-old college professor exudes confidence in photographs, whether paddling a weathered raft across an Andean river or posing in front of a tent at one of his digs. He played the part of explorer to the hilt, dressing in riding breeches and leather boots. Battered fedora shading his face, he seems a prototype for Indiana Jones. During the summer of 1911, when Bingham traveled to Peru on a surveying expedition, he also searched for traces of the Inca, a people who had created a 3,000-mile-long Andean empire that had lasted until the arrival of Spanish conquistadores in 1532.

Six days out of the old Inca capital of Cuzco, hiking a narrow and winding road, Bingham encountered an Indian who offered to guide him to ruins at a place he called Machu Picchu, all for the grand fee of 50 cents. Bingham accepted, and the next day they plunged through wet and miserably cold jungle to the Urubamba River. The guide led Bingham

Majestic and mystical even in black-and-white, this Hiram Bingham photograph of the Inca stronghold of Machu Picchu beckoned to NATIONAL GEOGRAPHIC magazine readers, spurring thousands of new memberships. Following his initial discovery, he led three Society-sponsored expeditions to the ruin, including one in 1915 (opposite, top). An earlier photograph shows Peruvian Army Sgt. Carrasco—who was with Bingham when he first saw Machu Picchu in 1911—and a local Indian boy at an *intihuatana*, or sun observatory (opposite, bottom).

Framed by history itself, Bingham interpreter Osgood Hardy stands within one of three monolithic doorways remaining from the ancient Bolivian city of Tiwanacu. Older than the Inca Empire, Tiwanacu dates to about A.D. 600; it was one of South America's first cities.

Alert even at rest, Hiram Bingham, left, and British naturalist Casimir Watkins relax after the first ascent of 21,074-foot Nevado Coropuna in 1911. Their successful climb followed an attempt on the peak by Annie Smith Peck the same year. After the discovery of Machu Picchu, expedition members explored other Andean peaks and ruins.

across its boiling rapids on a "shaky little bridge, made of four tree trunks bound together with vines"—a structure so flimsy that the archaeologist crawled over it. On the far side of the river the men hacked their way through more jungle growth and started up a steep slope. "On all fours," Bingham wrote, "we pulled ourselves up through slippery grass, digging with fingers to keep from falling. Far below, the Urubamba snarled angrily. The heat was oppressive.... Calling on every reserve, I clambered through thinning jungle to where the ground leveled. Drenched with sweat, I straightened and saw a grass hut. Indians approached with gourds of spring water."

The Indians told Bingham of more old houses a little farther away, and he set off with a local boy as a guide. Part of the path, he noted, was "ladders of vines and tree trunks tied to the face of the precipice." Rounding a knoll, Bingham caught sight of tier after tier of terraces. "In my excitement," he recalled, according to the 1963 Geographic book *Great Adventures,* "I forgot my fatigue and hurried the length of a wide terrace toward the...jungle beyond it. I plunged into damp undergrowth, then stopped.... A mossy wall loomed before me.... Huge stone blocks seemed glued together, but without mortar—the finest Inca construction."

The city clung to a narrow ridge between two dome-shaped crags. Beyond, clouds draped neighboring peaks; far below thundered the Urubamba. Bingham's hands traced ancient walls masked by centuries of jungle growth. Vines and mosses draped stair-stepped tiers and terraces surrounded by sheer precipices that had hidden them for at least three centuries. The houses, crowded closely together, were connected by an extensive system of narrow streets and more than a hundred stairways. Machu Picchu was the largest and most complete Inca city ever found in modern times, and it was well preserved.

With the Geographic's help, Bingham returned three times to Machu Picchu—in 1912, 1914, and 1915. His crew rebuilt the rickety Urubamba bridge, which had been swept away after his initial visit. Then they blazed a trail to Machu Picchu, felling trees, chopping away bushes, and burning the debris to reveal details of the ancient city. The Inca had tamed the steep slopes with terraced gardens fed by stone aqueducts, and had divided the city into wards, each with its own gateway. A flight of 150 steps formed the main thoroughfare.

Aware of the Inca custom of burying material possessions with the dead, Bingham searched for graves. His 1912 expedition opened more than a hundred tombs, unearthing the bones of 173 people as well as jars, dishes, and jewelry that provided information about Inca society. On foot and mounted on mules, Bingham and his party scrambled through adjacent canyons and over nearby mountains to uncover even more Inca ruins hinted at by locals. His discoveries, descriptions, and photographs, entitled "The Wonderland of Peru," filled the entire April 1913 magazine—186 pages.

Bingham's 1914 expedition surveyed previously noted ruins, and, despite clouds and rain most of the time, mapped much of the area around Machu Picchu, correcting errors in existing maps. Bingham was elated at finding an old Inca road leading into Machu Picchu, and when he returned in 1915 he located several more trails and new groups of ruins.

Although the professor willingly endured hardships to ferret out ruins, clearly he preferred planning and comfort whenever possible. He did not feel it was an explorer's duty to rough it, and commented that "some of the younger men on our parties sometimes feel that their reputation as explorers is likely to be damaged if it is known that strawberry jam, sweet chocolate, cheese, and pickles are...on the bill of fare!"

Bingham's popularity helped the National Geographic Society grow. By 1913 it boasted 234,000 members, making it the largest educational association and geographic society in the world. Never short on ego, Bingham parlayed his fame into a career. He had married an heir to the Tiffany jewelry fortune and was eventually elected governor, then senator, of Connecticut. Bingham's penchant for exploration, however, extended from Peru to women, and he was divorced in 1937.

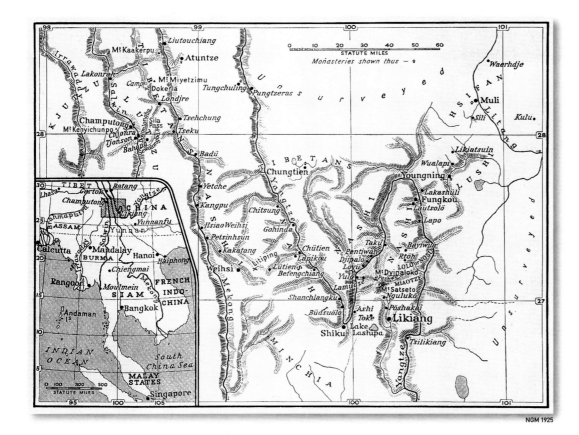

Botanist-explorer
Joseph F. Rock
roamed the remote
highlands of the
Tibet-China border
for more than 20
years, frequently
reporting his exploits
in the pages of
NATIONAL GEOGRAPHIC.
This sketch map
of that region graced
an April 1925 maga-
zine story about his
first trek there,
the 1923 Yunnan
Province Expedition.

JOSEPH F. ROCK—THE WONDERS OF CHINA AND TIBET

LIKE BINGHAM, Vienna-born scientist-
explorer Joseph F. Rock was ambitious. He
had a strong will and an even stronger ego, but
he lacked the archaeologist's urbanity and ease
with people. Rock's mother died when he was
six, and his stern and strict father raised an
introverted boy. Determined to travel rather
than become the priest his father wanted,
Rock studied languages on his own throughout his childhood. He was fluent in several
when he graduated from high school and left
Austria. He lived in Hawaii for a few years,
where he taught himself botany. In his first
article for the GEOGRAPHIC, which appeared in
March 1922, he wrote about his search for the
chaulmoogra tree, which produces an oil that
proved to be an effective treatment for leprosy.
Rock tracked the tree from Singapore to Siam,
to Burma, and into India. His own photographs of Bangkok shrines, Burmese natives,
and tiger traps accompany his text.

In 1923 the Geographic sponsored Rock's
first Yunnan Province Expedition, which
explored the Tibet-China border and reported
on the Naxi, a group of Tibeto-Burman people
who had lived in the area for more than 1,200
years. Headquartered in the Naxi village of
Nguluko in China's Yunnan Province, Rock's
group spent nearly two years exploring the
region. On one foray they set off through the

perpetual snows of what he called the Likiang
Mountains, a range of high peaks pierced by
the Yangtze River, seeking the Buddhist
lamasery of Muli. "The wind was howling furi-
ously and huge
masses of dry snow
were being whirled
hundreds of feet into
the air," he wrote.
"The gale from the
southwest fairly
pushed us along and
almost off our
horses." Growling
leopards kept Rock
awake one night in
a region "sparsely
settled and so moun-
tainous that hamlets
are perched on cliffs
like swallows' nests against a wall." It took ten
trips on a leaky boat to ferry his expedition
across the Yangtze. The morning after the sixth
night, they woke to sunlight—and, after riding
over a 15,000-foot pass, had a view of Muli,
perched on a distant hillside.

A settlement of 340 houses that sheltered
700 Buddhist monks, Muli gave its name to an
independent Buddhist kingdom in the
extreme southwestern corner of Sichuan

Harsh justice in the
Buddhist kingdom
of Muli: Confined to a
dungeon in shackles
and neck boards,
these purported
murderers saw
sunlight only when
Rock photographed
them in 1928.

Called Mount Mitzuga by Joseph Rock, rugged slopes sacred to members of the Muli Monastery cup a small lake shown here in a 1928 photograph Rock took at 14,750 feet. Rock was one of few photographers in the twenties who made Lumiére Autochromes; the NATIONAL GEOGRAPHIC pioneered the use of color photographs produced by that process. At a lamasery in what is now Yonming, the son of a Tibetan bandit chief donned the elegant robes and headdress of his office (above), and began to shake with convulsions and take on the voice and persona of the Tibetan deity Chechin.

Shoulder boards, tumplines, and bamboo canes help these Minchia porters bear heavy loads over the hills of Yunnan. Many of Rock's photographs, like this one from 1923, document Tibetan cultural groups previously unknown to Westerners.

Province. Its king ruled 22,000 subjects in a realm of 9,000 square miles—about the size of New Hampshire. Muli had lamaseries, not towns, and it became Rock's focus and home for nearly 20 years. In several of the ten articles he wrote for NATIONAL GEOGRAPHIC, Rock described the culture and customs of Muli. "A Tibetan tea party is, to say the least, a gastronomic endurance test which no squeamish soul could survive," he noted. Refreshments at one affair included gray buttered tea that tasted like liquid salted mud, antique and spotted yak cheese, and rocklike cakes like pretzels. The king of Muli presented Rock with a gift of dried mutton and yak cheese that was "literally *walking* all over the terrace of our house, being propelled by squirming maggots the size of a man's thumb." Taking tea would be one of Rock's tamer experiences, however.

In a 1925 letter to the Society he reported being stranded in a miserable temple full of coffins while bandits attacked the village. Believing he would be captured, Rock "wrapped up some extra warm underwear, a towel, condensed milk and some chocolate, besides ammunition for my two .45-caliber revolvers." Inexplicably, the outlaws disappeared with the night, and Rock and his crew proceeded safely.

He explored the Yangtze, Mekong, and Salween Rivers, taking photographs all the while and collecting 493 species of rhododendrons, more than 1,600 birds, and scores of mammals, all of which he sent back to the U.S. He especially recalled crossing the Yalung River, where natives had strung a cable equipped with a rawhide sling from bank to bank: Each man and animal in Rock's retinue dangled in turn above boiling rapids as someone on shore hauled on a wooden pulley to get them to the opposite shore.

In 1927 the Society sponsored Rock's second expedition to Yunnan Province. From his headquarters in a lamasery in the ancient principality of Choni, Rock made forays to

two mountain ranges—Amnyi Machen (now Anyemaqen, in Qinghai Province) and Minya Konka (Gonga Shan, Sichuan)—never before visited by Westerners. A local war pinned Rock in the lamasery, where 154 Tibetan heads were "strung about the walls of the Moslem garrison like a garland of flowers," but he finally pressed on in late spring with an epic caravan—20 armed men, 34 mules, and 60 yaks.

Often, Rock's expeditions involved caravans of heroic proportions. He dealt with blizzards, bandits, and rugged treks across mountain passes on an almost daily basis, but, as he noted in an August 1926 magazine story, "after a long day's march or ride, one cares little about surroundings as long as one has his own bed, table, chairs, and other necessary adjuncts brought with him from the civilized world." His cook prepared Austrian dishes based on Rock's own recipes, and Rock bathed daily in a folding tub from Abercrombie & Fitch. Presumably his many bearers and guides filled and cleaned it; Rock would never stoop to such a task.

A stickler for protocol, he dressed in white shirt, jacket, and tie to meet even the lowest-ranking Tibetan chiefs. He always faced the camera head on, making a short but solid presence. Indeed, all his articles reveal him as an outsider looking in—an observer, never a participant. He even speaks of "dying alone, as I have lived."

His pictures of towering icy mountains—first in black and white, then in pioneering color—evoke his loneliness. They are startlingly immense and empty panoramas of sharp angles and sheer slopes draped in blowing snow. At 18,000 feet he had to dry his negatives over yak-dung fires to keep them from freezing. Over the rivers and mountains his porters carried a black developing tent. Rock's photographs captured a land frozen in time, a place few Westerners had seen.

In 1949, as communists gradually gained control of China, they proclaimed Rock an enemy of the people and evicted him from the land he had loved and studied for more than 27 years. He finally returned to Hawaii, where he died in 1962. Today, hundreds of species of the rhododendrons he brought back from Asia bloom throughout the world, and his words and photographs chronicle peoples and cultures that have virtually disappeared since the Chinese Communist Revolution.

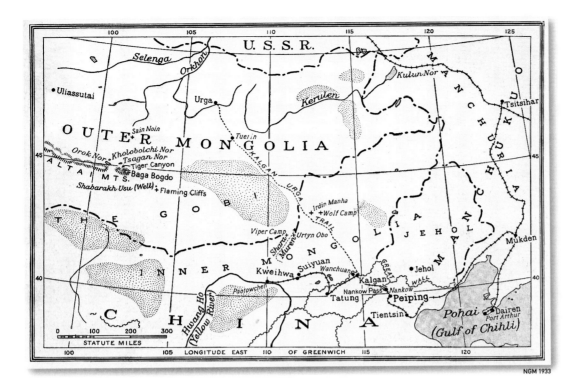

Known for its severe climate and vast distances, the Gobi stretches about 2,000 miles east to west through the heart of Mongolia. Roy Chapman Andrews traversed this desert of gravel and sand with motor vehicles. Between 1922 and 1930 he completed five expeditions to the Gobi, sponsored by the American Museum of Natural History.

NGM 1933

ROY CHAPMAN ANDREWS: EXPLORATIONS IN THE GOBI

NATURALIST ROY CHAPMAN ANDREWS, like Joseph F. Rock, also explored a little-known area of Asia. A zoologist employed by the American Museum of Natural History, he led five Central Asiatic Expeditions from 1922 to 1930, to probe Mongolia's geologic history. One goal was to determine whether the Gobi—the vast stony desert of Central Asia—had been an important zoological nursery.

Until that time scientific research in Mongolia had been very limited. Arctic temperatures there restricted research to April through October. There were no railroads, and transportation consisted of ponies, camels, and oxcarts. Andrews figured that camels could cover only ten miles a day; since cars could travel a hundred, scientists in cars could complete ten years' work in just one season!

Thus Andrews imported Dodge vehicles to traverse the Gobi's wastes, supported by a camel caravan that carried gas, food, and other supplies several months in advance of the rest of the expedition. The cars held only enough food and fuel to sustain them until the next camel rendezvous at a preselected site.

Each camel toted about 400 pounds of supplies packed in rectangular wooden boxes, which would hold fossils carefully swathed in camel hair when the expedition left the desert. The group was a catholic combination of scientists—geologists, paleontologists, topographers, and a botanist—because Andrews wanted expert knowledge available on the spot.

Andrews was 38 in 1922. Photographs show him wearing a campaign hat (standard issue U.S. Army wear of the time). He looks very young and very earnest, whether excavating a giant fossil or feeding pet eaglet chicks with chopsticks. A pistol in a leather holster often rests on his right hip.

"Brigands must be considered in every expedition to the interiors of Mongolia or China," he would write in his June 1933 NATIONAL GEOGRAPHIC article summarizing the expeditions. "They swarm like devouring locusts, even up to the walls of the cities." On one expedition the savvy and self-confident Andrews was able to negotiate a half-price fee for safe conduct—$2.50 per camel—because the bandit chieftain turned out to be an old friend.

It was bitterly cold when Andrews's camel caravan set out early in March 1922 on a 600-mile trek.

"Snow still lay on the desert and spring blizzards raged," wrote the leader. "Brigands were reported along the trail."

Nomads gingerly approach one of the Dodge vehicles Andrews used in the Gobi. None had seen such a machine before, and most were so frightened at first that they fled to the hills on horseback.

When sandy areas—comparatively rare in the gravelly Gobi—trapped the Dodges, expedition members simply pushed them onward, with Andrews's dog, Wolf, happy to hitchhike (below). At a dig called Flaming Cliffs, the team unearthed its most exciting find—fossilized dinosaur eggs (opposite, top) 95 million years old. A *Protoceratops* nest containing 18 eight-inch-long eggs now rests in Chicago's Field Museum of Natural History. Using a radio primarily to pick up time signals, scientists were able to establish the accurate longitude records necessary to map the Gobi; local Mongol nomads seemed to enjoy listening in (opposite, bottom).

Investigating the shore-whaling industry for his first NATIONAL GEOGRAPHIC article in May 1911, Roy Chapman Andrews ranged from Japan to Canada's Vancouver Island in British Columbia. Andrews shipped this 60-foot sperm whale, killed off Japan, to New York's American Museum of Natural History, where he was assistant curator of mammals.

A reclining Andrews and companion study the remains of a dinosaur known as a titanothere that was unearthed in 1925 at Urtyn Obo, central Mongolia. Titanotheres, gigantic herbivores resembling rhinoceroses, became extinct about 30 million years ago.

A month later, his vehicles started from the railhead in Kalgan, a rather dreary trading center west of Beijing.

Beyond the town they hit bogs that sank them to their hubs. In sandy spots the men used canvas strips and ropes to get traction, and sometimes even the scientists had to push. On the whole, however, the Dodges successfully navigated the fine gravel surface of the Gobi.

In the very first season the team unearthed one of the world's richest and most important fossil beds, at an area called Flaming Cliffs. Their most celebrated discovery was dinosaur eggs—the first found anywhere.

Two eggs contained partial, embryonic skeletons of *Protoceratops* fossils, proving what some scientists had surmised earlier—that the giant reptiles did lay eggs. Expedition members also dug up 75 skulls and 14 skeletons of *Protoceratops*.

Since the Age of Dinosaurs, climate changes have brought the Gobi to such a dry and cold state that it now shelters few reptiles. One night, however, a veritable army of pit vipers seeking warmth invaded the tents of Andrews's camp. The men woke to find snakes wrapped around the legs of their cots, in their shoes, lying on top of their guns, and even in a hat. They killed 47 vipers, and even the unflappable Andrews seemed shaken.

"This snake business got on our nerves," he wrote. "The Chinese and Mongols deserted their tents and slept in the cars and on camel boxes. The rest of us never moved after dark without a flashlight in one hand and a pickax in the other."

The explorers used finer equipment at Flaming Cliffs to brush sand from the 30-million-year-old bones of a *Baluchitherium,* the largest land mammal that ever walked the face of the Earth.

Andrews is quoted as describing it as "an aberrant browsing rhinoceros that must have looked like a grounded blimp—24 feet long, 17 feet high at the shoulders, 25 feet tall at its head."

Like the dinosaur eggs, the bones of "Baluch" helped prove that Mongolia was one of the places where dinosaurs flourished.

Even more exciting to Andrews was the discovery of seven rat-size skulls belonging to the most ancient known mammals. Only one mammal skull from the Age of Reptiles had ever been found before.

Expedition topographer Maj. L. B. Roberts made great strides in mapping the heart of Mongolia, a land so featureless that few natural landmarks exist. (Once, the group traveled 500 miles before seeing a tree; they promptly picnicked in its scanty shade.) Roberts overcame such lack of landmarks by using the Dodges as stadia rods and measuring distances by the cars' speedometers. In that way, he managed to survey more than a thousand miles of desert.

An outgoing and gregarious leader, Roy Chapman Andrews was refreshingly free of self-importance—unlike Rock or Bingham. When one expedition member played a practical joke on him, Andrews remained unruffled—but later trumped the trickster, an avid bird egg collector, by dyeing hard-boiled hen eggs and placing them as though they were in a crane's nest, leaving them for the joker to discover and analyze.

Andrews chronicled the bitter cold and the scorching sun of the Gobi, but he also noted its stark and alluring beauty. He remembered one campsite on a gravel beach near the edge of a lake.

"Just as the sun disappeared, Baga Bogdo was flooded with a wonderful lavender light which edged the lake with deepest purple. Then the moon rose in a splendor of gold from behind the sand dunes, drawing a glittering path across the water to the very door of my tent."

Andrews admitted to a wave of sadness upon leaving Flaming Cliffs for the last time. But the itch to explore urged him on. "The active years of an explorer's life are short," he wrote, "and new fields are calling for those that remain to me."

In 1931 the National Geographic Society awarded Andrews its highest honor—the prestigious Hubbard Medal.

His discoveries, said Editor Gilbert H. Grosvenor, "have pushed back the horizons of life upon the earth and filled in the gaps in the great ancestral tree of all that breathes."

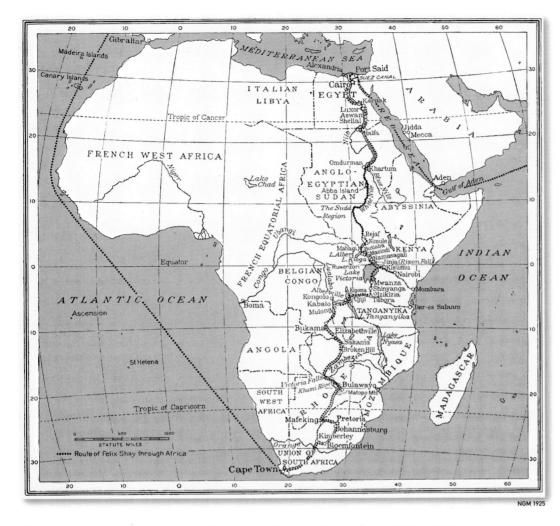

Cairo to Cape Town: Setting out from the Egyptian capital in 1924, American adventurers Felix Shay and his wife, Porter, took four-and-a-half months to reach South Africa, traversing the continent north to south by boat, train, and foot. Another African epic, the 1924-25 Citroën Central African Expedition, relied on cars equipped with tires and caterpillar treads. In Tanganyika, now Tanzania, the Citroëns rafted the 200-foot-wide Ruaha River on three leaky pirogues connected by boards (below).

NGM 1925

THROUGH AFRICA: CROSSING THE CONTINENT

UNLIKE ASIA, closed to Westerners for centuries, Africa was a known quantity when the Society was founded in 1888. European explorers had begun to sail Africa's Atlantic coast, and the legendary 19th-century journeys of David Livingstone, Henry Morton Stanley, Richard Burton, and John Speke had opened the continent and paved the way for European colonization. By 1900 most of Africa was administered by European nations. Railways and roads were few. Large sections were isolated by jungle and desert, peopled by tribes whose customs were strange to Westerners.

A trip of several thousand miles overland from Cairo to Cape Town began as the whim of inveterate globetrotters Felix Shay and his wife, Porter. It was an informal odyssey, not a scientific one. Boating along rivers and lakes, taking trains where possible, and hiking twice through tropical regions, the Shays reached Cape Town in 135 days. Felix reported every detail of the journey in the February 1925 NATIONAL GEOGRAPHIC, including being marooned in the desert while a sirocco blasted their train with sand.

He described ferocious Masai warriors wearing headdresses of lion's manes and Nairobi women with shaved heads and earlobes distended by huge earplugs, and he noted the thousands of animals—baboons, elephants, roaring lions, elands, antelopes, gazelles, and hyenas. For one section of the journey, they walked 250 miles in 16 days, mostly on a dirt path, at times stricken with fever. Shay's magazine article contained more pages—138—than the expedition did days. Today it reads rather like a Christmas letter about a family vacation, yet it gave GEOGRAPHIC readers an in-depth look at a fascinating continent and its people.

Feast of different cultures often greets the indomitable Geographic explorer. After traversing Africa in Citroëns, Georges-Marie Haardt captained a similar expedition across Asia—where he gained audience with Mir Mohammed Nazim Khan, in Hunza, India (left). The khan later treated Haardt's team to a gala evening at his hilltop castle, complete with dancing girls. After wading through several crocodile-infested rivers in Africa's Sudan, Porter Shay smilingly opted for an alternate mode of transportation (above).

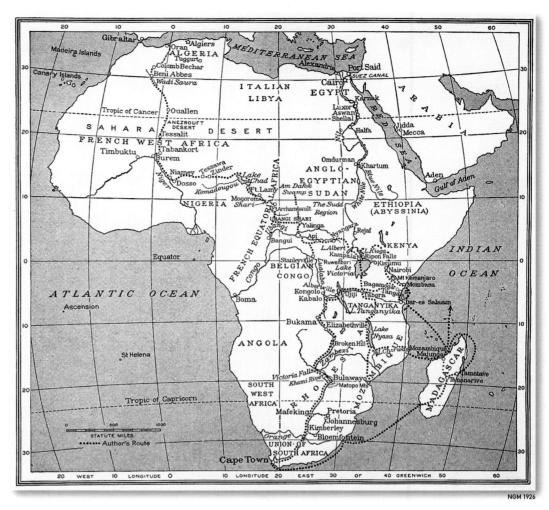

Embarking from a railhead south of Algiers, the eight cars in Haardt's Citroën Central African Expedition rolled south and east across Africa to Cape Town, covering some 15,000 miles in nine months.

AS AMERICA'S LOVE AFFAIR with the automobile blossomed in the 1920s, the NATIONAL GEOGRAPHIC carried the stories of two French expeditions to cross the African continent by car. The first, the Citroën Trans-Sahara Expedition, set out in December 1922 to traverse 2,000 miles of dunes, sharp rocks, boulder-strewn plateaus, and high crags. For traction, rollers covered in rubber and canvas replaced the rear wheels on five specially designed Citroën autos. Two vehicles were equipped with rapid-fire guns to repel marauders, and all five had huge headlights and outsize front tires that made them look like giant bugs.

The cars rolled south from dusty Tuggurt (now Touggurt), the terminus of the Southern Algerian Railway. Keeping to an average pace of a hundred miles a day, they stopped at two pre-established depots for supplies and fuel. Broiling by day and freezing at night, the expedition fought its way across waterless wastes and through a sandstorm.

Christmas was spent at a lonely mountain camp; New Year's passed at an ancient well. But the strange-looking caravan pulled into the sand-blown streets of the ancient trading center of Timbuktu (now Tombouctou, in

today's Mali) after only 20 days, completing a trek that normally took camels three months.

So isolated that it remains a symbol of remoteness even now, Timbuktu was founded on the desert's edge about A.D. 1100 by Tuareg nomads. It grew and prospered with the trans-Sahara caravan trade in salt and gold. By 1500 it was a commercial and intellectual center known throughout Africa; its population ranged perhaps as high as one million. When the Citroën Trans-Sahara Expedition arrived in 1923, Timbuktu contained only about 8,000 inhabitants, many of them nomads. Its total European population consisted of about 20 souls. The June 1924 NATIONAL GEOGRAPHIC notes that life in Timbuktu "passes like a slow moving picture through the narrow, tortuous windings of its sand-carpeted thoroughfares."

To prove that cars could cope with equatorial forests as well as deserts—and also to pioneer a possible railroad route through central Africa—Georges-Marie Haardt organized a second Citroën expedition in 1924. He led the group of seven other explorers and nine mechanics. Eighty tons of supplies had been shipped ahead and con-signed to supply depots along the route. Eight "caterpillar cars," each equipped with a trailer carrying extra water, gas, and oil, left the rail-head in Algeria on October 28, 1924, and proceeded south through the Sahara.

The first leg of their 15,000-mile journey paralleled the route of the previous Citroën caravan, with cars rolling across a stretch of 330 waterless miles, past the bleached bones of unlucky travelers who had died of thirst, to reach the Niger River in three weeks.

Like settlers circling their wagons on the American prairie, the men parked their cars each evening in the form of a hollow square and camped within, keeping a wary eye out for robbers. In the June 1926 NATIONAL GEO-GRAPHIC, Haardt describes the elaborate braids and hairstyles, the tattooed faces, nose plugs, and plate-size lip disks of native African women, and the veiled faces and flowing robes of Tuareg tribesmen.

In March 1925 the caravan entered thick equatorial jungle. "What surprised us most in the great forest," Haardt noted, "was its silence." For 375 miles the group followed a trail—cut for them by a 40,000-man crew in a month—roofed by thick foliage. The cars crossed rivers and ravines on bridges that were only slender branches lashed together with vines. They "creaked and swayed in a most alarming manner," Haardt complained, and "everyone breathed easier when they left the "region of eternal twilight." As planned, the caravan split at Lake Victoria to explore four different routes to the Indian Ocean. Haardt and a companion, with a second vehicle, motored south. The cars crossed one river on a raft made of three leaky native canoes, three men bailing constantly while natives pushed and pulled the makeshift craft to safety. It sank just after the second car made its precarious crossing.

Haardt's pride at reaching the east coast of the continent was evident. "Finally," he wrote, "after eight months of struggle through swamps, bush fires, rivers and jungles, a sea breeze brought us the invigorating tang of salt air." The expedition returned from its journeying with insights into Africa's terrain and geography as well as sketches, some 90,000 feet of motion pictures, and about 8,000 photographs. Haardt had proved that automobiles could negotiate the African wilds.

EXPEDITIONS OF PERSONAL FULFILLMENT:
PROBING CAPE HORN AND
CIRCLING THE WORLD ALONE

AS A BOY OF 14, Oregon-born sailor Amos Burg heard mariners tell of the fog and gales they had fought as they had rounded Cape Horn, the storm-ridden tip of South America that reaches toward Antarctica. Until the Panama Canal was completed in 1914, ships routinely negotiated the Horn as they crossed between the Atlantic and Pacific. Poised at the southern end of the Andes, the Horn occupies one of many mountainous islands that make up the Tierra del Fuego Archipelago at the continent's end. None of the old salts Burg listened to had ever bothered to explore the many ragged coastlines that exist between South America's mainland and the cape—a straight-line distance of some 300 miles. Burg dreamed of navigating that wind-whipped no-man's-land. Decades later the story of his personal quest appeared in the December 1937 NATIONAL GEOGRAPHIC.

Map shows present-day boundaries and names.

Buffeted by nonstop storms, the rugged islands leading from the mainland of South America to Cape Horn constitute a horrific maze—and a sailor's ultimate challenge. For eight months, Amos Burg explored these gale-swept waters aboard *Dorjun*, a modified 26-foot surf boat.

Burg bought a condemned 26-foot U.S. Coast Guard surf boat and modified it himself to withstand the rigors of the voyage. From Magallanes (now Punta Arenas), a town of 25,000 in extreme southern Chile, he and his

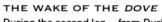
NGM 1970

THE WAKE OF THE *DOVE*

During the second leg—from Durban to the Caribbean—of Robin Lee Graham's journey (above, right), Graham tired of the sea and had to force himself to continue. By the time he completed the trip's final segment from the Caribbean Sea through the Panama Canal to Long Beach, California (above), Graham was 20, married, and captain of a new and larger vessel, *Return of the Dove*. During the first part of his journey (above right), while ashore in Darwin, Australia, Robin scrubbed *Dove*'s transom while his cat, *Avanga*, supervised (left).

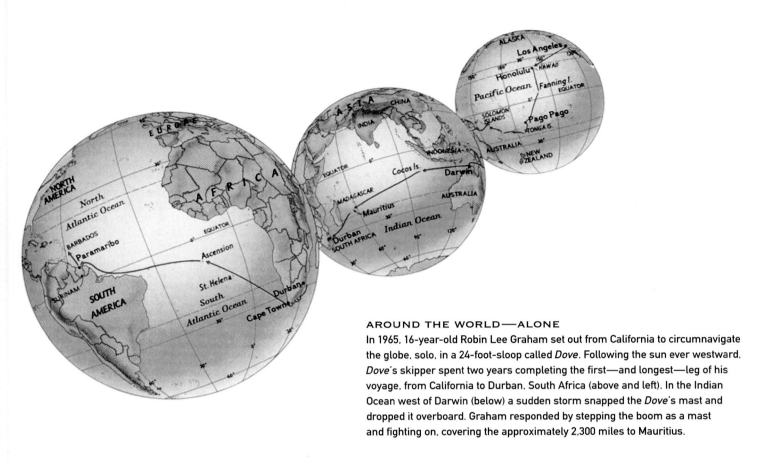

AROUND THE WORLD—ALONE

In 1965, 16-year-old Robin Lee Graham set out from California to circumnavigate the globe, solo, in a 24-foot-sloop called *Dove*. Following the sun ever westward, *Dove*'s skipper spent two years completing the first—and longest—leg of his voyage, from California to Durban, South Africa (above and left). In the Indian Ocean west of Darwin (below) a sudden storm snapped the *Dove*'s mast and dropped it overboard. Graham responded by stepping the boom as a mast and fighting on, covering the approximately 2,300 miles to Mauritius.

Taking a break from his solo sail around the world, Robin Graham flew to the interior of Surinam after reaching South America and motored upriver to an Indian village. His antics with a bird's disembodied feet inspired a sound he often missed on his lonely cruise—laughter.

companion, seaman Roy Pepper, sailed south into a labyrinth of wild glacier-covered mountains, narrow inlets, and small bays. It rained for an entire month—"a dismal downpour."

Through furious squalls and blinding snow the two men edged toward the cape, stopping at small settlements to visit seal hunters and anchoring in glacial fjords to photograph penguins and icy peaks. Never far from land—small islands covered with beech forests and carpeted with moss and vines—they fought the weather every day, anchoring in sheltered bays during the worst storms. The boat's four-horsepower motor beat against howling westerly winds, and the men could seldom raise sail.

When influenza struck Burg down, he dosed himself with "two of this and two of that" and struggled on. The men saw no sign of the ship that was supposed to resupply them, and their provisions dwindled. Eventually they ran out of gasoline while exploring glacial inlets of Darwin on Tierra del Fuego.

For nearly three weeks they rowed various fjords, averaging only a mile an hour. Perpetual mists and clouds shrouded the peaks and snowfields that surrounded them. One evening a gale blew them toward a glacier that was calving icebergs. "Our oars were useless," Burg reported. "We drifted nearer. Our fate— smothered by hundreds of tons of ice—seemed inevitable. Then suddenly the wind calmed."

Finally the men sighted their supply ship and, with 80 gallons of gasoline, fresh photographic supplies, salt, flour, and potatoes safely stowed on the little boat, they sailed east. After the longest calm of the trip—six days—they welcomed the rising shriek of

wind and enjoyed several days of good sailing.

Then, as drinking water ran short, another gale threatened to blow them out to sea. "The sail boom snapped and fell overboard," noted Burg. "Our lee rail went under," and the men struggled to a safe anchorage. After five raging days the gale weakened. "I was not surprised," Burg commented dryly. "It had used up all the wind in the world." The men hoisted anchor and steered south.

Pounding through the teeth of yet another storm, they anchored off an island just 12 miles from the Horn. The next morning Burg scrambled through ravines crowded with wind-warped beech forests and clambered his way up talus slopes past a glacier to the top of 2,211-foot Mount Hyde for a panoramic view of Horn Island and, at its tip, Cape Horn. It had taken him eight months to achieve that view. Even as he descended, fog and mists closed in.

ANOTHER SKIPPER WITH A DREAM so captured the imagination of GEOGRAPHIC readers that they followed his adventures in three sequential articles. Robin Lee Graham was barely 16 when he set out from Los Angeles, California, in July 1965 to circumnavigate the globe— alone. His was not the first solo circumnavigation—Joshua Slocum accomplished that feat in 1897—but Graham was the youngest ever to try.

In his 24-foot fiberglass sloop, *Dove*, Graham survived hurricanes, dismastings, weeks becalmed, and a near collision with a freighter. The greatest hardship, he reported, was the "agony of loneliness." Although he stopped numerous times to work, vacation, make repairs, take on supplies, and even get married, he was cut off from other people for weeks at a stretch and grew so depressed that he considered quitting.

Graham didn't quit, but grew in stature and strength as he sailed from California to Australia, South Africa, and on to the Caribbean. He then went through the Panama Canal and continued to California, completing his voyage.

In a journey of private growth he shared with millions of GEOGRAPHIC readers, Graham traveled almost five years, logged 30,600 nautical miles, and gained an appreciation for solitude: Soon after his return, he moved to an 80-acre homestead in Montana.

IN SEARCH OF VANISHING PEOPLES

FROM ITS EARLIEST YEARS, the Society published reports and sent explorers to the farthest reaches of the globe to chronicle various peoples and cultures, both in words and photographs. Many of them got an eyeful. In May 1903 a picture of two bare-breasted Filipino women appeared in the magazine, presenting the world's peoples *au naturel*. The decision to publish was not made lightly. Newly appointed Editor Gilbert H. Grosvenor explained that "the women dressed, or perhaps I should say undressed, in this fashion.... The pictures were a true reflection of the customs of the time in those islands."

The inclusion of naked women likely broadened the GEOGRAPHIC's audience. For years thereafter—at least until the proliferation of men's magazines—pre- and post-pubescent males ogled the magazine's pages. Truth be told, plenty of young ladies peeked, too, impatient for such endowments. The pictures, however, were a small part of the story. Hundreds of NATIONAL GEOGRAPHIC articles have immortalized peoples whose lives and cultures were rapidly changing forever.

The June 1963 issue featured one such group, the Bushmen—or San—of Africa's Kalahari Desert. Summing up seven expeditions to the 360,000-square-miles of low scrub and grass in southwest Africa, Elizabeth Marshall Thomas described the habits and lifestyle of these "small, slight people, as hard and strong and slender as the thorn trees among which they live." They were nomads, living in one spot until food was gone, then moving on. The Kalahari, she noted, contained almost no surface water for ten months of the year—yet the Bushmen survived by drinking fluids squeezed from melons and roots. They constructed simple branch-and-grass shelters and hunted with two-foot-long reed arrows tipped with bone points and a poison crushed from beetle pupae so lethal that a drop of it would kill a man if it reached his bloodstream. Even so, Bushmen were gentle people whose lives revolved around trust, cooperation, and peace.

By 1982 many Bushmen, long admired for their hunting and tracking skills, carried automatic weapons in a fight for South West Africa's independence. Only a few remained in the small nomadic bands Marshall had found in the Kalahari.

ON THE OTHER SIDE OF THE GLOBE, photographer Malcolm S. Kirk explored the world of a very different group—headhunters and other Stone Age peoples living in a region that is now part of Papua New Guinea. North of Australia, 1,500-mile-long New Guinea is the

Map shows present-day boundaries and names.

world's second largest island, after Greenland. Much of it is a wild mix of jungles, muddy deltas, mangrove swamps, and rivers that harbor man-eating crocodiles.

With two companions—research chemist Derek Skingle and mountaineer Maxwell Smart—Kirk began a four-month, 600-mile crossing of the island by canoe and on foot. Each man carried a 75-pound pack loaded with gear, survival rations, and trade goods.

Homeland of Africa's Bushmen—more properly called San—the Kalahari Desert faces increasing change as civilization continues to encroach. Elizabeth Marshall Thomas chronicled the simple lifestyles of these people—and warned of their dwindling numbers—in the June 1963 NATIONAL GEOGRAPHIC.

Faced for the first time with his own image, a Biami warrior in Australia-administered New Guinea (now Papua New Guinea) grins with pride and amazement. Malcolm S. Kirk photographed members of various Stone Age peoples of this South Pacific island before modern influences began to alter them forever.

Barely above the surface, research chemist Derek Skingle and two native guides pole across a rain-swollen stream in the wild Nomad River area of central New Guinea (left). Skingle and mountaineer Maxwell Smart joined photographer Malcolm Kirk to canoe and hike from south to north through the widest part of the island—taking nearly four months to make the 600-mile trek. Costumed to portray an evil spirit in a festival in Mount Hagen, now part of Papua New Guinea, a mud-smeared tribesman wears a dried-clay helmet; his bamboo stick serves as a spear.

Laced with crocodile-infested streams, the mosquito-ridden mud flats and tropical forests of the Asmat, on the southwestern coast of New Guinea, still shelter remnants of Stone Age cultures. Although Indonesia had declared head-hunting illegal, Kirk found the practice alive and well when he explored the Asmat by dugout canoe in the 1970s. An island divided, New Guinea answers to two governments: Indonesia continues to control Irian Jaya, as it has since the Dutch left in 1963. Papua New Guinea, administered by Australia when NATIONAL GEOGRAPHIC published this March 1972 map, became an independent nation in 1975.

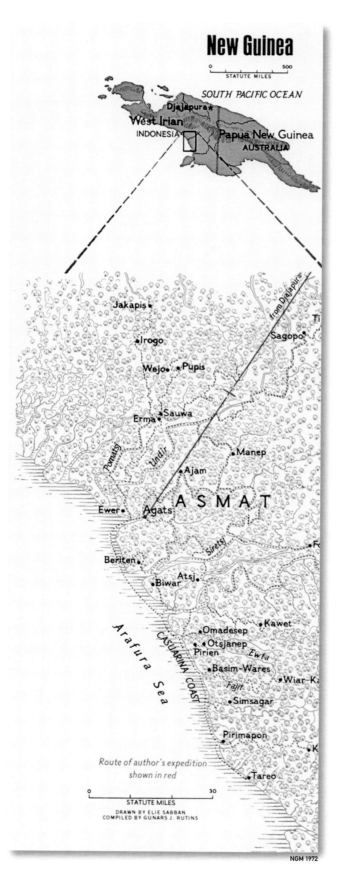

Kirk carried his camera gear; his two companions packed rifles. For Kirk the trip was "an opportunity to record a way of life civilizing influences must inevitably end." Smart would guide the group, and Skingle would collect medicinal herbs for later study. From Lake Murray the men canoed north to pick up a native trail. Then, led by two local guides, they began hiking through rain forest. It was eerily quiet. Kirk reported in the April 1969 magazine that "the green canopy of foliage closed over our heads. The trees became bars of some enormous prison.... We slipped and fell on damp tree roots. We stopped to pick off leeches." The men's legs wept with ulcerated sores, and their feet shriveled in their boots. But they would see a lifestyle, a culture, unfold: Island men hunting, children with their mothers, women working. One warrior, apparently in good health, claimed that a local sorcerer had marked him for death. A week later Kirk took pictures of his funeral, a ritual rarely witnessed by outsiders. As Kirk entered one village of headhunters, he realized that most of them, "even the young boys peering at us through the bushes—had eaten the flesh of slain enemies, and still were doing it." The attainment of manhood, he discovered, was marked by an initiation rite that included the piercing of the nasal septum. Warriors stretched the opening wider with successively larger plugs of bamboo or bone.

Kirk returned to New Guinea a few years later to photograph Asmat headhunters in the south-central part of the island, which he explored via a dugout canoe equipped with an outboard motor. Although headhunting had been outlawed by the Indonesian government several years before, in some parts of the Asmat a freshly-severed head was an integral part of a boy's ritualistic initiation into manhood. Asmat warriors baked and skinned the heads of enemies, then pierced the temples, shook out the brains, and ate them. "Once a man," Kirk wrote, "offered to trade me a human skull, quite fresh, for a jungle knife."

Soon, encroaching civilization—government officials, missionaries, tourists—would make inroads on native rites and beliefs in New Guinea. The journeys of Marshall and Kirk, along with many others reported in the pages of NATIONAL GEOGRAPHIC, chronicled what Kirk called "the old ways before they faltered and were gone."

Pushing Back the Horizons of Exploration:
Parachuting into the Vilcabamba;
Seeking the Source of the Amazon

On August 5, 1963, G. Brooks Baekeland and Peter R. Gimbel parachuted onto a 10,500-foot-high shelf in the Cordillera Vilcabamba, a spur of the Andes in southeastern Peru. To their knowledge, they were the first people ever to set foot there. Their high-altitude landings were made possible with recently developed experimental parachutes equipped with dozens of slits to direct air to the back of the canopy, lifting and slowing the chutes. Just in case, each man wore a crash helmet and football padding. As he pulled his rip cord, Baekeland noted in the August 1964 National Geographic: "The valley seemed dark and bristly, like the mouth of a Venus flytrap waiting to catch me."

Certainly the 9,000-square-mile drainage of the Vilcabamba was wrapped in jungle and mystery. Legends abounded of Inca gold and ruins in the area, and now vague reports of a 50-mile-long plateau suitable for colonization were attracting the interest of the Peruvian government. The main goal of this expedition was to cross the rugged and jungled mountain range from the Apurimac River on the west to the Urubamba on the east. Another aim was to collect plants and animals no scientist had ever studied before.

Initially, Baekeland and Gimbel had hoped to rough out an airstrip, but the ground was far too soggy and soft. They decided to rely instead on airplane supply drops. Four days later, two compatriots parachuted in, and the entire group started climbing. Each man carried a pack weighing up to 90 pounds. "We were in dense cloud forest," wrote Baekeland. "Moss-covered holes swallowed us to the thighs." In "permanent wetting cold" the four men slashed their way up with machetes. Specimens, including a strange tree frog, a hummingbird, a moth, and club moss, went into their packs.

Thirteen days later the group reached a lake at 13,000 feet, near the crest of the range and crossed the divide. With 15 day's rations they started their descent. "It was to take us not 15 days to reach our destination on the Urubamba," Baekeland recalled later, "but 61; most of these days were remembered now

as though in a nightmare." Air drops of food and supplies sustained the men—barely—as they trudged downward. Wasps attacked Baekeland one day. Temporarily blinded, he passed out—then plunged on an hour later, in typical superhero style.

Temperatures grew warmer as the men descended, and on October 13 they encountered the first people they had seen in two months—blue-tattooed Machiguenga Indians, who traveled with them for two weeks and helped them reach their goal—the Urubamba. This expedition, the first to penetrate the heart of the Vilcabamba on foot, resulted in an accurate map of the region. The explorers discovered its true contours—jagged peaks, muskeg-covered slopes, and steep-walled valleys. It took them almost three months to complete their 150-mile-journey, a feat impossible without modern equipment and airplane support.

Author-photographer Loren McIntyre, whose freelance career with the Society would span nearly 40 years, relied on stereoscopic aerial photographs to pinpoint the ultimate source of the mighty Amazon River. He used cunning as well as supreme self-confidence to bring off the trip, convincing friends at the Inter American Geodetic Survey to go, then advising the National Geographic

Diverse techniques help National Geographic explorers fill in blanks on the map. Parachutes bore one team to southern Peru's previously unexplored Cordillera Vilcabamba in 1963, while crampons and a compass took Loren McInytre (below) to the Amazon's most distant source—a tiny Peruvian lake high in the Andes.

Often considered a tropical Eden due to the raw beauty of its native people and its nature, the Amazon Basin spans an area three-fourths as big as the contiguous U.S. One hundred years ago, some 230 different forest tribes inhabited this region; since then, civilization has driven many to extinction. Loren McIntyre chronicled many Indian peoples during his decades of travel in Amazonia, including these Kamayura newlyweds (below), rejoicing in 1972 over signs that their first child is on the way. McIntyre also photographed this 877-foot-long waterfall upstream from Peru's Apurimac River, shrinking an airplane to toy dimensions (opposite).

Legendary refuge of Inca rulers, the 9,000-square-mile Cordillera Vilcabamba, or Vilcabamba Range, juts from a vast tangle of jungle on the eastern slope of the Andes. Data gathered over the course of a three-month traverse by the four explorers shown at right resulted in the first map to delineate the actual outlines of the range.

Four explorers surveyed the terrain from the air and on foot, collecting biological specimens and making notes for this map, the first to show actual outlines of the rugged Vilcabamba. The expedition achieved the first known traverse between the Apurimac and the Urubamba, tributaries of the Amazon.

G. Brooks Baekeland
Expedition Co-leader

Peter R. Gimbel
Expedition Co-leader

Peter A. Lake

Jack C. Joerns

THE
VILCABAMBA

0   10   20   30
STATUTE MILES

Main Party Route ——   Asheshov's Route ••••••••
Bush Settlements ⊡   Expedition Stations ⊡
Airstrips ✈   Elevations in feet 14800

© National Geographic Society   Map by John J. Brehm and John F. Dorr

NGM 1964

that he would be accompanying the IAGS survey. McIntyre and cartographers at the Society had already almost figured out the source; all they lacked was proof. The resultant 1971 expedition would travel up the longest branch of the Apurimac River, an Amazon tributary.

McIntyre and two others hiked 20 miles through the southern highlands of Peru to a semicircular crest of the continental divide. McIntyre hefted cameras, compasses, and altimeters; his companions hauled tent, stove, ice axes, crampons, ropes, other gear, and food. The men backpacked through terrain so barren it resembled a moonscape. Finally, roped together, they clambered onto an ice-edged ridge. A thousand feet below them—at 17,220 feet above sea level—lay a 100-foot-wide tarn that came to be called Laguna McIntyre (Lake McIntyre). "More a pond than a lake," McIntyre commented; a single landslide or earthquake could easily displace it. Still, it was the birthplace of the Amazon, a river so vast that Portuguese explorers had named it *O Rio Mar*—the River Sea. Countless tributaries, some larger than the Mississippi, feed the Amazon as it rolls to the Atlantic.

McIntyre, too, seems to roll on inexorably. Now in his 80s, he continues to make several trips a year to South America, ever watchful for images that capture a sense of wonder.

TIBET'S FABLED TSANGPO GORGE

ALTHOUGH TECHNOLOGY has made the world much smaller in the last century, there are still destinations beyond the horizon that beckon. And the National Geographic still helps explorers reach them. Since 1890, National Geographic's Committee for Research and Exploration has awarded nearly 7,000 grants. The Society's recently formed Expeditions Council has funded another 40 projects so far, around the globe. In 1998 the Expeditions Council gave grants to two expeditions to explore a gorge in southeastern Tibet, which were reported in the first issue of *National Geographic Adventure*.

Legendary since the 19th century, the waterfall lies on the Yarlung Tsangpo River, which boasts the world's deepest gorge and is a tributary of India's Brahmaputra River. The Tsangpo's drainage, called Pemako, is a wilderness of earthquakes, landslides, and monsoon rains considered sacred according to Tibetan scripture. Big and muddy for most of its journey across Tibet, the 1,800-mile-long Tsangpo hooks between two peaks of the Himalaya and makes a sharp U-turn in Pemako, creating its inner gorge. The gorge at the bend is three miles deep—three times the depth of Grand Canyon—while the river descends at about 65 feet per mile in some sections—eight times faster than the Colorado River does through Grand Canyon. Then it gets *really* steep: At times dropping 250 feet a mile, the Tsangpo takes just 200 miles to descend some 11,000 feet before joining the Brahmaputra.

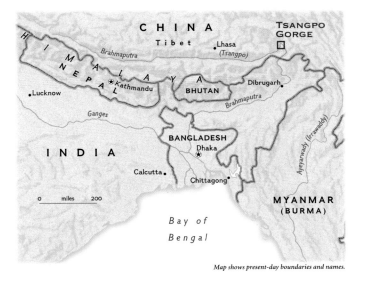

Map shows present-day boundaries and names.

Tucked into a tight turn between two Himalayan peaks, the inner gorge and falls of the Tsangpo River in southeastern Tibet evaded explorers for more than a century. In 1998, the National Geographic Society supported two expeditions to the canyon.

The existence of a major waterfall on the Tsangpo would explain its rapid drop, so Victorian-era explorers set out to find what they called "the lost falls of the Brahmaputra." In 1924, British botanist Francis Kingdon-Ward was the last European to seek the falls before China closed the area to foreigners. Fighting his way through forests of rhododendron and giant bamboo on near-vertical slopes, he sighted a cataract he named Rainbow Falls. The terrain defeated him, however, and Kingdon-Ward left a 15-mile gap of canyon unexplored. The story of his search, *The Riddle of the Tsangpo Gorges,* fueled speculation that an even larger cataract existed, adding to the mystery of the fabled "Lost Falls."

Looking forward to a world-class challenge, kayaker Doug Gordon, left, sought to shoot the Tsangpo (right). But roller-coaster waves cartwheeled his kayak, sweeping him away without a trace. Ian Baker and Ken Storm later hiked into the gorge. Storm (opposite) measured the waterfall's drop at 108 feet.

SOME 70 YEARS LATER, Wick Walker, a champion river kayaker mesmerized by the exploits of Kingdon-Ward, tried to run the Tsangpo. In 1985 he was denied a permit; not until 1992 did China reopen the area to foreigners. Walker and a team reapplied, and he won a Society grant in 1998. Unfortunately, the expedition ended in disaster: Lead kayaker Doug Gordon drowned in backwash after going over an eight-foot drop in the river; his body was never found.

A second expedition, also sponsored by the Society, arrived several weeks later to explore the stretch of canyon that had eluded Kingdon-Ward. Buddhist scholar and adventurer Ian Baker, who lived in Nepal, was that team's leader. He had made several trips to the area, the first in 1993 as a translator on another expedition. His group found the Pemako untouched by the modern world.

They fought off pit vipers, giant leeches, and stinging nettles, winning the respect of the local Monpa people. In May 1998 Baker's long-time guide finally led him to the edge of a cliff overlooking a distant waterfall—almost certainly the Lost Falls of the Brahmaputra. Lacking time, supplies, and equipment, he vowed to return.

In October of that year Baker and three companions trekked back to the Tsangpo's inner gorge, clawing their way through thick jungles of rhododendrons, hemlocks, and magnolias. Mosses and ferns carpeted the thick slopes, and the men clung to tree branches as the river churned 1,000 feet below them. Late one afternoon they emerged from the forest. Upstream from Francis Kingdon-Ward's Rainbow Falls, Baker saw

"a broad veil spread across the river."

He and his team hiked into the canyon and camped at a cliff that even the Monpa guides had never visited. In the morning they found a break in the jungle; before them lay the fabled Lost Falls, visible from top to bottom. After crashing over Rainbow Falls, the Tsangpo shoots through a 50-foot-wide flume, then drops into space. Halfway down, the water thunders against a rock outcrop and dissolves into mist. Blasted by spray and deafened by the raging water, Baker and companion Ken Storm rappelled 80 feet down the cliff to gauge the falls with a laser rangefinder and clinometer: It measured 108 feet. Baker and Storm named the cataract Hidden Falls of Dorje Phagmo, for the goddess who protects the inner gorge. Standing on slippery, moss-covered rocks at its base, Baker noted, "felt like being at the bottom of the Earth."

When his description of Hidden Falls became public, other people stepped forward to claim the find. Although Baker freely admits that others had seen part of the falls earlier, he remains adamant that seeing it from a distance and standing at the base to scientifically measure it were experiences poles apart.

And what of local knowledge? Monpa guides had known where the falls lay, and Baker could not have navigated the jungled cliffs of the Tsangpo without their help. Similarly knowledgeable Inca descendants had guided Bingham to the "Lost City" of Machu Picchu—though Bingham got the credit. Is the "discoverer" the person who first sights a find, or the person who first publicizes it?

Perhaps what's important is not determining who was first, but understanding that discoveries still wait to be made, for it is this yearning that drives explorers—then and now—to search beyond the horizon. The National Geographic Society continues to help them get there. Whether the expeditions are archaeological, as Bingham's was; geographical, like Baker's; or voyages of fulfillment like Burg's, the Society helps make them possible and shares them with millions of readers.

Like Bingham, some explorers are egotists who meet the world on their terms; others, like McIntyre, are self-reliant individualists determined to make their dreams come true. All of them, confident and self-driven—have inspired larger-than-life heroes who enrich our lives and enliven our imaginations.

THE MORDEN-CLARK EXPEDITION ACROSS ASIA

Relying on camels to ferry men, equipment, and supplies, the Morden-Clark American Museum of Natural History Expedition Across Asia set out in 1926. In the foothills of the Altai Mountains the men picketed their animals and made camp in the cold air and blowing snow. Mongols later captured, bound, and tortured the crew, holding them captive for 36 hours. Released, they completed their 7,900-mile journey, a nine-month ordeal. An account of their expedition appeared in the October 1927 NATIONAL GEOGRAPHIC.

LIFE IN THE BUSH

After traveling all day through dust and intense African heat, members of the Weeks Expedition unwind beside the Barya River (now called Nanai Barya) in the Central African Republic (left). They are enjoying such amenities as a tablecloth, folding chairs, and pith helmets. A caption in the August 1956 NATIONAL GEOGRAPHIC notes that villagers here (the town here is now Markounda) considered the group—a bird-and-mammal collecting safari sponsored by the National Geographic Society and the American Museum of Natural History—"a kind of traveling circus" that erected definite barriers between itself and local peoples. Four decades later, in a photograph published in the NATIONAL GEOGRAPHIC in February 1996, photographer George Steinmetz exudes a more contemporary approach with Yali tribesmen—clad in rattan hoops and modesty gourds—in Irian Jaya, Indonesia, on the island of New Guinea (above).

TIM SEVERIN: TRACING ANCIENT VOYAGES

Squalls in the South China Sea strip the sails of *Sohar*, bringing a seaman to his knees in prayer (right). In this full-size replica of an eighth-century Arab merchant vessel, Tim Severin and crew re-created the travels from Oman to China of legendary adventurer Sindbad the Sailor. They entered Canton on July 11, 1981, capping a 6,000-mile, seven-and-a-half-month trip. Their triumph relied, in part, on 400 miles of *coir*—coconut-fiber rope hand-rolled and twisted—which secured *Sohar*'s timbers, and on applications of vegetable oil (below) that helped preserve those lines. Severin later set out in the aptly named, 54-foot-long *Argo* (bottom), retracing Jason's mythical quest—from Greece to the present-day Republic of Georgia—for the Golden Fleece.

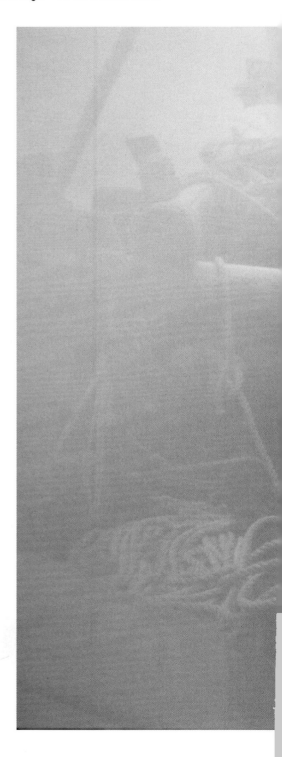

ACROSS AFRICA ...ON FOOT

J. Michael Fay wades through a stream in the Central African Republic during a lowland gorilla study that was published in the March 1992 NATIONAL GEOGRAPHIC. Mike is now on a yearlong walk through central African forests to survey plants and animals that may become threatened. "We're looking at another day or two of hell," he noted on January 10, 2000. Digital cameras and a lightweight computer system enable scientists in his group to transmit regular updates to Fay's online audience at www. nationalgeographic.com.

THE DEEP

TO DIVE IN THE OCEAN
IS TO IMMERSE YOURSELF
IN LIVING HISTORY...
—MARINE BIOLOGIST SYLVIA EARLE

I love the sea, born of an inconceivable deluge, because it is made of water. Water, as fluid as our souls, shapeless, enslaved to none but gravity. Water, welcoming our bodies in a total embrace, setting us free from our weight. Water, mother of all life, fragile guarantor of our survival.

—Jacques-Yves Cousteau

By
CATHERINE HERBERT
HOWELL

Despite our land-based existence, we remain creatures of the sea. The salt solution of our ancestral home continues to flow in our veins. Our bodies bear the same proportion of water as the surface of the Earth—70 percent. No wonder, then, that for millennia we humans have sought ways to return to the sea, to wander, and explore.

In many ways undersea exploration is like exploration in space—vast uncharted expanses, few clues to direction, and often a lack of a good gut sense of up and down. Yet, instead of the feeling of eternal nothingness—the great void—explorers of the deep become keenly aware of the pervasive somethingness of the medium they explore. At a depth of only 100 feet, the ocean exerts enough pressure to compress a person's lungs to one-fourth their normal volume. At 35,000 feet, the lowest point yet reached in the ocean, water pressures reach an incredible 8.5 tons per square inch—enough to crush an unprotected explorer into shapeless tissue.

Off Bermuda, deep-sea pioneers William Beebe, right, and Otis Barton stand beside the bathysphere that carried them to a record-breaking depth of 3,028 feet in August 1934.

Previous pages: Red sponges cover a gun barrel of the *President Coolidge*, a luxury liner converted to troop ship during World War II. Mines sent her to the seafloor in October 1942 off Espiritu Santo, New Hebrides (now Vanuatu). Here, Australians Allan Power and Kev Deacon explore the wreck as an angelfish plays with their air bubbles.

BEEBE, BARTON, AND BATHYSPHERE OFF BERMUDA

SUCH PRESSURES—as well as the elemental need of humans to breathe air, of course— place ordained limits on our capacity to survive in the deep. When naturalist William Beebe began his underwater exploration in the 1920s, dive-sustaining technology had not much passed the Jules Verne stage. Cumbersome copper helmets and all-encompassing diving suits connected by rubber hoses to a surface air supply were still the norm.

According to Beebe, his inspiration for deeper-sea exploration came from an unexpected source. That source was a late-night conversation with Theodore Roosevelt. Their discussion, he said, produced a drawing of a sphere suspended by a cable, a variation of the then-popular diving bell. Beebe later took the design to the engineer and adventurer Otis Barton, who had both the funds and the technical know-how to see it to completion.

In 1930 Beebe and Barton took their newly created two-ton bathysphere ("deep ball") to Bermuda, where Beebe had often collected specimens for the New York

Zoological Society. On June 6 the bathysphere's mother ship, the *Ready*, left Nonsuch Island, heading eight miles out to open water.

On the deck stood the sea-blue ball, only 4 feet 9 inches in diameter, loaded with oxygen tanks and chemicals for absorbing carbon dioxide and excess moisture. Beebe and Barton wriggled through the small hatch and adjusted their lanky frames to the bathysphere's curved and cramped space.

The 400-pound door was slammed shut, 11 nuts screwed down and hammered into place. "The terrific reverberation almost deafened us," they reported. Winched over the side of the *Ready*, they began their descent.

A trickle of water under the door at the 300-foot mark that remained steady at 800 feet became reason enough to abort the dive. Within a week, though, Beebe and Barton were on their way down again. They peered out through the fused-quartz windows at sea life attracted by luminous hooks hanging on the outside, baited with squid.

As Beebe later wrote: "Jellyfish, large and small, drifted past.... Fifteen-inch bonitos darted past in trios.... At four hundred feet there came into view the first real deep-sea fish...lantern fish and bronze eels.... At five hundred feet...I saw strange, ghostly dark forms hovering in the distance.... At six hundred feet...I saw my first shrimps with minute but very distinct portholes of lights."

At 1,426 feet Beebe and Barton "dangled in mid-water," setting a record. Having no cameras, they relied on their own observational powers to mentally record the life-forms they saw.

Later, they debriefed, talking with artist Else Bostelmann, whose own gifts transformed the explorers' descriptions and scribblings into renderings that would prove eerily accurate when compared years later to photographs of the same kinds of creatures.

Three years after this success, Beebe approached the National Geographic Society for funding to take the bathysphere down for another look. The Society responded with $10,000 and a stipulation for descents to one-half mile.

On August 15, 1934, again off Bermuda, the pair reached 3,028 feet—a record that would hold for more than 15 years—in a ball now painted with the Society's name and soon to hoist its tricolor flag, of which the bottom

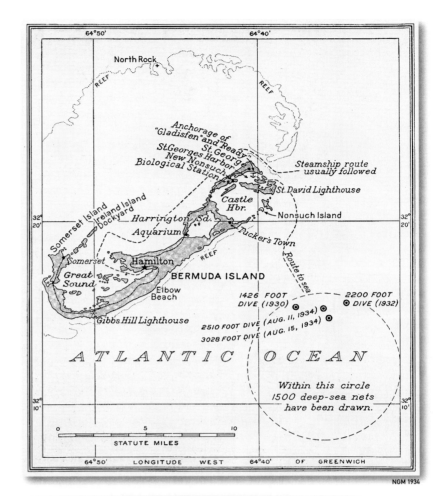

green stripe represents water.

As they dangled gently from the cable, Beebe observed, "Here it seemed as if all future nights in the upper world must be considered only relative degrees of twilight. I could never again use the word 'black' with any conviction!"

Beebe and Barton took the bathysphere on four different dives off Bermuda (above). the latter two under Society sponsorship. Beebe (left) peers from one of three portholes that served as windows on an undersea world never before glimpsed by human eyes.

JACQUES-YVES COUSTEAU: MASTER OF THE DEEP

HIS PROFILE IS ARRESTING: the hawklike nose jutting from the gaunt cheekbones, framed by thick coal-black eyebrows above and a wide, toothy grin below. Add his signature scant black swimsuit and you have perhaps the world's most recognizable explorer—Jacques-Yves Cousteau. Cousteau was a decorated French naval officer who married an admiral's daughter. He responded to water at an early age. "When I was four or five years old," he has said, "I loved touching water. Physically. Sensually."

In 1936, while recuperating from an automobile accident, he donned his first pair of goggles and stuck his face into the Mediterranean. The impact was enormous: "Sometimes we are lucky enough to know that our lives have been changed, to discard the old, embrace the new, and run headlong down an immutable course. It happened to me at Le Mourillon on that summer's day, when my eyes were opened on the sea."

Obsessed with diving to the point of dreaming about it, Cousteau wanted to swim free, not in the bulky gear of suit-and-helmet divers, but like a fish. To realize his dream, he drew on the inventiveness that would mark the rest of his career. The result was the Aqua-Lung, a self-contained portable cylinder that would feed pressurized air to the diver by means of a valve that opened only on inhalation. But how to get such a valve? In 1942 engineer Émile Gagnan showed Cousteau just the thing: a demand valve being used in wartime France that allowed cooking gas to fuel automobiles during the gasoline shortage.

After experimenting with several prototypes, Cousteau and Gagnan were satisfied. In the summer of 1943, with French Navy buddy Philippe Taillez and expert diver Frédéric Dumas, Cousteau put the Aqua-Lung to an extensive test in the Mediterranean. As he recorded, "I experimented with all possible maneuvers—loops, somersaults, and barrel rolls. I stood upside down on one finger and burst out laughing, a shrill distorted laugh.

The master checks out diving gear that is a more sophisticated descendant of the Aqua-Lung he invented in 1943 with French engineer Émile Gagnan. Designed to deliver a mixture of helium and oxygen, it served the divers in Cousteau's Conshelf Three project, an experiment in underwater living.

Nothing I did altered the automatic rhythm of the air. Delivered from gravity and buoyancy I flew around in space."

By autumn, the trio had made some 500 dives, Dumas reaching a depth of 210 feet in October. At the hundred-foot mark he experienced "a queer feeling of beatitude. I am drunk and carefree." His confusion increased with depth. It was a case of nitrogen narcosis, also known as "rapture of the depths."

Excess nitrogen and carbon dioxide in the human body—forced into the bloodstream by the great pressures under sea—produce a kind of inebriation. As Cousteau described it, "Mild elation grows into ecstasy; danger reactions fade. The diver may pass out, lose his mouthpiece, and drown."

Diving's other common physiological malady, the bends, also stems from the build-up of nitrogen in the body. When a submerged diver ascends too quickly, the rapid reduction of water pressure causes nitrogen gas to form bubbles in his bloodstream. This can result in extremely painful joints, even coma and death. Divers soon learned to prevent the bends by ascending in stages, allowing their bodies to adjust to the pressure at each depth before rising to the next stage. In time, decompression chambers were developed to create the same results artificially.

The Aqua-Lung, better known today by the acronym "scuba," for "self-contained underwater breathing apparatus," made "fish men," as contemporary NATIONAL GEOGRAPHIC articles touted, of Cousteau and his companions. When World War II ended, Cousteau turned his attention full-time to the pursuit of undersea exploration and the making of documentary films. But the Captain, as he would be known for the rest of his life, needed a ship that would take him where he wanted to go.

Cousteau remodeled an American-built minesweeper then in surplus, fitted it with a laboratory and an interior diving well, and christened it *Calypso*, after the sea nymph who held Odysseus captive for seven years. Cousteau's *Calypso* would make willing captives of her crew, including Taillez, Dumas, and master diver Albert Falco, for many years to come. The *Calypso* sailed from Toulon in November 1951.

Not long thereafter the 45-year-long

Routes of the Calypso
outbound _ _ return ...

© National Geographic Map
Drawn by Gilbert H. Emerson

NGM 1956

In 1955 the Society helped send *Calypso*, Cousteau's oceanographic vessel, on a 15,000-mile cruise from the Mediterranean port of Toulon to Assumption Island, in the Indian Ocean. There, "the Captain" filmed his underwater classic, *The Silent World*, a screen version of his popular book.

association between Cousteau and the National Geographic Society began. During this time staff members and photographers would join the Captain on expeditions that Society funding, totaling almost a half-million dollars, helped make possible.

One such staff member was Luis Marden, a polyglot and bon vivant who'd begun his career at National Geographic as a writer-photographer in 1934. He revolutionized photography at the magazine, introducing 35-mm cameras and Kodachrome film, once scorned as the playthings of amateurs.

An avid scuba diver, Marden joined a 1955 *Calypso* expedition to the Red Sea and Indian Ocean. Cousteau planned to make a full-length motion picture and Marden to experiment with underwater color photography.

Marden immediately took to life on the *Calypso*: "I saw at once that she was a well-organized ship. She carried two tons of red wine in stainless steel tanks and twenty tons of fresh water. With irrefutable Gallic logic, the water was rationed but the wine was not." Marden also admired the Captain's petite wife, Simone, a surrogate mother to the crew who could also put an errant crew member in his place "in terms that would have blistered the shell off the crustiest sea dog."

In those days each sailing of the *Calypso* charted new territory in undersea exploration. As Marden writes, "Those were halcyon days when the undersea world was new and lay all before us, waiting to be discovered. Every dive was like a visit to another planet: The landscape, the flora, the fauna, even the atmosphere, all were alien. At several uninhabited islands we were the first to breach the water film, and every dive might yield something new."

Altogether, Marden shot 1,200 photographs during the expedition with an ultra-wide-angle Leica and a standard Rolleiflex

enclosed in a watertight housing. Since the ship had no onboard photo lab, none of the still photos or movie film could be processed until the ship returned to France. Marden's 39-page article in the February 1956 NATIONAL GEOGRAPHIC showcased stunning images from that expedition, including a portrait of Ulysses, a 60-pound grouper with a Churchillian mien that followed Marden around like a puppy while he photographed. Ultimately, Ulysses became such a pest that he had to be locked up in a shark cage for two days so that Marden could complete his work.

Marden made underwater exploration history of his own in 1957 when he found the site of the wreck of Captain Bligh's *Bounty*. Almost nothing remained of the hull, but by studying the unusual shapes on the lime-encrusted seafloor, he identified metal fittings that he was able to pry out with a hammer

Cousteau launches his souped-up *soucoupe plongeante*, or diving saucer, in 1959 (right). Lacking either rudder or tail fins, the vessel was deftly maneuvered with water-jet nozzles that allowed it to approach an undersea feature and retreat quickly, if necessary. Inside the three-fourths-inch-thick, fused-steel hull, a pilot and an engineer lay prone on rubber mattresses (above) as they dove as deep as 1,000 feet. Instrument panels surrounding them monitored depth, pressure, and direction, as well as distances to the surface, the bottom, and various underwater objects. Today's submersibles—both manned and unmanned—continue to expand the capabilities of undersea explorers.

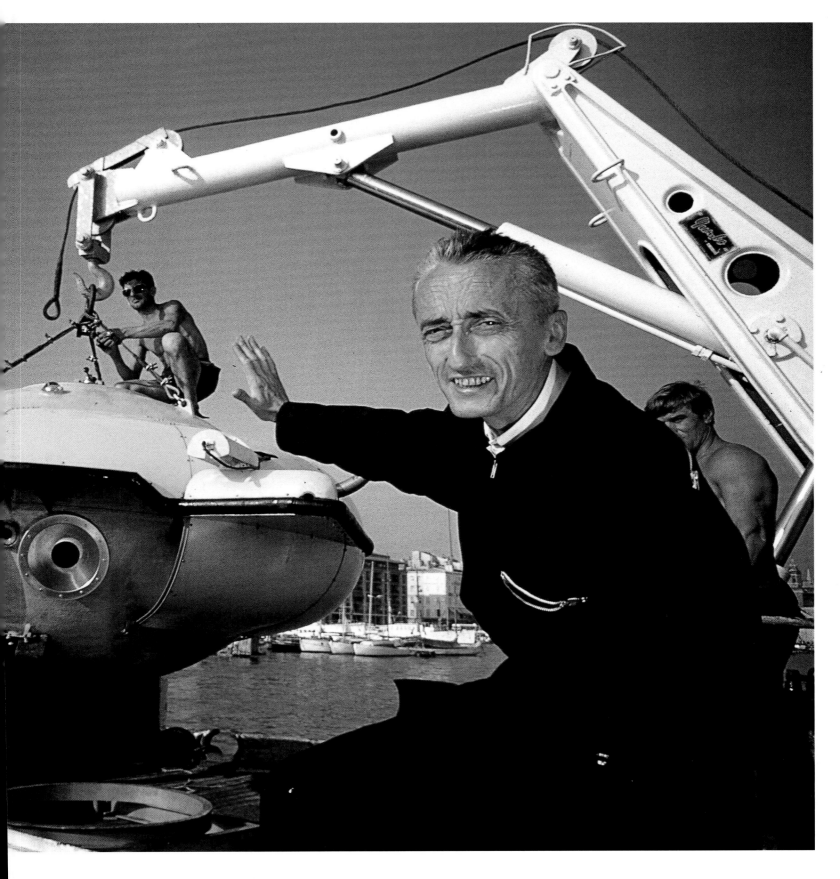

and chisel. The film Marden produced on his find inspired the creation of National Geographic Television, now a for-profit subsidiary of the nonprofit Society.

Marden's uncanny ability to find things no one else could find surfaced again in 1986 when, along with his wife and navigator, Ethel, he sailed in the wake of Columbus, determining by extensive research and computer calculations the explorer's possible course and landfall. Throughout his long and varied career—he remained a regular NATIONAL GEOGRAPHIC magazine contributor for more than two decades after his 1976 "retirement," with his 61st article appearing in 1998—Marden made other discoveries, including a new species of orchid and a new species of sea flea, both named after him. But it was as Cousteau's lensman that Marden made some of his most memorable contributions.

Nearly each new Cousteau expedition brought some advancement in underwater photography. Lack of light—total beyond a depth of 1,200 feet or so—and the need for pressurized housings for cameras and other equipment tested the ingenuity of many professionals. One was Harold E. Edgerton of MIT, whose pioneer work in high-speed photography included unforgettable images such as the splatter-built crown of a drop of milk, and the trajectory of a speeding bullet through the thin edge of a playing card.

With Society help, "Papa Flash," as the Calypso crew called him, developed cameras and lighting systems that could withstand the 5.5 tons of pressure that exists at 24,000 feet, as well as an amazing nylon line only three-eighths of an inch thick that could lower the equipment to such depths without snapping. Edgerton and Cousteau used the rig in the mid-Atlantic's 24,600-foot-deep Romanche Trench. Although the transducer designed to locate the ocean's bottom failed, Edgerton's camera system provided useful images—the first taken at this incredible depth.

In the late 1950s Cousteau realized that scuba diving could take his fish men only so far. The time had come to develop a vehicle

that would extend human capacity for exploration even deeper. Trial-and-error led him to a flattened sphere powered by water forced through nozzles on either side of the hull.

Cousteau's diving saucer was put to the test for the first time off Puerto Rico. Falco, chosen to be the test pilot, returned from the first shallow dive and pronounced: "Ça c'est de la bagnole!" or, roughly, "What a hot rod!" Eventually the saucer would take Cousteau and others to a depth of a thousand feet.

In 1966 the National Geographic Society and television producer David Wolper created "World of Cousteau," an hour-long program documenting Cousteau's Conshelf Three project—a venture that put six carefully selected men into a 140-ton structure anchored at 328 feet below the surface of the Mediterranean.

The oceanauts lived and worked for three weeks in the sea, demonstrating that subsea stations were extremely practical for oil exploration and recovery.

The television program was a wild success. Landlubbers throughout the world became hooked on the Calypso's adventures. In addition to regular specials produced by the Society, Cousteau later entered a deal with ABC that created The Undersea World of Jacques Cousteau, enjoyed by millions during its nearly nine-year run.

From his research Cousteau began to realize that the ocean, despite its vastness, was an extremely threatened environment. The Mediterranean, in particular, was ailing. Cousteau put his by then very famous name to use to establish the Cousteau Society in 1973 to support his advocacy of the sea. He also sent Calypso to oceans and river systems all over the world to document their decline.

Cousteau remained very active. At his death in 1997 at the age of 87 he received one of his country's highest accolades, usually reserved for heads of state—a funeral mass in Notre Dame Cathedral.

The next year his close friend and colleague Luis Marden eulogized him in the February 1998 issue of NATIONAL GEOGRAPHIC, referring to the inscription he had penned for the Special Gold Medal of the National Geographic Society that Cousteau received in 1961 from the hands of President John F. Kennedy:

*To Earthbound man he gave
the key to the silent world.*

New generation: Equipped with Cousteau's liberating Aqua-Lung, French divers swim circles around a "hardhat" sponge diver encumbered with helmeted suit, heavy boots, lifeline, and air hose—gear with origins in the 19th century.

DESCENT TO THE DEEPEST DEPTH

AUGUSTE PICCARD'S MOTTO could rightly have been, "Whoever goes up must go down." The Swiss designer of the first balloon to sail up into the stratosphere also invented, in the 1940s, the vessel that would reach the lowest point on the Earth's crust: the Mariana Trench, almost seven miles down in the western Pacific. This bathyscaph ("deep boat"), named *Trieste*, was a kind of deep-sea dirigible consisting of two hollow floats supporting a steel-hulled observation chamber. Instead of hot air the floats used lighter-than-water gasoline, which condensed in cold water to make the vessel sink. Unlike bathyspheres, Piccard's bathyscaph could descend and ascend without a surface tether; various models had proved their mettle down to depths of 24,000 feet.

With 60 dives to its credit, *Trieste* was ready for the assignment that would ferry Piccard's son Jacques and U.S. Navy Lt. Don Walsh to the depths of the deep. On January 23, 1960, the Navy's unsonorously named tug *Wandank* pulled the bathyscaph into the open Pacific, more than 200 miles off Guam. The seas roiled and pitched in high winds that day and damaged and destroyed some nonessential parts of *Trieste* as she was being towed. With all efforts poised for the moment when she was to descend, however, the pressure to keep on schedule was enormous.

Jacques Piccard had final say. He checked *Trieste*'s main electrical circuits. These controlled, among other things, electromagnets that released iron-pellet ballast, allowing the bathyscaph to rise.

Piccard gave the go-ahead. No fanfare accompanied the descent, only the closing of the heavy steel hatch with the single bolt that would seal it hermetically, relying on water pressure to keep it shut.

Trieste descended at the pace of "an elderly elevator." The diving duo scarcely used the craft's searchlights so they could observe bioluminescent creatures. Little life of any kind appeared, though, and Piccard surmised that the falling craft had scared it away.

An undersea telephone kept the two in touch with vessels on the surface. But their sense of well-being evaporated at 32,500 feet when they heard dull cracking sounds soon followed by a cabin-trembling shock. They

More than a mile deeper than Mount Everest is high, the western Pacific's Mariana Trench plunges nearly seven miles beneath the ocean's surface. In January 1960 the bathyscaph *Trieste* delivered Jacques Piccard and USN Lt. Don Walsh to the bottom of the Challenger Deep, the trench's low point at 35,800 feet.

hadn't hit bottom and there was no sign of malfunction on their instrumentation. They turned off anything that made noise and listened carefully.

Piccard recalled in NATIONAL GEOGRAPHIC magazine: "In the heavy silence we hear only tiny cracking sounds, like ants in an ant hill, little crackling sounds coming from everywhere, as if the water were being shattered by our passage. Could it be shrimps? Is the cabin's paint cracking? We do not know yet, but the descent itself is regular, reassuring."

They grew preoccupied with the

Italian mechanic Giuseppe Buono hangs onto Lt. Lawrence Shumaker as the two teammates help Jacques Piccard, far right, replace *Trieste*'s towline. The original had snapped during a four-day haul from Guam in choppy seas. Despite the loss of a current meter and a topside telephone that normally communicated with *Trieste*'s observation sphere, the record-breaking expedition stayed on schedule.

approaching bottom. After a nearly five-hour descent they were within 300 feet of their goal—already they had dived deeper than anyone else. The laconic Walsh uttered, "Finally." Piccard's own response was more poetic: "At 1306 hours the *Trieste*, in my sixty-fifth dive, made a perfect landing, on a carpet of uniform ivory color, that the sea had laid down during the course of thousands of years."

They stayed only 20 minutes on the bottom. Walsh searched for the source of the noises and determined the viewing port of *Trieste*'s entry tube had cracked—not a life-threatening incident but one which made a daylight return to the surface all the more necessary. Before ascending, however, Piccard and Walsh viewed through the porthole, illuminated by a powerful beam of light, a sole-like fish—proof that life *does* exist nearly seven miles beneath the waves.

GEORGE BASS: RECLAIMING CULTURES FROM THE DEEP

IN 1960, AS A STUDENT of Mycenaean civilization at the University of Pennsylvania, George Bass was offered an opportunity he could not refuse: to direct the excavation of a pile of bronze artifacts off Cape Gelidonya, off the southwestern Turkish mainland. It would be unlike any dig the young archaeologist had ever encountered. To begin with, the site lay in 91 feet of water. Bass would need to learn to scuba dive, so off he went to the local YMCA to take lessons. Then he left for Turkey.

In those days, planned underwater excavation was an entirely new enterprise, although the salvage of wrecks for their cargo was nearly as old as the wrecks themselves.

Gold doubloons, jewels, and other treasures had been luring salvagers to sunken ships for centuries, their only objective to retrieve the loot. In the 1950s, even Jacques Cousteau pulled amphorae helter-skelter from the remains of a 2,200-year-old Greek ship in the Mediterranean with no thought to the overall wreckage in which the ancient jars were found.

The Cape Gelidonya dig turned out to be not a random pile of artifacts but the remains of a ship dating to the Bronze Age, about 1300 B.C. While trying to be as thorough as on a land-based dig, Bass nevertheless had to improvise. First, divers photographed the wreck underwater and sketched the position of artifacts on the rocky seafloor, using ordinary pencils on sheets of frosted plastic. Since corrosion and undersea growths had caused the ship's cargo to fuse, Bass had to loosen chunks with a jeep's jack and then winch them to the surface to be pried apart on shore.

Pottery styles and radiocarbon dating determined the age of the ship; its cargo determined the provenance. Copper ingots weighing 44 pounds each must have originated in Cyprus; other artifacts resembled wares from Syria and Palestine. Bass then deduced that the ship was Canaanite or Phoenician and had picked up the ingots after sailing from Syria to Cyprus. The era and legitimacy of underwater archaeology had been established.

The waters of the Aegean and the Mediterranean off Turkey had witnessed centuries of war and commerce between Mycenaean Greece, Troy, and other cultures, and they proved fertile ground for underwater archaeologists. Many excavators owe their success to the Turkish sponge divers who log

Founding father of underwater archaeology, George Bass takes a break during his excavation of a Byzantine wreck off Yassi Island in the Aegean during the 1960s. Under four decades of Society sponsorship, Bass has created and refined, almost singlehandedly, the methods and techniques of undersea archaeology.

thousands of hours in coastal waters, becoming attuned to every bump or bulge that might suggest unnatural structures. Modern echolocation techniques, such as side-scan sonar, are used today as well, but throughout the years sponge divers have been just as effective at spotting wrecks—if not more so.

For his next project, Bass planned an excavation of a Byzantine ship also wrecked in the Aegean. Supported by Society funding that continues today, he put in place equipment and methods that soon would become standard in underwater archaeology.

The site off Yassi Ada—Flat Island—lay at 120 feet, a mound of rounded amphorae with corroded anchors at one end. Bass set up a mapping frame by laying wire grids over the entire site. Divers tagged each item, and artists plotted each artifact *in situ* before it was carried to the surface. Piles of muck were sucked up by a big "vacuum cleaner," called an air lift, onto a dive barge, where they were sifted for additional artifacts.

To document the site, Bass set up two underwater photographic towers. For the scattered timbers of the ship's hull—reduced by centuries of deterioration to a density resembling that of balsa wood—Bass devised an ingenious solution: He staked them into the seafloor with 2,000 sharpened bicycle spokes. An assistant recorded the position of each timber, each nail hole, bolt hole, score line, and mortise, and later used this information to sketch the outlines of the vessel.

In subsequent excavations, including one of a Roman wreck at the same site, Bass added improvements and innovations to his methods. One was a "telephone booth," a kind of transparent stationary diving bell, under which divers could rest and talk to each other and to the surface without having to go up.

At the depths at which they were working, 20-minute stints on the wreck were often the limit due to the risk of the bends. This made decompression an issue and so Bass set up air-filled stations at several points along the ascent route. Divers could hang by straps and breathe air at the proper pressure. To combat boredom, reading material was stashed in a bucket dangling at the stations. Bass would later add a four-person submersible decompression chamber. He also installed a number of devices to bring artifacts to the surface, including balloons that ferried items up

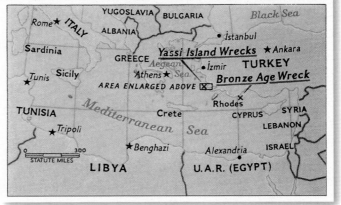

NGM 1963

at a constant rate of speed.

Four decades after first donning a mask and tank and slipping into the Aegean Sea, George Bass remains the dean of underwater archaeologists, working now from the Institute of Nautical Archaeology he founded at Texas A&M University. His excavation in the 1980s of a Bronze Age wreck off Ulu Burun, Turkey, which had borne the products of at least seven cultures, remains his most famous. It took four years and some 4,000 dives to recover the treasures from this 50-foot-long ship, which added much to our knowledge of trade more than 3,000 years ago.

Vessels of myriad cultures have plied the shipping lanes of the Aegean Sea for millennia, leaving a plethora of wrecks that attract salvors, looters, and—most recently—underwater archaeologists like George Bass. He and his crews have focused on numerous sites in Turkish waters, including sunken ships off Yassi Island and, farther east, off Ulu Burun, a wreck that dates to the Bronze Age.

Dangling from a weighted barrel, archaeologists peruse a soggy magazine as they decompress, gradually exhaling the excess nitrogen absorbed by their bodies while at greater depth and pressure. By making decompression stops at various depths as they make their way to the surface, they can avoid the bends, a painful—and potentially fatal—risk all divers face.

Relying on air rather than muscle, archaeology team member Susan Phipps (opposite) exhales from her tanks into an upturned amphora, so that she can float it to the surface. But recovering such artifacts from below waterline is just the first step in a lengthy process of identification, cleaning, and restoration. Laboring on land as well as in the sea, George Bass and his wife, Ann, apply plastic preservative to wooden fragments from the Ulu Burun wreck (below), while Turkish seamen hoist ox-hide-shaped copper ingots onto a launch for shipment to a nearby museum (bottom). The ingots probably originated from foundries in Cyprus. They represent a crucial Bronze Age commodity, as copper is a primary ingredient of bronze.

Like a living marker on an immense, underwater chessboard, a diver hovers above an iron grid erected over the skeletal remains of a medieval shipwreck off the island of Rhodes. The grid enabled excavators to precisely plot every find at the site and thus gain the most information from each fragment. Remnant ribs of the thousand-year-old ship's hull appear in this view, interspersed with artifacts that range from amphorae and glass tumblers to fishing weights and even a plate with chicken bones. One amphora housed an obstreperous octopus that snatched back artifacts removed by the divers.

Her Deepness, Sylvia Earle

Encased in the wearable undersea environment known as a Jim suit, Sylvia Earle ascends to the surface tethered to a minisub after her historic solo stroll on the seafloor off the Hawaiian island of Oahu in 1979 (right). Earle rode the sub to a depth of 1,250 feet, then stepped off to begin a two-and-a-half-hour exploration, connected to the sub by an 18-foot cable. During four decades as a pioneering scientist of the ocean realm, marine biologist Earle has led a number of Society expeditions, including a study of Truk Lagoon (opposite). This seagrowth-encrusted ship's mast belongs to one of some 60 Japanese vessels sunk by the U.S. at Truk during World War II, shipwrecks that now make up the world's largest collection of artificial reefs.

Sylvia Earle: Guardian of the Water Planet

A smiling Sylvia Earle reaches out to close the Jim suit's hatch, while underwater photographer and longtime collaborator Al Giddings offers encouragment during a dress rehearsal for her walk on the ocean floor. Together, Giddings and Earle have logged many thousands of diving hours, in locations ranging from California's Santa Catalina to the South Pacific.

THE YEAR WAS 1970. Lunar exploration was in full swing, almost becoming commonplace. Astronauts were the heroes of the times. But on a momentous day that year, five women rode triumphantly up Wall Street and lower Broadway, accepting the uniquely American accolade of a ticker-tape parade. Later, they would be feted at the White House. What had these women done to deserve these honors, usually reserved for the likes of returning moon walkers or local baseball clubs when they win the World Series?

The answer may surprise: They had spent two entire weeks living in a four-room dwelling 50 feet under water some 600 miles off the U.S. Virgin Islands. The all-female mission, the sixth team of an eleven-team project called Tektite II (after tektites, glassy meteoric nodules found on land and on the ocean floor), ate and slept minimally, learning things that only inhabitants and not merely visitors to the sea can learn: the dynamics of spiny lobster populations, the vulnerability of reefs, and how fish communicate sonically. That they had the opportunity to participate in Tektite, similar in many aspects to Cousteau's Conshelf projects but with a strong link to the U.S. space program, was owed to the tireless crusading of their team leader, whose hours logged on or near the bottom of the sea would eventually encourage the media to bestow on her such titles as "Her Deepness" and "The Sturgeon General."

Sylvia Earle grew up on a New Jersey farm until, at the age of 12, her family moved to Clearwater, Florida. With the Gulf of Mexico as her new backyard, Earle's interest in nature focused on the marine. She entered Florida State as a precocious 16-year-old, learned to scuba dive, and soon began to specialize in the study of marine plants. Marriage and motherhood did not deter Earle from joining or organizing undersea expeditions throughout the world. In partnership with her, underwater photographer Al Giddings has captured innumerable images of her pioneering work.

The weeks in Tektite II demonstrated to

Earle the benefits of remaining at a constant depth where one could explore without the need for decompression. But it seems axiomatic that all explorers of the deep want to continue going deeper—and deeper. Earle was no exception, except that the idea of being a mere voyeur in an underwater vehicle did not appeal to her.

Enter the Jim suit. Named for Jim Jarrat, a diver who, in 1935, used an early version of this spacesuit-like creation, it was a hundred-pound, wearable undersea environment. It was cumbersome; it had a surface tether—like an old-fashioned helmeted diving suit—but it enabled divers to go deeper by combating the effects of pressure and providing atmosphere, surface pressure, and a rebreather that added oxygen and chemically scrubbed out carbon dioxide. Special liquid-filled joints and pincer-like hands enabled the wearer to grasp objects. Other divers had used the suit, mostly for salvage and offshore oil operations, always while tethered to the surface.

Earle was eager to take a Jim suit down for a test of her own, to check out its capabilities for research—but only if she could do so unfettered. In 1979, with support from the National Geographic and the University of Hawaii, among others, Earle obtained use of a suit from its owner, Oceaneering International, Inc., setting in motion the most risk-filled scientific adventure of her career.

She chose a site six miles off the Hawaiian island of Oahu, planning to descend while strapped to the front of the University of Hawaii's research sub *Star II*. Communication problems between Earle and the sub scrapped the first two attempts, but the third worked, and Earle finally stepped off the sub, attached to it, rather than to a ship at the surface, only by an 18-foot nylon tether around which was wrapped a communications wire.

With her first step on the ocean floor at 1,250 feet, Sylvia Earle became the only person then or since to walk at that depth untethered to the surface. Carrying a Society flag identical to one carried to the moon's surface, she likened her surroundings to a lunar landscape, although one teeming with life: "A small circle of light from *Star II* illuminated for the first time a dozen or so long-legged, bright-red galatheid crabs swaying on the branches of a pink sea fan; a small, sleek, dark brown lantern fish darting by with lights glistening; an orange fish and several plumelike sea pens clinging to the rocky bottom near the edges of visibility."

Throughout her career, Earle has used her expertise to advocate the protection of the planet's watery realm. As chief scientist for the National Oceanic and Atmospheric Administration (NOAA) in the early nineties, she monitored the health of the nation's waters. Now in the middle of a five-year term as a Society explorer-in-residence, she has again submerged herself, this time in a program sponsored by the Society, NOAA, and the Richard and Rhoda Goldman Fund—the Sustainable Seas Expeditions. It marries cutting-edge deep-sea technology to the study of ecosystems in the United States' 12 marine sanctuaries, the underwater equivalent of national parks. At 64, having accumulated more than 6,000 hours of diving time and been named *Time*'s first "hero for the planet," Sylvia Earle still possesses the curiosity and enthusiasm she had as a girl of 18 diving for the first time in the Gulf of Mexico.

HOUSE CALLS UNDER ARCTIC ICE

SIMULTANEOUSLY, TWO DIVERS realize that it is time to surface. Each presses a round valve on his inflatable suit, and like human helium balloons, both begin to float to the surface. One picks up speed, ascending too quickly. But he doesn't reach the surface in a propulsive splash. Instead, with a buoyant thud, he hits a ceiling—a ceiling of Arctic ice.

Only a very few M.D.s become guinea pigs for the well-being of their patients. Joseph E. MacInnis is one of them. The Canadian physician has spent more than three decades painstakingly—and often painfully—exploring the parameters of the physiology of diving, then converting his hard-earned knowledge into greater safety for other divers. He has checked out the efficacy of equipment and tested the limits of human endurance in one of Earth's most inhospitable environments, the frigid waters of the northern polar sea.

In 1972 MacInnis took 15 scientists and underwater photographer William R. Curtsinger, a frequent contributor to NATIONAL GEOGRAPHIC, to ice-choked Resolute Bay, then only 125 miles from the north magnetic pole. He wanted to test the utility of Sub-Igloo, a portable, plastic, air-filled bubble similar to Bass's "telephone booth," which divers could use for respite during numbing exploration under ice. Assembled, it looked like a transparent spider that had eight pairs of metal struts for legs.

Working in water temperatures of 28.5°F, which can bring death in only five minutes to a person not clad in specialized wetsuit, MacInnis also offered the functions of his own body to the endeavor. A swallowed electronic pill containing a transmitter measured his core body temperature and sent out that information in a continuous radio signal. Another device sensed heart rate and sent this measurement to a surface receiving set.

MacInnis's credentials as an underwater explorer are no less authentic than his medical ones. In 1980, after a six-year search, he located the *Breadalbane*, a British bark lost in 1853 in Canada's icy Northwest Passage, the northernmost shipwreck ever discovered on the seafloor.

The H.M.S. *Breadalbane*, her hull punctured by storm-driven ice, sank off Beechey Island, coming to rest under 340 feet of water. Sidescan sonar revealed, tantalizingly, an intact hull, preserved by the absence of wood-boring insects in the frigid water. But her depth dictated she was way out of reach for recovery or exploration. MacInnis was undaunted.

Three years later, with Society funding, he returned with the WASP, a yellow "wearable" one-man submarine, similar in appearance to Sylvia Earle's Jim suit. But WASP was designed for transport, moving by means of six thrusters powered by cable from the surface. A National Geographic camera, riding on an RPV, or remotely piloted vehicle, recorded the WASP's sub-arctic "flight." The *Breadalbane* revealed many secrets, adding to the contributions of an intrepid M.D. with a penchant for well-chilled adventures.

Closely related to the Jim suit, the one-man rover known as WASP is readied to take Phil Nuytten to the H.M.S. *Breadalbane*, lying in 340 feet of Arctic water. Six surface-powered thrusters drive WASP wherever the diver wishes.

Project FAMOUS: Journey to the Cauldron of Continental Creation

PROJECT FAMOUS AREA

Part of a mountain range more than 46,000 miles long that snakes through all the world's oceans, the Mid-Atlantic Ridge attracted the attention of Project FAMOUS— the French-American Mid-Ocean Undersea Study—in the 1970s. Through remote sensing and direct inspection by submersibles, FAMOUS scientists learned how lava flowing from a rift in the center of the Mid-Atlantic Ridge creates new seafloor, driving the continents apart.

FOR MORE THAN 65 YEARS, much of the pathbreaking news of ocean exploration and research has emanated from a small village on southwestern Cape Cod in Massachusetts. Woods Hole Oceanographic Institution (WHOI) has sent vessels and researchers to nearby waters and to the ends of the Earth in the name of oceanography. In the early 1970s WHOI served as a primary sponsor of Project FAMOUS, the French-American Mid-Ocean Undersea Study that, despite its name, involved scientists of Canada and Great Britain as well. Their task would take them to the crucible of one of Earth's most spectacular natural features— the Mid-Atlantic Ridge, a 12,000-mile-long mountain range that runs the length of the Atlantic Ocean, from Iceland to Antarctica. Its crests rise an average of 10,000 feet above the seafloor, and some of its peaks even poke above the waves—forming the Azores and other islands of the North Atlantic. We now know that the Mid-Atlantic Ridge is part of a submarine mountain chain that winds more than 46,000 miles through all the oceans of the globe.

Aided in part by Society funding, Woods Hole sent its first expedition to the Mid-Atlantic Ridge in 1947. Scientists aboard the ketch *Atlantis* zigzagged between the Old and New Worlds, taking core samples of the ocean bottom, collecting soundings and other measurements, and making major advances in undersea color photography.

By the time Project FAMOUS got underway in the 1970s, scientists were beginning to grasp more of the intricacies of modern plate tectonics theory, which holds that Earth's continents and oceans ride on rigid plates of rock that are slowly but continually moving. To observe tectonics on a smaller scale, FAMOUS sent its scientists to find out what kind of changes go on in a distinctive rift that runs through the center of the Mid-Atlantic Ridge. Ranging from 3 to 30 miles wide, the rift marks the boundary between the African and North American plates, which are currently moving away from each other.

FAMOUS zeroed-in on a 60-square-mile segment of the rift some 400 miles southwest of the Azores, crisscrossing the site with remote sensing gear that measured seismic activity, magnetism, gravity, and heat. Naval and civilian organizations contributed photographic and sonar technologies to produce extremely detailed maps of the ocean floor.

As impressive as these measurements were, they were acquired from a distance. Phase Two called for a much closer inspection that would involve travel and retrieval some 9,000 feet below the surface by using a small and versatile pressurized submersible that could maneuver among the irregular features of the rift.

The indisputable star of the various vessels enlisted for the expedition was the U.S. Navy's *Alvin*, commissioned at Woods Hole in 1964. The 22-foot-long *Alvin* cradles a spherical passenger compartment with a lightweight titanium-alloy hull only two inches thick. More than mere transport, though, it is a floating research station. Equipped with a remote-controlled manipulator arm, *Alvin* can gently retrieve rocks and other objects, dropping them into a rotating sample basket. It sports flood and strobe lights and both still and television cameras to capture the action of the deep. Sonar, a compass, and a current meter take vital statistics of the environment.

Led by Woods Hole's J. R. Heirtzler, the American scientists of FAMOUS included geologist Robert D. Ballard, whose discovery of the *Titanic* a decade later would make "Bob Ballard" a household name. Ballard rode shotgun to Heirtzler in *Alvin* down to the rift, sampling and testing at various designated work stations.

Near bottom they became aware that the forces they were witnessing were both tectonic, such as faults, and volcanic. Lava in myriad forms, including massive pillow lava ornamented with glassy buds—evidence of newness—was everywhere, especially along the axis of the rift. As the massive tectonic plates move, then, new lava wells from fissures in the rift. For the first time, explorers could witness firsthand the undersea cauldron of continental creation and renewal.

Robert D. Ballard:
Deep-sea Geologist Turned Archaeologist

Titanic. Today that name may conjure up the image of a fair-haired actor, new heart-throb of a generation. A decade ago the image it conjured belonged to a fair-haired scientist who guided the most famous expedition in search of the most famous shipwreck in the world, the R.M.S. *Titanic*, sunk after striking an iceberg on her maiden voyage in April 1912. For five dramatic weeks in the summer of 1985, Bob Ballard and his work often dominated the evening news, captivating viewers with the first photos of the fractured luxury liner, lying on the ocean floor. Within 22 months, National Geographic published three of Ballard's articles.

How did a marine geologist, a former member of Project FAMOUS, and the man who had discovered new life-forms and natural features at the ocean's bottom become involved in such a sensational, non-geological undertaking? The answer lies in technology.

As a kid growing up in California, Ballard often visited Disneyland, where he rode a come-to-life version of the *Nautilus* from *20,000 Leagues Under the Sea*. As a teenager he was more interested in scuba diving than in surfboarding; like Cousteau a generation before, Ballard was fascinated by what went on beneath the waves. During his years as a junior scientist at Woods Hole and a naval officer, Ballard signed on with the *Alvin* group, which would push the frontiers of undersea scientific exploration.

Alvin's ability to dive to 13,000 feet enabled it to reach the crest of the Mid-Atlantic Ridge, and also gave it the potential to dive in the area where the *Titanic* rested. Ballard came to believe that *Alvin*'s capabilities, including a beefed-up visual-imaging system, could help secure funding for the search for the *Titanic*. And a *Titanic* expedition could, in turn, be used to develop technology for interactive deep-sea exploration.

It was a decade-long quest, during which Ballard, like an auditioning actor, heard "no" many more times than he heard "yes." In the meantime, however, *Alvin* and Ballard continued to develop their partnership, making scientific history in the process.

The National Geographic Society did not need much persuasion to support a 1977

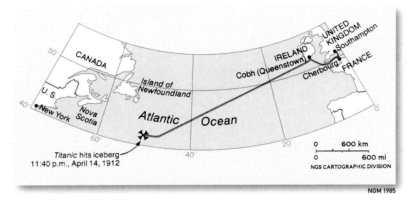

Titanic hits iceberg
11:40 p.m., April 14, 1912

NGM 1985

scientific trip to the Galápagos Rift on the East Pacific Rise that included Ballard and 24 other scientists. Its purpose was to look for the thermal springs that scientists believed must occur where seawater enters cracks in the ocean's crust, becomes superheated, and returns to the sea through vents in the crust. Research vessel *Knorr* was accompanied by *Alvin* and ANGUS, a deep-towed camera system. A cable dragged the sled-like ANGUS back and forth just above the seafloor, while its down-pointing still camera photographed the target site. No remote system monitored ANGUS's observations; what it saw was not witnessed until its film was processed. ANGUS's passive nature and means of travel inspired the unflattering nickname "dope on a rope." But in the end, ANGUS had the last laugh.

On board ANGUS was a sensor that recorded a rise in temperature, noted by Ballard aboard the *Knorr*. Later that night, as he came upon the corresponding location in the 3,000 frames that were all in a day's work for ANGUS, Ballard found giant white clams flourishing at a depth of more than 8,000 feet.

Anxious to learn more, Ballard dived in *Alvin*. What he saw would forever change the scientific view of life on this planet. In the utter darkness of the near-freezing deep, warm

Missing for 73 years, R.M.S. *Titanic* sank on her maiden voyage in 1912 (map). On September 1, 1985, Robert D. Ballard (below, in cap) and his colleagues aboard the research vessel *Knorr* celebrated their discovery of the luxury liner's location.

Finding and documenting *Titanic* proved a mammoth undertaking, jointly sponsored by Woods Hole Oceanographic Institution and a French counterpart, Institut Français de Recherches pour l'Exploitation des Mers (IFREMER), with cooperation from the U.S. Navy and the National Geographic Society. In 1986, Bob Ballard rode to the ship's two-mile-deep grave in the versatile submersible *Alvin* (left) a veteran of Project FAMOUS. These haunting views, photographed from *Alvin* and the underwater robot called *J.J.*, reveal *Titanic*'s encrusted bow (below) and the pedestal that held her wheel (bottom).

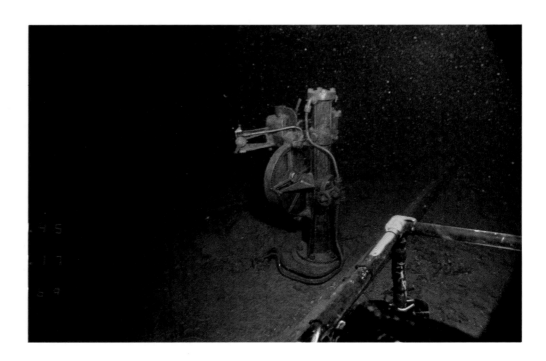

springs or vents were nourishing an astonishing assortment of life-forms: The foot-long giant clams, red-plumed tube worms as tall as 12 feet, enormous never-before-seen spectral crabs, white thread-like worms, mussels, anemones, and fish.

Why such a diverse array of life-forms at the dark bottom of the sea, so far from the sun that powers most ecosystems? Water samples from the vents bore the strong stench of sulfur—the product of hydrogen sulfide. But that wasn't all: Vent water also contained more than 250 types of bacteria. These bacteria turned out to be the lowest creatures in the underwater food chain. They fed on the energy created when the oxygen in seawater combines with hydrogen sulfide, using that energy to transform carbon dioxide dissolved in seawater into the carbon compounds vital for all life. In short, in this sunless undersea world, chemosynthesis had replaced photosynthesis. This incredible discovery posed a central question: Were these vents unique?

A year later, in 1978, an international team using a French submersible explored the East Pacific Rise, just off Mexico, where they answered that question. An oasis of similar life surrounded tall stony chimneys spewing opaque clouds of black particles. A thermometer dipped into the center of one of these "black smokers" melted; later measurements revealed a temperature of 350°C.

While nearly casually discovering new life-forms, Ballard continued his push for support to find the *Titanic*. He enlisted the help of GEOGRAPHIC photographer Emory Kristof, a colleague and friend from Project FAMOUS days, who made many contributions to the technological aspects of underwater photography. Ballard also began to lean heavily on the Office of Naval Research, *Alvin*'s owner, which agreed to support plans for a two-part vehicle for deep-sea exploration. Named *Argo/Jason*, it combined a remotely controlled video apparatus with a "swimming robot" complete with lights and stereo cameras that was tethered to *Argo* by a cable "leash."

By 1985 *Argo* was ready for the big test. Ballard enlisted the cooperation of the French, always ready for undersea adventure and exploration, especially if it involved advanced technology. The official partner was the Institut Français de Recherches pour l'Exploitation des Mers (IFREMER); Jean-Louis Michel, a

colleague from Project FAMOUS, would be the French co-leader.

Michel went looking first in a French ship, dragging its state-of-the-art side-scanning sonar back and forth with no luck. It was left to the *Knorr* to find the *Titanic*, and if successful, to document it, using *Argo*'s cameras.

It was the graveyard shift on September 1, 1985, during the fifth week of the search, with just five days left in the mission.

From the control van on the starboard deck an engineer was "flying" *Argo* in the usual systematic fashion when it began to send back pictures of debris. Suddenly, a large round shape came into view. Someone recognized it as a ship's boiler, unmistakably of the type installed in the *Titanic*.

The next afternoon the main piece of the hull was detected. For four days, in choppy seas, *Argo* and ANGUS were towed over the wreck site, obtaining the first images of a ship not seen for more than 73 years. Who owned those images would soon become a major source of difficulty between the Americans and the French.

Ballard was anxious to explore the wreck more intimately, testing the mettle of the deep-sea submersibles. In July 1986 *Atlantis II* sailed again to the site, without any French team members. Along with the indomitable *Alvin*, *Atlantis II* carried *Jason Jr.*—J.J. for short—an underwater robot Ballard nicknamed the "swimming eyeball."

Alvin dove on July 13. During its descent, salt water started to leak into its battery packs. Alarms sounded, but with news from the surface that *Titanic* lay merely 50 yards away, *Alvin* continued. As Ballard recalled in NATIONAL GEOGRAPHIC, "Ralph [Hollis] eases

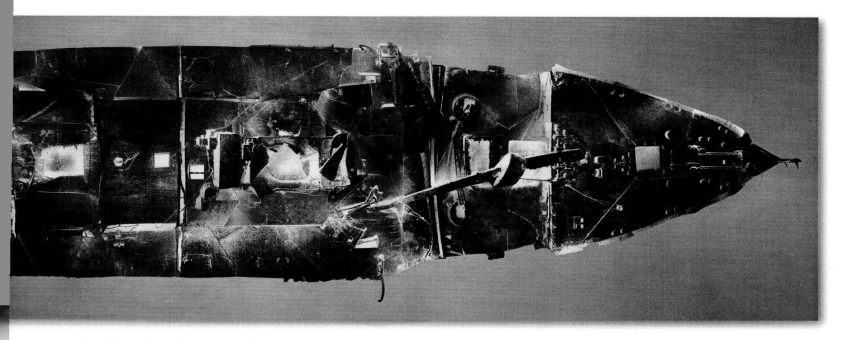

Alvin forward until he is stopped by an endless slab of black steel rising out of the bottom. Our journey at long last has reached its goal. *Titanic* is a few inches away. In that brief instant we become the first ever to actually see *Titanic* in her grave. Then Ralph pulls the plug, and we lift up from the ocean floor."

In 11 more dives both *Alvin* and *J.J.* would peruse every corner of the once-elegant liner, and the world would become familiar with the fate of the ship and—through many personal artifacts—the 1,500 souls who perished in the sinking. Upon the first view of *Titanic*'s debris in 1985, Ballard had pronounced to himself, "The quest for *Titanic* is over."

Today, what happened after *Titanic*'s discovery remains a painful subject for Ballard. Co-discoverer Jean-Louis Michel and others began to salvage artifacts from the wreck despite a tacit agreement to leave the shattered ship intact. "Never in my wildest imagination did I believe they would…salvage it," recalls Ballard. "I never even thought to claim it. There's a big difference between doing something to fill in a missing chapter in human history and doing it for personal greed."

In the wake of *Titanic*, Ballard would again carry the Society's banner as he successfully located various casualties of war: the German battleship *Bismarck* (1989), the *Lusitania* (1994), and the *Yorktown* and other ships of the Battle of Midway (1998). In addition, he has made the submersible *Jason*, completed in 1986, a familiar presence in schools all over the world through Project Jason, which each year enables hundreds of thousands of students to follow the craft's explorations, through interactive hook-ups.

Ballard, now president of the Institute for Exploration, has taken *Jason* to the Black Sea. There, by discerning and following ancient trade routes, scientists hope to find the remains of ships buried and preserved in the oxygenless mud caused by a flood—possibly of Noah's time—about 7,500 years ago.

Today the Society continues to channel resources into deep-sea exploration, including the promising technologies of the future. The versatile *DeepWorker 2000* is one example. Used extensively in the Sustainable Seas Expeditions, a joint venture between the Society and NOAA, *DeepWorker* is a lightweight, one-person sub capable of diving to 2,000 feet and maintaining life support for 80 hours. No more complex to operate than a golf cart, *DeepWorker* turns scientists into pilots in short order, allowing them to retrieve objects weighing up to 150 pounds by means of highly dexterous arms. The vessel boasts several kinds of sonar, can record sounds with a directional hydrophone and make video recordings, and maintains contact with the surface through wireless communications— functions that someday may transform the once-frustrating and fearsome task of exploring the deep into a commuting profession.

We know much more about the deep than we did a half-century ago, or even in the last decade. But we are still, in William Beebe's words, in the "kindergarten stage" when it comes to our knowledge of the oceans.

Having committed early to the support of undersea exploration, the National Geographic Society has recognized the brilliant achievements of four of its deep-sea pioneers with the presentation of Centennial Awards, in 1988, to Edgerton, Cousteau, Bass, and Ballard as true heroes of underwater exploration.

Stark photo-mosaic of *Titanic*'s bow section, produced under Society supervision, shows its current condition. In April 1912 as the ship took on water, she broke in two. Bow and stern portions sank separately, ultimately coming to rest some 600 yards apart.

CONSHELF TWO: VILLAGE UNDER THE SEA

Onion-domed underwater garage houses Jacques Cousteau's diving saucer 36 feet below the surface of the Red Sea. It and other seafloor structures, including a residence and laboratory known as Starfish House, formed part of Conshelf Two, Cousteau's experimental underwater colony. In June 1963 five men lived at Starfish House, joined there in the last week by Mme Cousteau.

Researcher Valerie Taylor (above) appears to be sparring with a blue shark off San Diego as she tests a custom chain-mail suit designed by her husband, Ron. Society funding supported the Taylors' work with such fearsome—and often misunderstood—creatures. While the 15-pound suit, constructed of some 150,000 stainless steel rings, survived this assault, a later test with reef sharks in Australia revealed a potentially fatal flaw: the gap where hood and suit meet. To this day Taylor harbors in her jaw an embedded shark tooth, reminder of her too-close encounter. Gaping jaws of a great white shark clamp down on photographer David Doubilet's shark cage off Australia (right). Recalled Doubilet later, "I wasn't really afraid until I put down the camera and realized how close the teeth were."

Ichthyologist Eugenie Clark, at right, approaches the world's largest fish, a bus-sized whale shark, during a research trip to Baja California. Long a Society grantee, Clark has spent a life-time with sharks, sea dwellers that have changed little over the past 300 million years. Despite their size, whale sharks pose no threat to divers; they dine only on plankton. This pregnant female even allowed Clark to catch a ride on her dorsal fin.

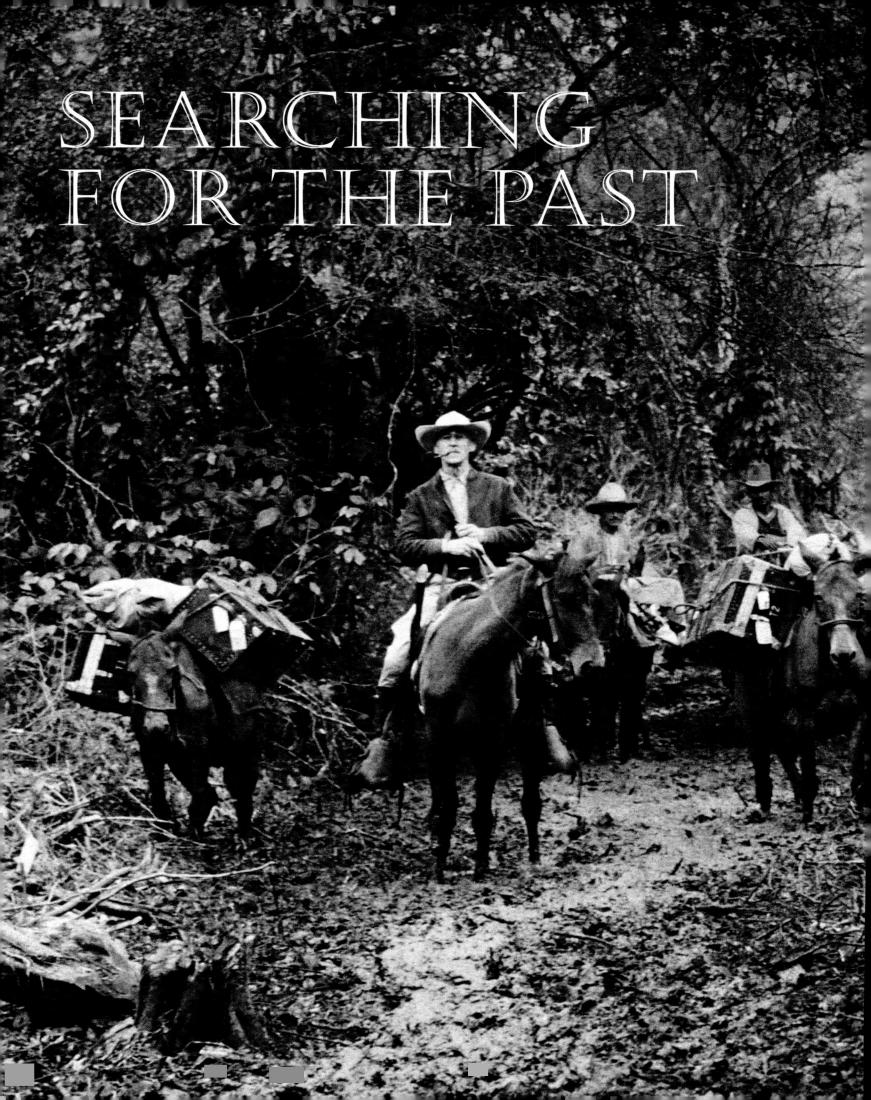

SEARCHING
FOR THE PAST

WE WERE REVEALING AN ENTIRE
CULTURE HITHERTO BARELY SUSPECTED
BY THE OUTSIDE WORLD.
—ARCHAEOLOGIST MATTHEW W. STIRLING

BY GEORGE E. STUART

The mound was the largest I had ever seen, and what was emerging from it was nothing less than amazing. The year was 1958, I was a young student of archaeology, hired as part of the National Geographic Society-Tulane University archaeological expedition to the ancient site of Dzibilchaltún, in the northern part of Mexico's state of Yucatán. I had just arrived at the ruined city in the company of the archaeologist in charge—and my new boss—the late Dr. E. Wyllys (Bill) Andrews IV of Tulane's Middle American Research Institute. We stood in the scant shade of a flimsy tree regarding a mound the size of a small mountain, all dazzling white limestone rubble. A throng of excavators and stonemasons, some on scaffolding of cut and tied saplings, others on the slopes, worked around its summit.

All their efforts, carried out in the mild heat of a tropical February morning, slowly revealed the regular form of a buried stone building—a spectacle that even my untrained eye could recognize and appreciate. Archaeologically speaking, I had arrived. I would spend the next three years of my life at Dzibilchaltún, whose Maya name means "the place of writing on flat stone."

Bill Andrews's investigation of this site between 1958 and 1962 is one of many scientific expeditions sponsored by National Geographic, in its continuing quest for knowledge of the human past. In just over a century since its founding, the Society—mainly through its Committee for Research and Exploration—has made nearly 7,000 grants, including those for archaeological research on all the inhabited continents and at all manner of ancient sites, from the buried remains of Ice Age hunting camps to glorious cities such as Greco-Roman Aphrodisias, an architectural miracle of marble in Turkey; from ancient ships sunk in the ocean depths to eternally frozen shrines on the loftiest summits of the Andes; and from the arid lands of the tombs and temples of the pharaohs to the dark, buried cave-crypts of Maya kings deep in the tropical rain forests of Central America.

My three-year stint at Dzibilchaltún was my own first direct experience in the kind of field expeditions funded by the National Geographic in pursuit of its stated mission: "the increase and diffusion of geographic knowledge." On that first morning, Bill Andrews quickly gave me my assignments: to make a detailed map of the vast system of mounds, roadways, and other ancient remains that stretched over some 20 square miles of arid northern Yucatán; and to make architectural drawings of any structures brought to light by the project. I was to begin with the great stone building emerging from the big mound.

That building, it seems, had been covered by a later platform "pyramid" and building that hid the original structure, but the newer one had totally collapsed into a meaningless heap, revealing part of the past. The nearly pristine temple and platform pyramid that soon emerged proved to be one of the most interesting ever found in the Maya area. Today it is called the Temple of the Seven Dolls, because Bill and I excavated a ceremonial cache of buried clay figurines from its central chamber. Andrews had noticed a curious feature once the plaster floor had been cleared of debris—a carefully made plaster-lined hole in the floor of the room. Only an inch or so in diameter, it was clearly not a drain, for it was slightly higher than the surrounding floor surface, so Bill decided to see for

Hundreds of ancient Maya sites crowd the Mexican state of Yucatán (right). Society-supported archaeologists have probed Dzibilchaltún, Chichén Itzá, and other Yucatán ruins over the past half-century, revealing valuable data on one of the most brilliant civilizations of American antiquity. Today, some six million descendants of the Maya occupy the Yucatán Peninsula.

Previous pages: Matthew and Marion Stirling follow a jungle track in search of a vanished civilization. In eight Society-sponsored expeditions to southern Mexico beginning in 1938, the Stirling team rewrote the early history of the Americas.

himself what lay below. He began excavating while I removed the fill to a distant pile. Barely two feet down Bill suddenly saw the reason for the hole: Seven crude clay figurines, each barely four inches tall, lay in a pocket of rubble fill. Clearly this was a cache of enormous importance ritually buried with the opening left above it, perhaps so the living could communicate with whoever—or whatever—was represented by the small figures.

Positive identification of the seven "dolls" remains a mystery, partly because of their crudeness. Several appear to be physically deformed—two hunchbacks, another with exaggerated limbs, suggesting a medical reason for the offering. Whatever the seven dolls meant to their maker, the building they came from proved to be a unique example of Maya architecture for its combination of windows, turning corridors, and a hollow vaulted tower rising from its center, above the secret chamber where we found the dolls.

The Temple of the Seven Dolls, its central tower now rebuilt—it had been truncated when the outer structure was added—once again stands proudly as it did some 1,500 years ago, dominating the eastern hub of this ancient city. At that time the temple's upper facades were covered with eight great supernatural countenances, perhaps gods of rain or earth, and other images of carved and brightly painted stucco, including stingrays, fish, and other creatures of the sea in sharply modeled relief. Some of this sculpture was miraculously preserved by the burial of the structure, but most had cracked and fallen into a great puzzle of tiny fragments.

Font of history, the central cenote, or ceremonial well, in the heart of Dzibilchaltún has yielded thousands of artifacts to divers, including the shards of numerous pots accidentally dropped—or intentionally thrown—into its depths. Archaeologist E. Wyllys Andrews, at left, and Manuel May examine pottery fragments whose dates, based on style and comparison to other sites, helped establish that this site has been occupied for at least 3,000 years.

We know now from the work of Andrews and his team that the archaeological zone of Dzibilchaltún that I helped map held a succession of sites which together were inhabited for at least 3,000 years. Dzibilchaltún proper—the area dominated by the plaza holding the Temple of the Seven Dolls and the complex of huge structures around the great cenote, or ceremonial pool, flourished throughout the Classic and Postclassic Periods, from around A.D. 500 to the Spanish Conquest of Yucatán a thousand years later.

In 1542, Francisco de Montejo founded the city of Mérida. Half a century later, the Maya still living in the vicinity of Dzibilchaltún erected a stone chapel near the cenote and adorned its interior with a mural depicting a Roman Catholic bishop. The shell of the chapel still stands, its paintings faded beyond recognition, surrounded by quiet mounds and other ancient structures—a monument to the final use of the heart of the old city.

By virtue of its size and character, Dzibilchaltún once must have dominated much of the northern Yucatán Peninsula. One eroded hieroglyphic inscription suggests it held sway over the neighboring city of Tiho, which occupied the site of present-day Mérida. From the standpoint of sheer political power, the sacred precinct dominated by the Temple of the Seven Dolls must have formed one of the great focal points of both religious and political power in the northern Maya realm.

SPLENDORS OF ANCIENT APHRODISIAS

Focal point of a city, the marble odeum, or concert hall, of ancient Aphrodisias once drew crowds with its musical concerts, readings, mime performances, and lectures. The city council met here as well. The odeum's ornate decor included marble armrests carved in the shape of dolphins— such as the damaged example at far right—and portraits commissioned to honor family, friends, and benefactors of the theater.

Kenan T. Erim's Expeditions to Ancient Aphrodisias

Even as Dzibilchaltún ran its course, another city of note thrived some 8,000 miles to the east, across an ocean and a sea, in what is now the southwestern corner of Turkey. We

Bathed in beneficial waters, the marble face of a second-century Aphrodite found at Aphrodisias peeks from modern protective wraps. Keeping the sculpture wet helps conservators loosen damaging encrustations and impurities that have penetrated the porous stone, thus furthering its preservation for future generations.

know its name from the annals of Greco-Roman antiquity—Aphrodisias—and we know that when both these places were in their heyday, neither knew of the other. In our present age of archaeological investigation, however, both places share at least one thing: Aphrodisias, like Dzibilchaltún, was revealed to the world through a series of Society expeditions. These took place between 1966 and 1990, under the enthusiastic direction of Kenan T. Erim of New York University.

Although Aphrodisias had been known since some excavations in the early 20th century, Kenan Erim first visited the site in 1959, two years after local farmers uncovered parts of a large relief carving in marble. The carving included six elegant and elaborately garbed life-size figures, and its discovery absolutely captivated archaeologist Erim.

"This western region of my native Turkey was, I knew, rich in the husks of vanished cities—Ephesus, Pergamum, Smyrna, Sardis, Priene," wrote Erim. "What would I find here

within these unmanned ramparts and columned edifices, long untenanted and tumbled down? What lay under this raucous arena of chickens, dogs, and children? Under this jumble of peasant houses with marble inscriptions and chunks of statuary peeking from their walls…?" What indeed? In more than 20 years of research, Kenan Erim slowly unearthed a city of marble, surely one of the most spectacular places in all the vast reaches of the Roman Empire.

This city, devoted to and named after Aphrodite, the Greek goddess of fertility, love, and beauty, thrived from the first century B.C. to the sixth century A.D.—roughly from the reign of Julius Caesar to Justinian—although its original habitation dates to the deep mists of the Stone Age, some 8,000 years ago. At its peak, Aphrodisias held an estimated 50,000 people.

It's difficult to judge the most spectacular find in this superlative city of magnificent art. Some would cite the original slabs unearthed by the farmers nearly half a century ago. Thanks to the efforts of art historian R. R. R. Smith, we now know that those pieces went together to form the frieze of the opulent marble mausoleum of distinguished citizen C. Julius Zoilos, a former slave who won self-government for Aphrodisias. Zoilos joined the gods around 20 B.C. The frieze, Smith showed in his rearrangement of the slabs, depicts the honor and esteem granted to Zoilos: The allegorical composition of six-foot tall figures sculpted in nearly the full round show the figure of Bravery extending a shield to the hero, who is also about to be crowned by Honor. At the same time, Demos, representing the people of Aphrodisias, greets the heroic Zoilos; and Polis, a woman representing their city, proffers him a crown.

Others seeking superlatives among the treasures of Aphrodisias might point to the information revealed by the discoveries. A prime example lies in the inscription—one of the most complete ever discovered—detailing an edict of Roman Emperor Diocletian in A.D. 301. That proclamation set the prices for virtually every commodity in the markets from food to wagon parts, in an attempt to stem inflation—a reminder frozen in stone showing that the nature of human economics has changed very little in the last 1,700 years.

Kenan Erim's excavations of the acropolis of Aphrodisias, the 75-foot mound that formed the highest part of the ruins, revealed the city's long and complex past. From the present habitations of the contemporary village of Geyre, the quest led downward through layers of human settlement that were the milestones of Aphrodisias's history. As Erim put it, "past the day when Alexander the Great marched by here to the Indus…past invasions of the Persians, the fall of Homer's Troy, and the rise of the Hittites, of Egypt's Pyramids, and of writing in Sumer—back to Stone Age habitations of 8,000 years ago."

Consider the attractions of this city: The great agora, or market, where teeming throngs once bargained for goods; the nearby opulent Baths of Hadrian, for the respite of the public; the Temple of Aphrodite, the architectural crown of the cult of the fertility goddess that gave the city its name and drew the citizens to worship; the odeum, or concert hall, where Aphrodisians enjoyed mime, music, and readings; and everywhere, the marble portraits of gods, goddesses, priests, scribes, and politicians—all produced in local studios. So brilliant were these that they created a demand that reached throughout the Roman world. The beauty of Aphrodisias itself inspired the emperor Augustus to state: "I have selected this one city from all of Asia as my own."

At the center of the city lie the ruins of a graceful semicircle of marble whose seats once held as many as 8,000 spectators. They celebrated the feast days of the Roman imperial calendar by attending a variety of events—pageants and plays— and at the stadium enjoyed contests such as foot races, javelin throwing, or boxing and wrestling bouts. The glory of Aphrodisias continued even after the fall of Rome, as a brilliant outpost of empire into Byzantine times. It began to fade only in the 12th and 13th centuries, when earthquakes and invasions by the Seljuk Turks occurred.

Yet human settlement continued here, as the ever changing trappings of the eastern Mediterranean world slowly covered the city's past splendor—until Kenan Erim and the National Geographic helped bring life once more to the ruins of a city Erim described as "the remains of where people lived and loved, were happy and unhappy, and died."

Set on a lofty plateau near the Menderes Valley of present-day Turkey. Aphrodisias thrived from the first century B.C. to the sixth century A.D. as the principal city of the Roman province of Caria. Later renamed Stavrapolis (City of the Cross) in order to eradicate remnants of the pagan cult of Aphrodite, the city fell to raids by Seljuk Turks and others during the 13th century and was abandoned.

EARLY ARCHAEOLOGICAL GRANTEES: BINGHAM, JUDD, AND OTHERS

NATIONAL GEOGRAPHIC EXPEDITIONS of the sort that helped reveal Dzibilchaltún and Aphrodisias to the modern world had their beginnings long before the generation of Bill Andrews and Kenan Erim.

Specifically, the Society's involvement with "lost cities" began in 1912, when Hiram Bingham's arduous trek into the precipitous mountain country of south-central Peru's Urubamba Valley with a local guide ended at the long-forgotten Inca city of Machu Picchu.

For many, Machu Picchu epitomizes the notion of the lost city, a romantic vision that has long symbolized the journey's end of the ultimate adventure. The popular literature of lost cities ranges from the exploits of Tom Swift in popular juvenile novels of the early 1900s—doubtless stimulated by Bingham's work—to the living lost city of *Shangra-La* in literature and cinema. While Machu Picchu comes about as close as one can to the concept, most places so designated have never been "lost" in the true sense. Local inhabitants of the regions in which they are located almost always know of them. In the end, however, it matters little the degree to which an ancient ruin is lost; the importance of any such place lies in the treasury of information it holds

Masonry walls at least eight centuries old define some of the 800 rooms occupying the four-story ruin of what archaeologists named Pueblo Bonito—Beautiful Town—in northwestern New Mexico (below). With funding from the National Geographic Society, archaeologist Neil M. Judd spent eight seasons excavating this unique self-contained structure, beginning in 1921. His analysis of differing masonry styles helped date the sequence of wall construction, while dendrochronology, or tree-ring dating, helped establish the span of occupation to between A.D. 900 and 1200. Circular room plans (opposite) mark Pueblo Bonito's numerous kivas, or underground ritual chambers. Judd's success in Southwestern archaeology depended on close collaboration with local Native Americans, whose ancestors built Pueblo Bonito and other ancient towns in the area.

Photograph by O. C. Havens

The Society's man in Pueblo Bonito, Neil M. Judd surveys the nearby contemporary town of Santa Clara Pueblo with its Native American governor, Santiago Naranjo.

Map shows present-day boundaries and names.

about its inhabitants and the world they knew.

Beginning barely a decade after Bingham's trek to Machu Picchu, Neil M. Judd of the Smithsonian Institution would lead no less than eight Society-sponsored expeditions to a remote corner of New Mexico that has proved to be one of the most intriguing archaeological sites in our Hemisphere. Its modern name is Pueblo Bonito—Beautiful Town—and it lies with dozens of other ruins strewn through Chaco Canyon, a broad, arid valley that has been designated a national cultural historical park since 1907, bounded by 100-foot-high sandstone escarpments in the semi-desert of northwestern New Mexico.

Early on, Pueblo Bonito and neighboring ruins were recognized as obvious works of pre-Columbian ancestors of the Indians of the North American Southwest, mainly various Pueblo groups who lived along the Rio Grande upstream from present-day Albuquerque and Santa Fe. The rest of the story, however, remained a mystery. When was Pueblo Bonito built? How many lived there? How did its farmers survive in such a harsh area? And, finally, when was it abandoned, and why? Answers began to emerge in 1921, when the Geographic funded Judd's first expedition. In the summer of that year, a tent camp was set up for the archaeologist and crew. "Our corner grocery at Gallup," Judd later recalled, "was separated from our kitchen at Pueblo Bonito by 106 miles of happened-by-chance road. When this road was dry the one-way trip could be made in seven hours; during the midsummer rains our drivers always carried their bed-rolls and a week's rations."

Slowly Pueblo Bonito yielded to meticulous excavation by Zuñi and Navajo workers. D-shaped in plan, it consisted of a huge self-contained structure, four stories high and holding more than 800 rooms. Until 1882 it was larger than any single building constructed in what is now the United States!

Judd's analysis of superimposed masonry styles and other architectural features showed that Pueblo Bonito had grown in stages, and with continuous renovation. Its rooms served as dwelling places, as storerooms, and as kivas,

circular chambers on or below the ground floor, where secret ceremonies took place.

By 1925, Neil Judd was able to determine that Pueblo Bonito had had a relatively brief life, beginning with its construction around A.D. 900. Nearly three centuries later, at a time roughly coincident with the demise of Aphrodisias—a world away—the inhabitants abandoned their remarkable settlement forever. Precise reasons are yet unclear, but archaeologists generally agree with Judd's speculations that prosperity in such a capricious environment is fragile at best, even for a people skilled both in hunting and horticulture. More recent evidence points to a prolonged drought and perhaps warfare among various groups in Chaco Canyon as factors that helped trigger the ultimate decision to abandon the city.

Aside from the statistics of the stones and architecture of ancient Pueblo Bonito, Judd's work brought that previously unknown place to life, revealing a precious glimpse of a thriving community that once held perhaps 1,200 people. Among them were skilled potters, whose black-and-white wares of eggshell delicacy possess an excellence seldom surpassed; talented lapidaries who worked hard turquoise as if it was putty; and hunters, gatherers, gardeners, and farmers who sustained the village in the face of nature's constant threats. Men and women of Pueblo Bonito pursued the various tasks of domestic life, social duty, and religious service with distinction, much as their descendants today do in the same region.

Neil Judd's expeditions into Chaco Canyon were the beginning of the Society's intense interest in the land of the pueblos. Between 1958 and 1964, the Geographic and the National Park Service jointly sponsored five archaeological investigations of cliff dwellings and other settlements at Wetherill Mesa, part of Mesa Verde National Park.

Douglas Osborne, Park Service archaeologist and project leader, supervised teams of scientists who investigated virtually every aspect of ancient life at Wetherill Mesa. In the course of their investigations, they turned to dendrochronology—tree-ring dating—to establish absolute dates for the history of the Pueblo peoples who had inhabited the area. The method was developed in the late 1920s with the Geographic's help; the grantee was Andrew Ellicott Douglass, director of Steward Observatory at the University of Arizona.

The principle behind dendrochronology lies in a simple fact: Each year, every living tree adds a layer of new wood over its entire living surface of trunk and branches. If every year were the same in terms of rainfall and other factors, then each addition to the tree would be the same thickness, and a cross-section of the trunk would show uniformly spaced concentric rings, whose number would equal the age in years of the tree when cut—interesting, but not very useful.

In actuality, of course, years are not identical; hard winters, for example, or dry summers can cause tree-ring growths to vary greatly from year to year. Douglass realized that, in the American Southwest, the type of pine tree used by ancient Pueblo-builders for beams and rafters was particularly sensitive to annual differences in rainfall: dry years produced thin layers of new wood; wet years, thicker—and the pattern of years was neither regular nor predictable. Thus, each sample of ancient wood used in construction held a set of rings reflecting a certain span of years, much like a modern bar code. This being true, two different beam poles cut a few years apart should overlap in a way that Douglass could use in order to expand the range represented by either pole alone.

What Andrew Douglass needed to make dendrochronology work was a large sample of cut beams, both ancient and modern. If only ancient beams were used, the years represented in their overlapping ring patterns would, in effect, "float in time" with no anchor to any known date. To fill the gaps, Douglass led the National Geographic Society Tree-Ring Expeditions to sites and villages throughout the Southwest. At Betatakin ruin in northwestern Arizona he found a thick Douglas fir log containing rings for the years between A.D. 1073 and 1260, when it was cut. That beam proved to be an important missing link that bridged the gap between the latest samples Neil Judd had found at Pueblo Bonito and a point in time 586 years later, near the end of the prehistoric period. For more recent beams, Douglass and his team lived among the Hopi, and with their permission sampled beams found among their dwellings, further closing all but one gap. The end of the long quest came with a partially burned beam found at Show Low ruin, Arizona, in the summer of 1929. Reading its rings in an old tool shed commandeered for the purpose, Andrew Douglass carefully traced the visible rings from the outside toward the center. When he finished, the years 1237-1380 lay before him and provided the final missing link in the sequence.

"The history within that carbonized bit of beam held us spellbound," he reported. "Its significance found us all but speechless; we tried to joke about it, but failed miserably. We felt that here was the tie that would bind our old chronology to our new and bring before us undreamed-of historic horizons."

Aided by the tree rings, the archaeologists on the Society's Wetherill Mesa expeditions eventually produced a securely dated history of the ancient Pueblo occupation of the area. It showed that by A.D. 700 the earliest inhabitants had dwelt on the flat mesa top, in semi-subterranean pit-houses. Around 1150, with an ever-expanding population, they had begun to build larger and larger complexes of rooms. Their final building stage saw a shift in location, when buildings such as the famed Cliff Palace were constructed in sheltered hollows beneath the overhang of the mesa edges, perhaps for defense. In 1276 a severe drought began in the region. It would last 24 years, eventually causing the failure of farming and the end of ancient Pueblo occupation.

In 1976, Ray Williamson of St. John's College in Annapolis, Maryland, and his colleagues who study ancient astronomical practices added another dimension to our knowledge of the ancient pueblos. Helped by Society funding, he discovered that certain stone structures in Chaco Canyon and other Southwestern ruins marked key solar alignments that would have helped mark solstices—an obvious aid in determining the precise length of a solar year. At Pueblo Bonito itself, Williamson found that at least two corner doorways—features rare in ancient Southwest architecture—allowed views of sunrise at winter solstice.

Temporarily mired in the quicksands of Chaco Canyon, the Society's Pueblo Bonito expedition vehicle succumbs to one of many natural challenges that can beset field archaeologists in search of new knowledge. It took ten men, a team of horses, and another truck—sent for by a runner—six hours to finally free this one.

Photograph by O. C. Havens

Viewed from Chaco Canyon's north rim, the empty rooms and kivas of Pueblo Bonito look out upon a sere escarpment (left). At various times during the six or so centuries following A.D. 750, Pueblo Indians built more than a hundred settlements in and around this canyon. Pueblo Bonito, which harbored successful farmers, traders, and craftspeople, was by far the largest. A remarkable turquoise necklace found in 1924 at the site (below), contains more than 2,500 beads and four pendants, reflecting the enormous talent and labor of its maker.

Matthew and Marion Stirling and the Giant Olmec Heads of Veracruz

ON RARE OCCASIONS, explorations funded by the Geographic have resulted in the discovery and definition, not merely of cities, but of entire civilizations. By far the best example lies

At Tres Zapotes—translatable as "Three Chickens"—in 1939, Matthew Stirling's team carefully raises an ancient stone monument from its muddy bed. Carved some 2,500 years earlier, such discoveries helped Stirling reveal ancient Olmec culture, the earliest great civilization of the Americas.

in the expeditions led by Matthew W. Stirling of the Smithsonian Institution's Bureau of American Ethnology between 1938 and 1946. These took place in the dense and relatively unexplored tropical rain forest in the low, humid lands along Mexico's Gulf Coast, in the states of Veracruz and Tabasco. Stirling, his wife, Marion, and NATIONAL GEOGRAPHIC photographer Richard H. Stewart traversed this area by foot and on horseback in one of the greatest epics of expedition teamwork in the history of archaeology.

Matt Stirling was drawn to the region by curious and inexplicable things he had seen elsewhere. One was a strange jade mask of a snarling feline in a Berlin museum exhibit; another, the brief notice in an old Mexican journal of the accidental discovery of a colossal stone carving of a human head by a farm laborer—he thought at first it was a buried kettle—at the small settlement of Tres Zapotes, Veracruz. The focus of both these finds lay in a land noted as far back as the time of the Spanish Conquest as the location of the "Olmeca," or "people of the rubber country" in Nahuatl, the language of the Aztec, whose empire collected tributes of rubber balls from the area—these for the ritual games played in the Aztec capital.

The Stirlings and Stewart departed for Veracruz late in 1938 with the blessing of the Society's Committee for Research and Exploration and the Smithsonian Institution, and the first step was taken in the revelation of one of the most remarkable of all the early cultures of the Americas.

During a survey trip earlier in 1938, Stirling had excavated the colossal head at the farmstead of Tres Zapotes, based on a reference to it in an 1853 Mexican journal. Upon his return, he excavated mounds in the surrounding area. There he came upon more intriguing things, including part of an ancient stone monument. Its front bore the face of a snarling jaguar, and its flat back face held, in low relief, a series of bars and dots—representing the numbers 5 and 1, respectively, as was the custom in some parts of ancient Mesoamerica, particularly the Maya area.

Here Matt Stirling, aided by flawless instinct, took a leap of faith, a small chance in interpretation: Realizing that the general pattern of the numbers he found before him matched that used hundreds of miles away in Maya hieroglyphic dates, he made the assumption that the two cases reflected an identical calendar system. Then, using the customary "correlation factor" employed by Mayanists to convert their dates to Christian equivalents, he converted the Tres Zapotes date. The date came out earlier than any known example from the Maya area by some three centuries!

The news came as a bombshell to Stirling's colleagues in Maya studies. Some questioned his partial reconstruction of one of the numbers on the stone—an obviously correct reconstruction for the few who had actually examined the stone, and one that was verified decades later when the other fragment of the monument came to light. In time, most agreed that Matt Stirling had found what was then the earliest recorded date in the Americas—equated by the present correlation factor to September 3, 32 B.C. Although it falls long after the peak of the Olmec phenomenon, this date helped confirm Stirling's conclusion that the Olmec were on the Mesoamerican scene earlier than anyone had previously thought.

Stirling's expeditions into the remote

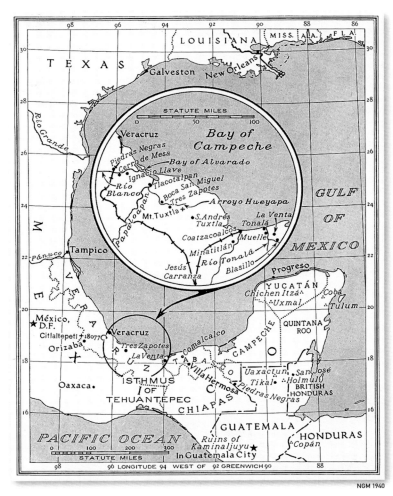

STATUTE MILES

NGM 1940

cultures of virtually all its neighbors, from those of Central Mexico to the highlands of Guatemala. Matthew Stirling's basic notion that Olmec culture contained virtually every element that marked the Maya, Zapotec, and later Mesoamerican peoples and civilizations has proven correct. So have most of the conclusions reached by this remarkable scientist.

Excavations funded by the National Geographic saw later expeditions follow up on Matt Stirling's initial finds. In 1955 Philip Drucker and Robert Heizer showed that the Olmec center of La Venta was a carefully constructed series of parallel platforms symmetrically arranged around a gigantic earthen mound. That central structure, 100 feet high, probably represented a sacred mountain—some say a volcano, because grooved gullies give it the aspect of a fluted cone.

In one astonishing find at La Venta, excavators uncovered a set of standing figures mostly of jade, one of a rougher stone, each measuring about eight inches tall. This miniature ensemble had been carefully placed to represent a set of actors engaged in a ritual of some kind that apparently took place in a structure with stone columns—represented by narrow axes of jade—perhaps with the figure wrought in the lesser stone as victim or prisoner. Whatever the meaning—and that will never be known with any certainty—the discovery helps us glimpse a vignette of ancient Olmec life.

Putting Olmec archaeology on the map (left). Stirling's Veracruz expeditions deduced the basics of Olmec history by analyzing its artifacts. Distribution patterns showed that these people once traded across Mesoamerica for jade and other raw materials, which they used for figurines, ear ornaments, and other luxury goods. A gigantic stone head (below), one of three unearthed at the Olmec site of La Venta, probably portrayed a powerful chieftain or god.

mound sites of southern Veracruz and Tabasco continued to reveal new information about their builders. His last expedition to Veracruz and Tabasco took place in 1946, when he, Marion, and Dick Stewart journeyed to the village of San Lorenzo Tenochtitlan. Nearby, on the flat summit of a broad plateau overlooking the Coatzalcoalcos River, lay a large number of overgrown mounds. Ravines that cut into the edges of the site yielded more colossal heads like those at Tres Zapotes and La Venta. One San Lorenzo head measured nine feet in height and weighed an estimated 30 tons. Stirling's test excavations revealed other enigmatic sculptures as well—many blended the features of humans and jaguars; others depicted serpents or other animals. All were rendered in hard, volcanic basalt—some pieces weighing many tons—which the Olmec somehow had transported over rivers and rough terrain from quarries up to a hundred miles away. The superb sculptures produced by these astonishing people more than 2,500 years ago represent America's first great art style.

Olmec culture first began to flourish about 1200 B.C., and started to fade after 400 B.C. While its main center of activity lay along the Gulf Coast, its influences permeated the

EXQUISITE MAYA RUINS OF PALENQUE AND CHICHÉN ITZÁ

Partially cleared of its dense forest shroud, a courtyard of the so-called Palace at the Maya ruin of Palenque stands revealed in this 1891 photograph from the Maudslay Expedition (left). Stucco relief carvings on stone piers miraculously survived some 1,200 years of tropical rains, as did a unique masonry tower overlooking the ancient royal precinct. Later expeditions followed Maudslay's example of carefully documenting ruins through photographs and drawings. Early images of the serpent columns at Chichén Itzá's Temple of the Jaguars (below) and its Red House (bottom), for example, greatly benefit current archaeologists studying the Maya area.

Properly shaded by a parasol, Anne Cary Maudslay inspects broken Maya stelae in Quiriguá, lowland Guatemala, in 1894. She traveled with husband Alfred Percival Maudslay, who spent months meticulously surveying the site and making molds and photographs of its sculptures. The first serious scientific study of this important Maya center, Maudslay's work eventually helped later experts decipher Maya inscriptions.

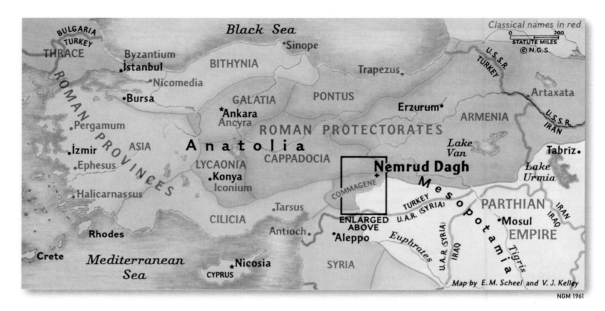

Map by E. M. Scheel and V. J. Kelley

NGM 1961

THERESA GOELL AND THE MIDDLE EAST KINGDOM OF COMMAGENE

ABOUT THE SAME TIME that Drucker and Heiser were exploring La Venta, archaeologist Theresa Goell was leading a set of five expeditions supported by the Geographic and others to still another forgotten kingdom of antiquity, this one half a world away. Her discover-

Some 2,000 years ago, Antiochus I of the Kingdom of Commagene built a memorial to himself at Nemrud Dagh (above). In the 1950s, archaeologist Theresa Goell (right)—here flanked by colossal sculptures of the king and a bearded god— mounted five Society-sponsored expeditions that helped reveal the former splendor of this once-forgotten site.

ies took place in southeastern Turkey, once home of the all-but-forgotten kingdom of Commagene. The site that drew Goell to this remote region was called Nemrud Dagh, "Mount of Nimrod," an arid promontory overlooking the Euphrates River. On the rubble slopes of Nemrud Dagh, Theresa Goell unearthed a treasure trove of sculpture.

Unlike the art of Aphrodisias, the monumental portrait sculptures that Goell found seem relatively unrefined, possessing the raw strength of a somewhat earlier time and style. She interpreted that style as "a dramatic amalgam of East and West, of Greece, Persia, and

Anatolia." In her seasons of research at the remarkable mountain, Goell also brought recognition to one of the greatest rulers of antiquity—the god-king Antiochus I. At Nemrud Dagh, artisans, architects, and planners under Antiochus "had hewn three great courts out of living rock." Two, the East and West Terraces, held "similar arrays of statues"—up to 29 feet tall—of the king and his supernatural companions. A gigantic guardian eagle is on the North Terrace.

"Looking up at Antiochus and his gods— a ruined pantheon presiding over a ruined Olympus—none of us could escape a sensation of awe," wrote Goell after workers had cleared away the rubble of ages. "These gods combined the deities worshiped by the king's Greek and Persian ancestors." Among those portrayed in the great gallery of seated statues were the Sun God, the Fortuna, or Fertility Goddess of Commagene, the "Thunder Shaker" Zeus-Ahuramazda, Hercules, and Antiochus himself. "The implacable ravages of the centuries," Goell noted, "had decapitated all but one: The goddess had kept her head."

At its height in the first century B.C., the small kingdom of Commagene had served as a buffer between Rome and the powerful Parthian Empire. Its capital, Samosata, lay 34 miles to the southwest of the great silent shrine at Nemrud Dagh, at a strategic crossing point on the Euphrates. When the worker-subjects of Antiochus created the courts of Nemrud Dagh and the statuary that brooded over them, the rubble they removed was used to cover the great conical mountain-top that rose behind the shrine and its rows of

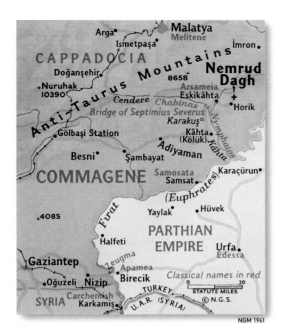

sculptures. Theresa Goell became convinced early in her study that this mountain held the tomb containing the remains of Antiochus I, but all efforts to start exploratory tunnels ended when avalanches of stone forced a halt. Goell departed the site, hoping to await the development of better methods of tackling this formidable engineering problem, but her ambition was never realized. Mount Nimrod in all likelihood will continue to protect the tomb and remains—if in fact they are here— that were entrusted to it so long ago.

FORAYS INTO EGYPT: CARTER AND WEEKS

LIKE ANTIOCHUS I, the pharaohs of ancient Egypt and Nubia also sought a kind of immortality in the security of secret tombs. More often than not, their intent was thwarted by the ever-present problem of tomb robbers. Nowhere was the situation more acute than in a narrow dead-end canyon that lies between high sandstone cliffs just beyond the necropolis of Western Thebes, in the middle reaches of the Nile Valley: the Valley of the Kings.

When it comes to the romance of archaeology, no name resonates with more meaning in the conversations of scholars and lay-persons alike. The Valley of the Kings represents the very epitome, almost the stereotype, of the never-ending race between scientists and tomb looters. Indeed, tomb robbing may well be the second oldest profession. In the Valley of the Kings, tombs more often than not were sacked within days of their closing. No one wanted the mummies, only the trappings—the ornaments of gold, precious stones, and other items of intrinsic value.

In this century, more than a dozen royal mummies were found crammed together in a crevice in a cliff, abandoned ages before by tomb robbers. Authorities from Cairo rescued the remains from their ignominious fate, taking them by boat to the Cairo Museum for safekeeping. Thus did some of the most powerful pharaohs ever to rule ancient Egypt make their final journey down the River Nile.

Of all the royal tombs in the Valley of the Kings, only that of the young Pharaoh Tutankhamun escaped the looters, probably because its entrance remained invisible below

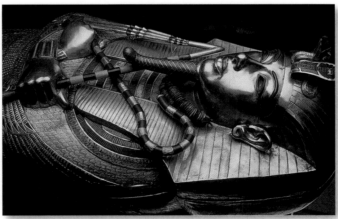

In 1922, Howard Carter's milestone discovery in Egypt's ancient Valley of the Kings (map) rocked the world: He found the unlooted tomb of "missing" Pharaoh Tutankhamun. Carter recovered innumerable treasures, including this lavishly decorated and superbly worked gold coffin.

the rubble until 1922. That year, archaeologist Howard Carter, who had sought the tomb for many years after noting Tutankhamun's name on an artifact from the vicinity, narrowed the most probable location to one tiny area— the site of his workers' tents. These were removed, the rubble cleared, and a stairway was revealed.

Jumbled accoutrements of the young god-king Tutankhamun—chests, chariots, a royal throne, and much more—overflow the antechamber of his tomb (right) in this 1922 photograph, taken at the time of Carter's discovery. While most royal tombs in the Valley of the Kings had been looted by tomb robbers long before, paintings and reliefs remained, often revealing much about these long-departed monarchs— and their egos. A royal temple dedicated to Ramses II (above), for example, depicts a procession of his many sons while he towers above, facing primary god Amun-Re.

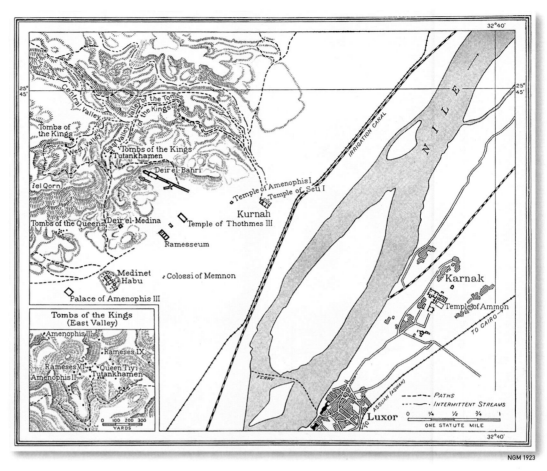

Located just west of Egypt's lifeblood river, the ruins of ancient Thebes marks a giant necropolis that includes the Valley of the Kings and the Valley of the Queens. On the Nile's opposite shore stands the living city of Luxor and the great Temple of Karnak.

NGM 1923

AFTER CARTER'S FIND, it was firmly believed that Tutankhamun's tomb would be the last major discovery in the Valley of the Kings, since all pharaohs had now been accounted for. But more than 70 years later, in 1995, Egyptologist Kent R. Weeks of the American University in Cairo made a stunning coup—

and it happened beneath the road at the valley entrance.

Kent Weeks had first come to Western Thebes in the early 1970s, as a graduate student at the University of California at Berkeley. He headed the Theban Mapping Project, which plotted the incredible inventory of known ruins that lay between the Nile and the cliffs, including the Temple of Hatshepsut and the Ramesseum, the palace of powerful Ramses II, legendary pharaoh of the Exodus.

Later Weeks began to devote himself to compiling a thorough and accurate inventory of all the discoveries in the Valley of the Kings—a database that would enable him and other archaeologists to conduct and plan their own research more effectively. The effort, partly funded by National Geographic, led to Weeks's amazing rediscovery of KV 5, the fifth tomb to be found in the Valley of the Kings, the designation assigned through a system developed by John Gardner Wilkinson, an early Egyptologist, in 1827.

At first it appeared to be only a rubble-filled room, one that had been mentioned in an obscure journal of the late 1800s. A British tourist-explorer had entered its narrow opening and noted partly buried columns and a statue in 1825. Weeks excavated with a small crew, clearing enough concrete-hard rubble

Dead man walking? No, just a lifelike portrait statue of Pharaoh Tutankhamun—or perhaps one of his wives—being borne from his tomb site by a laborer in 1923. Some speculate that the bust may once have been used by the king's tailors as a fitting dummy for making his clothes.

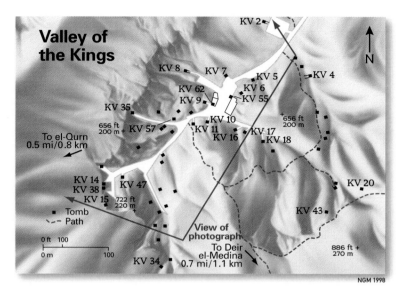

Valley of the Kings

KV 2
KV 8
KV 7
KV 5
KV 4
KV 62
KV 6
KV 9
KV 55
KV 35
656 ft
200 m
KV 10
656 ft
200 m
To el-Qurn
0.5 mi/0.8 km
KV 57
KV 11
KV 17
KV 16
KV 18
N
KV 14
KV 38
KV 47
KV 20
KV 15
722 ft
220 m
Tomb
Path
KV 43
0 ft 100
View of
photograph
0 m 100
To Deir
el-Medina
0.7 mi/1.1 km
886 ft
270 m
KV 34
NGM 1998

fill to see that KV 5 was not merely a room, but an entire system of rooms that appeared to have been filled by flooding.

Fragments found on the floor revealed two main things: First, KV 5 had probably been pretty thoroughly emptied long ago, and second, those artifacts that were left pertained to the Pharaoh Ramses II, since hieroglyphic inscriptions bore the known names of several of his children.

Soon, Weeks had uncovered not only a system of rooms with side chambers that may have functioned themselves as tombs, but several levels of room systems.

The whole, it appeared, was directly connected by tunnel to the nearby tomb of the Pharaoh himself, looted in the deep past.

The only conclusion Kent Weeks can reach at this point is that KV 5's gigantic system of chambers was carefully constructed by the architects, sculptors, and masons of Ramses II to hold the remains of the Pharaoh's 30 or more sons. Thus did a relatively small amount of assistance from the Society help solve a lingering mystery of ancient Egypt.

Repository of royalty, the Valley of the Kings holds more than 60 tombs of ancient Egyptian royalty, including Ramses II (KV 5) and Tutankhamun (KV 62). While all Egypt's kings have been accounted for, tombs of some lesser nobles may yield important discoveries in the future. "KV" on the map stands for "Kings' Valley" and precedes a number to indicate the sequence in which the tombs were found.

RICHARD ADAMS EXPLORES MAYA TOMBS AT RÍO AZUL

ROYAL TOMBS—EVEN LOOTED ONES—tell us much about a culture. Guatemala's Río Azul demonstrates the concepts behind the funerary customs of Maya nobility as perhaps no other place has done. It was discovered by oil prospectors in 1962 in a remote corner of rain forest beside a seasonal waterway near the point where the borders of Guatemala, Mexico, and Belize meet.

Reports of extensive looting of tombs at Río Azul reached archaeologist Richard E. W. Adams, of the University of Texas at San Antonio, in 1981. Determined to salvage what information he could from the site before it was too late, Adams conceived a plan of exploration and excavation, and with Society support, began work there in 1983. In four seasons, Adams mapped the ruined city and determined that it was closely related politically to the huge Classic Maya metropolis of Tikal, some 50 miles to the southwest.

Arriving in the wake of the looters, Adams saw the burial chambers they had emptied, and these were remarkable in themselves. Each of the 20 or so tombs at Río Azul consisted of a subterranean room centered beneath a ruined pyramid-temple. Most had smooth plastered walls, many of which still held brilliant painted hieroglyphic inscriptions or imagery connected with the Maya underworld. Thankfully, the looters had not destroyed them.

I arrived at Adams's field headquarters in early May 1984, for he had sent the Geographic word that, miracle of miracles, an unlooted tomb was about to be opened. Grant Hall, Adams's graduate assistant, had dug down into a mound and encountered the top of a row of capstones—the slabs with which the Maya customarily covered their vaulted crypts. I had arrived just in time to watch Hall and another member of the crew carefully chip the plaster holding the long stone in place, then slowly tilt back the heavy slab. Before us lay a black opening.

A ladder was lowered carefully so as not

Nearly as fresh today as when they were painted some 1,500 years ago, the elaborate murals of Tomb 1 at Río Azul, Guatemala (right), submit to careful measurement by archaeologist Richard Adams (right). The curving motifs symbolize water and the Maya Underworld, as does the cavelike tomb itself, which was discovered and emptied by looters in the 1960s. Hieroglyphs on the rear wall, behind Adams, refer to September 29, 417—apparently the birth date of the chamber's original occupant, probably a ruler of the local city-state. Unlooted burials nearby have yielded various carvings, including an effigy whistle-figurine (below).

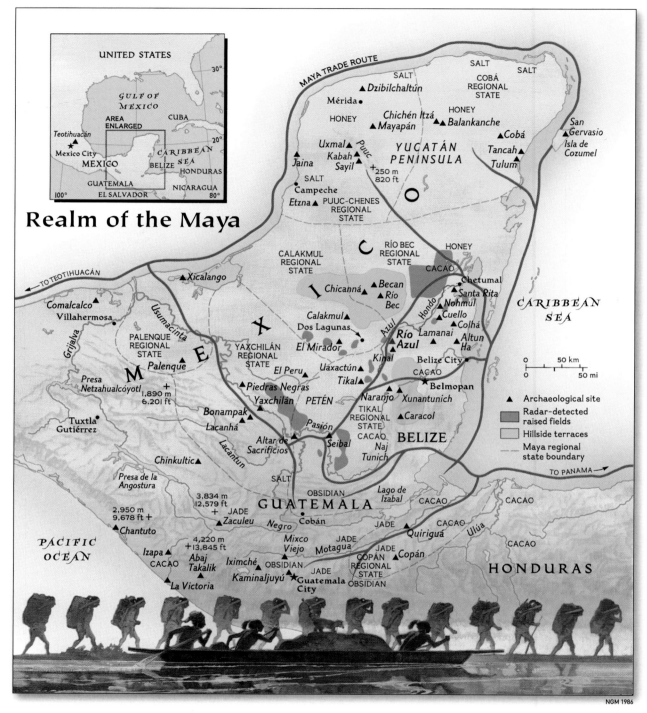

Varied resources and established trade routes helped the Maya sustain a series of prosperous city-states for more than 2,000 years, from the time of the region's first cities, around 600 B.C., to the coming of the conquistadores.

Realm of the Maya

NGM 1986

to disturb anything below. Hall, as discoverer of the tomb, was the first to descend into the narrow opening.

He returned about five minutes later and silently beckoned me to go next.

The floor of Tomb 19 lay only about eight feet below the level of the capstones. After a slow descent, I seated myself with great caution on the smooth surface as my eyes adjusted to the gloom. What I saw amazed me. Virtually every tomb interior I had ever seen or heard of had contained a thick layer of fallen debris obscuring most of the tomb

floor. This one was perfectly clean, as if it had just been swept. That unique circumstance somehow created for me an awesome feeling of intimacy with the other human being present, the 1,500-year-old corpse that rested on the floor barely two feet from where I sat.

The floor covered an oval area roughly eight by ten feet—not particularly large by Maya royal standards. This suggested that the person interred was a member of the Río Azul nobility—perhaps a relative of the occupant of Tomb 1, whose empty and looted burial chamber lay beneath the mound next door.

My companion in Tomb 19 lay wrapped in a dark, decayed mass of material, through which much of the skeleton could be seen. The offerings accompanying him consisted mainly of pottery vessels, still standing where they had been placed with reverence some 1,500 years earlier, each sealed with lids topped by small human heads of clay. A round jar with a stirrup handle was particularly intriguing, for not only did it bear painted hieroglyphs, but also it turned out to have a "lock-top" lid, skillfully rendered by an anonymous artisan genius. The unusual vessel had fallen off the clay ring base where it had been placed so carefully during the burial ceremony. Perhaps an earthquake, I mused.

The aura of the tomb soon overcame me when I realized that the body and the objects that lay before me had rested here for the last millennium and a half—a span that witnessed the demise of the Roman Empire, the flourishing of Aphrodisias, the flowering of Ming China, and the industrial revolution.

Richard Adams was able to verify the fifth century date of Tomb 19 by its ceramics and by its close relationship to nearby Tomb 1, upon whose wall was painted the hieroglyphic birth date of its missing occupant—September 14, 417. Like Tomb 1, Tomb 19 had been

Wriggling into a just-opened tomb, a Río Azul researcher checks its condition with a flashlight while his companions— including Richard Adams, center— anxiously await his report. The evidence, unfortunately, showed that this chamber had been looted in ancient times.

carved out of soft limestone bedrock, doubtless in imitation of a natural cave, which the Maya regard to this day as sacred entryways to the Underworld.

Later analysis of the contents of Tomb 19 resulted in yet another discovery. My son, David Stuart—an epigrapher at Harvard University's Peabody Museum—was able to read the syllable set ka-ka-w, or "cacao" among the hieroglyphs on the round jar I had seen. David's reading was confirmed when residue in the sealed vessel was analyzed by the Hershey Company laboratories in Pennsylvania and found to be that of chocolate.

THE SAGA CONTINUES: SOUTH AMERICAN SITES

EACH NATIONAL GEOGRAPHIC archaeological expedition inevitably leads to others. We have seen how Neil Judd's eight seasons at Pueblo Bonito led to Andrew Ellicott Douglass' travels across the Southwest in search of what he called "talkative tree rings," and how these discoveries encouraged the investigations by Douglas Osborne and others at Mesa Verde National Park, as well as Ray Williamson's work on the archaeoastronomy of the region.

In much the same manner, each year sees increased progress in virtually every area of the world, along with an increase in the quality of research as each new adventurer learns from and builds upon the discoveries of those who went before.

In South America, the tradition of exploration and the quest for knowledge embodied by Hiram Bingham nearly a century ago continues to influence the interests of the

Society, particularly in the ancient cultures and civilizations of Ecuador, Peru, and Bolivia—the heart of the fabled Inca Empire. The Geographic's archaeological expeditions in this region have ranged from the arid Pacific coastline to the lofty snow-covered ridges of the Andes, visible only a relatively short distance inland.

Between 1969 and 1974, National Geographic grantees Michael E. Moseley and Carol J. Mackey investigated the great adobe city of Chan Chan, desert capital of the kingdom of Chimor, which by A.D. 1400 had become the largest city ever built in the Andean area.

The superbly detailed map of Chan Chan produced by Moseley reveals a system of residences, sunken gardens, and cemeteries, as well as enormous compounds that served the Chimú rulers until the conquest

Lavish tombs of Peru's Chan Chan and Sipán sites reflect the magnificence of cultures that preceded the Inca Empire.

SPECTACULAR REMAINS AT A MOCHE SITE

Silhouetted security guards watch over archaeologists as they work at the tomb of a warrior priest at Sipán, Peru (above). Beginning in 1987, excavation of this Moche site revealed a succession of spectacularly rich burials. The dense green of oxidized copper adornments blankets the bones of a warrior-priest (right), as excavators gently lift out the remains, revealing numerous emblems of power beneath, including immense crescent-shaped plates of gold. The Sipán finds revealed remarkable craftsmanship and artistry—for an Andean culture that preceded the Inca by 1,200 years.

JOHAN REINHARD AND HIS QUEST FOR THE INCA MUMMIES

Explorer-anthropologist Johan Reinhard's 1995 trek to the summit of Peru's 22,000-foot-high Nevado Ampato might not have been such a dramatic success if the nearby volcano, Sabancaya, hadn't awakened at the same time. Drifting ash darkened Ampato's snows, causing more absorption of the sun's heat and thawing some of the ice. This process helped expose a 500-year-old shrine containing the mummified remains of a teenage girl and caused her corpse to plummet to an icefield below. Reinhard found the body there, still frozen and intact, with perfectly preserved clothing and other artifacts that, upon detailed analysis later, should reveal new information on the Inca, ranging from ancient diet to religious beliefs.

Reinhard, a Society grantee, reaches out to another Inca mummy (left)—this one partly burned by a lightning strike that penetrated more than four feet underground. His team found the remarkably well-preserved girl atop Chile's Cerro Llullaillaco, in a bedrock crevice near the summit. Close by in other crevices lay the remains of a teenage girl and a boy about eight years old. All had been sacrificed. Yet beneath her carefully plaited hair, the teenager's face (above) still wore a placid expression. Reinhard surmised that the youths probably had been rendered unconscious by the chill altitude and alcoholic drink during a ceremony and had died expecting immortality as participants in a sacred rite honoring the spirit of the mountain. Interred with them were numerous Inca statues, some elaborately costumed, along with delicately woven sandals, pottery, textiles, and dozens of other artifacts.

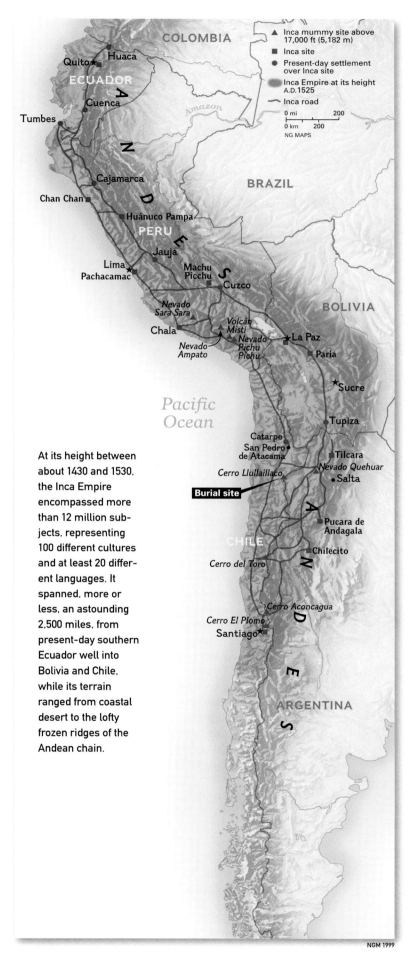

At its height between
about 1430 and 1530,
the Inca Empire
encompassed more
than 12 million sub-
jects, representing
100 different cultures
and at least 20 differ-
ent languages. It
spanned, more or
less, an astounding
2,500 miles, from
present-day southern
Ecuador well into
Bolivia and Chile,
while its terrain
ranged from coastal
desert to the lofty
frozen ridges of the
Andean chain.

of the city by the Inca around 1470.

In 1987, Society funding helped archaeologist Walter Alva secure the great mound at
Sipán, Peru, from looters who had already
begun to sack the rich burials there. Alva's
subsequent excavations revealed the treasure-
filled tomb of a warrior priest of the Moche
culture, which had flourished from about
A.D. 100 to 800. The opulent burial contained
gold beads made in the form of large peanuts,
as well as a gold-and-turquoise ear ornament
showing a human figure in full regalia,
equipped with a movable nose piece, gold
headdress, and war club. It is perhaps the
finest example of pre-Columbian jewelry ever
found in the Americas.

MORE RECENT SOCIETY-FUNDED expeditions
in this region include the remarkable exploits
of anthropologist and mountaineer Johan
Reinhard. I shall never forget the afternoon in
1995 that Reinhard telephoned me at National
Geographic headquarters to say that, only
hours before, he had found the 500-year-old
frozen body of a young Inca girl near the summit of Nevado Ampato, near Arequipa, Peru.
He needed emergency funding to keep the
body safely frozen until scientists could study
it. The money was granted that afternoon.

Later analysis indicated that this girl
of perhaps 13 years had been sacrificed to the
sacred mountain. The event took place around
the time that the conquistadores first
approached the shores of the New World.

Reinhard has since found other amazingly
well-preserved discoveries on some of the
highest summits in the Hemisphere, and will
doubtless make many more.

In the meantime, the Society's other
archaeological work continues. Ann Cyphers,
of the National Autonomous University of
Mexico, carries on Matthew Stirling's pioneering work at the Olmec center of San Lorenzo,
while other archaeologists with National
Geographic funding pursue their goals
throughout the globe.

One Society grantee looks for clues on
social organization in Germany during the
Iron Age, while another seeks ceramic samples
that will help reconstruct ancient human
migrations in the Pacific Ocean. Still another
attempts to assess ancient earthquake damage
to medieval Silk Road cities in Kazakhstan.
The list goes on and on.

NGM 1999

Archaeologist and author George Stuart visits Río Azul's Tomb 1 during Adams's exploration of the site in 1984. Entry to the subterranean chamber was made through a narrow opening in its roof dug years earlier by looters who had sacked the tomb.

YOU CAN GO HOME AGAIN

I RETURNED RECENTLY to Dzibilchaltún, the place where my first Maya archaeological adventure began, and walked some of the old trails. They remained much as I had first seen them; many of the same patches of cactuses and thorn trees still concealed parts of old staircases and walls. I climbed partway up one rubble slope to see if the vaulted room I remembered was still there. It was, although the debris had grown deeper where a tree root had dislodged part of a doorjamb.

At one point I reached a favorite spot, a tangle of brambles partly guarded by a cluster of bullhorn acacias—the kind whose giant thorns serve as the dwelling places for countless tiny stinging ants. Gently I pushed one aside and entered a small darkish clearing I had come upon in much the same manner 40 years before. In the clearing—the smooth gravel surface of an ancient terrace—the Maya had placed a large boulder of white limestone—at least that's what I thought at the time. Closer inspection brought me to the realization that it was not a boulder at all but a gigantic sculpture of a frog, rendered almost unrecognizable by a millennium of seasonal rains since the unknown artisan created it.

For me, that now-crude stone embodies the thrill of discovery, and I was glad to see that it still lay in its original place.

In the times to come, some of these mounds—perhaps even the great frog carving itself—will be excavated by archaeologists. Some will even be restored. Others will remain hidden in tropical growth and slowly become once more part of the ground whence they came. Still others will be suddenly and mercilessly obliterated by highways, houses, and other encroachments of modern times.

A museum at Dzibilchaltún now displays the whole story of the Maya people clearly and well, from the earliest times to the present, in all the areas they occupied. The campus and graceful buildings of the Universidad del Maya now sprawl over an area where I once walked, stepping over columns of leaf-cutter ants as I searched for mounds to map. Thus do places and perceptions change, and that is basically what archaeology is all about.

Someday another archaeological expedition may return to Dzibilchaltún with new problems to solve. If so, it is quite likely to be another National Geographic adventure in the making—one more attempt to help fulfill the Society's mission of learning about the endlessly varied, ever surprising human past.

CASTS OF THE PAST:
RECORDING ARTISTRY FOR THE AGES

Because nothing—not even rock—lasts forever, proper documentation of archaeological remains is key to understanding the past. A rock face at Nemrud Dagh inscribed with the holy law of Antiochus I gets the latex treatment (below): After painting the wall with liquid latex, Kermit Goell—brother of Commagene archaeologist Theresa Goell—and others peel off a hardened, sheet-like cast. Similar techniques used in North Africa by rock-art expert David Coulson on a carved Saharan outcrop yielded an incredibly expressive casting of ancient giraffes (right). Such methods allow scholars access to texts and works of art that they might otherwise never have an opportunity to visit, even if the originals survive intact.

THE FAMILY
OF MAN

I KNOW THE GORILLAS AS INDIVIDUALS, EACH
WITH HIS OWN TRAITS AND PERSONALITY....
—RESEARCHER DIAN FOSSEY

BY LESLIE ALLEN

"Dear Boy," they called him. Proud as any new parents, Louis and Mary Leakey carried their little treasure, a fossil human skull, out of Tanzania's Olduvai Gorge, swaddled him in cotton-wool wrappings, and set out in 1959 to show him off to astonished scientists in Africa, Europe, and North America.

In late fall, Louis arrived in Washington, D.C. When he showed a cast of the skull to the National Geographic Society's Committee for Research and Exploration, its members reacted in much the same way everyone else had: Their jaws dropped.

Dear Boy's own massive jaws, Leakey said, anchored "the largest molars ever found in a human." The skull also boasted a huge dished face, flaring cheekbones, practically no forehead, and a bony head crest like a gorilla's. "He is a fabulous creation," Louis had exulted. He estimated its age at 600,000 years, and had coined a controversial scientific name for this newly discovered hominid, *Zinjanthropus boisei.* The genus name meant "East African man," while the species name honored a benefactor, Charles Boise. Impressed, the Committee voted that very day to award the Leakeys more than $20,000 to expand their three-decade-long search for human fossils in Olduvai Gorge. By coincidence, 1959 also marked the centennial of the publication of *On the Origin of Species,* by Charles Darwin, who made the controversial claim that humanity's past lay in Africa. In 1959, however, Asia—not Africa—was thought to be the home of earliest man. But Asian contenders such as Peking Man or Java Man were fossils of the much more recent *Homo erectus,* predecessor to our own species, *Homo sapiens,* thought to have arisen about 100,000 years ago. Yet here was the flamboyant missionary's son, Louis Leakey, brandishing "Zinj," as he was called, and claiming that Africa—East Africa, precisely—was the human cradle.

At home amid the sunbaked strata of Olduvai Gorge in Tanzania (formerly Tanganyika), Louis Leakey and family search for fossil fragments in a place occupied by hominids some 1.8 million years ago.

Previous pages: Rain-soaked researcher holds a young mountain gorilla at Rwanda's Karisoke Research Centre, founded by the late Dian Fossey.

LOUIS AND MARY LEAKEY AT OLDUVAI GORGE

ALTHOUGH AN ANCIENT FOSSIL of the more apelike genus *Australopithecus* had surfaced in South Africa in 1925, practically no scientists other than the Leakeys had searched for early hominids in East Africa's Great Rift Valley. By the mid-1960s, few would be prospecting elsewhere. Slashing the Earth's crust from Turkey to Zimbabwe, the Great Rift ripples into a series of parallel fault lines in East Africa.

Over the course of eons, land between the faults sank, forming a broad valley crowned by volcanoes. Well-defined strata rose on the Rift's margins. A series of ancient lakes, watering holes for many prehistoric creatures, dried

into fossil-rich lake beds. At Olduvai, a river later sliced through 300 feet of Serengeti sediments—two million years' worth—as it cut to the dusty old lakeshore. Louis Leakey called the mile-wide gorge "a gigantic layer cake" of datable strata.

The Leakeys' new grants brought them assistants and more field time in 1960 and 1961 alone than they had counted in the previous 30 years. Louis often tended to his duties as curator of a Nairobi museum, so Mary, sometimes helped by their sons, ran the Olduvai operation as a permanent camp.

To move hundreds of tons of earth and

fully excavate the *Zinjanthropus* site, she recruited a field staff of Kamba tribesmen; one of them, 20-year-old Kamoya Kimeu, would go on to become Africa's most successful fossil hunter. There were also frequent visitors: giraffes, rhinos, hyenas, and zebras from the surrounding Serengeti plains. At night, curious lions padded around the camp, green eyes glowing in the dark. Mary kept a supply of firecrackers on hand to scare them off, and she never went anywhere without her five Dalmatians to sniff out danger.

Shaded by a well-worn, wide-brimmed hat, a cigarette often dangling from her mouth, Mary Leakey swung a pick, sieved, and washed dirt in the 100-degree heat alongside her Kamba assistants.

At most times, though, she steadily bent to her work on hands and knees. In addition to fossils, she would, over the years, record the location and characteristics of some 37,000 stone flakes, cobbles, cleavers, choppers, hand axes, and other ancient tools at Olduvai. Her work provided the world with glimpses of the earliest stirrings of culture, and her methods became a model for other archaeologists.

Stunning new fossil discoveries in 1960 and 1961 came from a site lower, and therefore possibly even older, than the *Zinjanthropus* floor. There, many hominid bones began turning up. Then, 19-year-old Jonathan Leakey found a hominid lower jaw, with several intact molars; it had belonged to an 11- or 12-year-old and soon became known as "Jonny's Child."

Though they were only fragments, all these pieces of the past pointed to a previously unknown hominid, strikingly different from *Zinjanthropus*. But what?

Soon, more startling news arrived, thanks to a brand new method for dating fossils. By measuring the rate of decay of radioactive potassium in volcanic deposits such as Olduvai's, this method, potassium-argon dating, could determine the age of fossils within those deposits. Louis dispatched samples from both the Zinj and Jonny's Child sites to a lab at the University of California's Berkeley campus. Preliminary results put both fossils at 1,750,000 years. That made Zinj—Dear Boy—three times older than even Leakey himself had supposed.

It seemed that not one but two very different hominids had stood on Olduvai's

ancient lakeshore at about the same time. More discoveries beginning the following year confirmed this. They included the teeth, jaws, and skull fragments of several more hominids, playfully named Cinderella, George, and Twiggy by the Leakeys. Like Jonny's Child, they had smaller teeth than *Zinjanthropus's* mighty chompers. Their roomy skulls had encased brains much larger than either *Zinjanthropus* or South Africa's more apelike *Australopithecus africanus* had possessed.

Though only half the size of modern human brains, their brains were large enough to cross a "cerebral Rubicon" into humanness, as Louis Leakey put it.

Just as important, their delicate, agile fingers were capable of a grip precise enough to fashion and use primitive tools. This, Leakey decided, was the early human toolmaker whose implements lay at Olduvai. *Zinjanthropus* was merely an australopithecine, Louis decided, not a real man. Without a backward glance, Leakey orphaned Dear Boy and all his kind.

At a 1964 press conference at the National Geographic Society, Louis announced the discovery of a new member of our own genus. Scientists settled on the name *Homo habilis*—the human with ability.

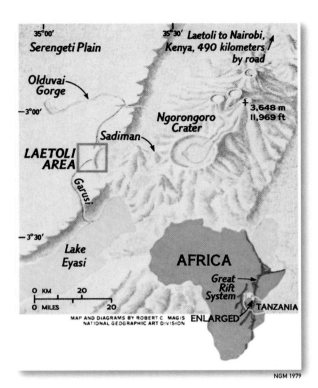

Led by Mary Leakey, Kamba tribesmen sift an Olduvai dry wash for fossils in the 1960s (below). During the 1970s, the archaeologist shifted focus south to Laetoli, another Tanzanian site (map), where her team would discover hominid footprints made 3.6 million years ago in damp volcanic ash.

Dispensing treatments for bodily ills, anthropologist Louis S. B. Leakey—an honorary member of the Kikuyu people—operates a makeshift clinic, attended here by Masai in a photograph published in the February 1965 issue of NATIONAL GEOGRAPHIC. The Kenyan-born scientist attributed his legendary success as a fossil hunter to survival skills such as patience and observation, gained from tribal elders. The former saw him through his early years of meager rewards at Olduvai; the latter taught him to recognize subtle but significant anomalies: "a glint of white in the face of a cliff, an odd-shaped pebble, a tiny fragment of bone." Born in 1903, Leakey grew up in his missionary family's mud-walled home (opposite, bottom), leaving Kenya only to attend school in England. On leave from Cambridge in 1924 (opposite, top), he set out on his first dig—for dinosaurs.

Cranial fragment no bigger than a matchbook (above) ignited a determined search for other, scattered remains of a single ancient individual. A thorn tree offers precious little relief to Richard Leakey and longtime colleague Kamoya Kimeu as they probe the barren wastes of West Turkana with dental tools (right). Their search eventually yielded the most complete skeleton yet found of an early hominid, generating a remarkable portrait of a young *Homo erectus* about age 12, who had lived some 1.6 million years ago. Five feet four in height and strikingly modern in appearance, Turkana Boy shattered the once-widespread belief that humans have grown steadily taller during our time on Earth.

Homo habilis stretched humankind's time on Earth from a mere hundred thousand years to a breathtaking two million.

Years of tedious labor—as well as several NATIONAL GEOGRAPHIC articles about their fossil finds—helped make Leakey a household name. Now, like the evolutionary tree, the family itself seemed to be branching in unpredictable directions. For Mary, ever the thorough scientist, celebrity was an intrusion on her devotion to her fieldwork. Louis, on the other hand, basked in the spotlight. Exchanging baggy coveralls for black tie, he crisscrossed the United States raising money, collecting honorary degrees, inspiring starry-eyed students, and pulling so many little fossils from his pockets that colleagues began calling him the "Abominable Showman."

Say what they might, they envied his ability to cultivate publicity and popularize the arcane, technical world of paleoanthropology. Above all, they envied the fabled "Leakey luck."

LIKE FATHER (AND MOTHER), LIKE SON

IN TIME, RICHARD LEAKEY would prove even luckier than his parents. Louis and Mary's lanky middle son, nicknamed "Ostrich," had endured merciless bullying at Nairobi's Duke of York Secondary School before dropping out to run a safari business. He later returned to the fossil-hunting fold but was not content to remain in Louis's shadow.

In 1968 Richard asked the Geographic for his own grant, staking his fledgling reputation on an unexplored area by Lake Rudolf, now known as Lake Turkana, in northern Kenya. He had spotted the site from a helicopter when detouring around a thunderstorm.

Though maps showed a region of volcanic rock, Richard could see that dramatic changes in the lake's level over millions of years had left vast sedimentary deposits, ideal fossil-hunting grounds.

A few months later, Richard and his small team of scientists and assistants were on their way from Nairobi to Turkana's windswept badlands, on the first of many Society-backed expeditions to the area. A 34-man armed detachment accompanied the convoy, for, as Richard warned one would-be team member, the area where they would be working "is officially termed 'hostile.' There is a long history of…raiding, murdering, and mutilating…."

Leakey's party seldom even glimpsed either bandits or the region's nomadic, spear-carrying Gabbra people—or anyone else. On the other hand, several team members nearly came to grief with the slender little carpet vipers that slithered around their tents. Crocodiles' eyes stared out from the otherwise inviting turquoise water of the 155-mile-long lake. But at the end of workdays that commenced at dawn, the overheated field staff learned to ignore them as they bathed before dinner.

When Richard hired camels to ease travel over Turkana's broken terrain in 1969, he and three other team members used them for days-long outings far from the main lakeside camp. It was the balkiness of a camel named George, Richard claimed, that led to his first major discovery, on an expedition toward the Ethiopian border. Tired of hearing George "complaining noisily," he recalled, the party dismounted and made camp near an eroded ledge studded with the bleached, fossilized bones of ancient elephants and pigs. The next

The long and the short of it cross paths in Uganda, as lanky Richard Leakey visits Pygmies. Here, as seen in the NATIONAL GEOGRAPHIC in February 1965, he examines a lizardskin harp. His safari business took Richard far afield, just as fossil-hunting later would. The remote, previously unexplored site he chose by Kenya's Lake Turkana proved to be a trove of various hominid fossils.

morning, he found himself staring at a domed object lying in the sand a few feet away. "For years I had dreamed of such a prize," he later wrote, "and now I had found it—the nearly complete skull of an early hominid."

Taking the fossil with them, the group decamped, urging their mounts back to the main camp. There, the sight of four distant figures on camelback, turbans flapping as they raced nearer, alarmed the camp's occupants—Richard's team wasn't expected back for a week. Richard tenderly unpacked his find from its nest of sheepskin and newspaper. It was the remains of *A. boisei,* like Zinj, but it was almost intact, though even older than the Olduvai fossil.

By coincidence, Mary Leakey was then visiting the Lake Turkana camp. "It's beautiful, Richard," she said. Ten years earlier, almost to the day, she had found Zinj at Olduvai.

Not yet 25, Richard Leakey already had the kind of important discovery his parents had waited almost 30 years to make. By the end of his fourth season at Lake Turkana, in 1971, his team had found a stunning 49 hominid fossils, scattered in every direction from their lakeside base, Koobi Fora. Then, in 1972, a shattered cranium, whose myriad pieces were first spotted by fossil-hunter Bernard Ngeneo, were discovered.

"We have a jigsaw puzzle with no edge pieces," said Richard's wife Meave, a zoologist who went to work reassembling the skull, known dryly by its field number, KNM-ER

1470. As she sat at Koobi Fora day after day, with her infant daughter, Louise, beside her, Meave saw the likeness of our own genus, *Homo,* begin to emerge. The reassembled skull was remarkable: more complete, in better shape, and capable of holding an even larger brain than the elder Leakeys' Olduvai specimen. Here was confirmation of what many scientists still doubted after the Olduvai finds: *Australopithecus* and the more advanced *Homo habilis* were living in the same general area at the same general time, about two million years ago.

How did *Homo* come to replace *Australopithecus?* Not by evolution, according to Louis Leakey, who died in 1972—the year that KNM-ER 1470 was discovered. To the end, Leakey believed that one genus evolved independently of the other.

While most other scientists argued—and continue to argue—about which species of *Australopithecus* evolved into *Homo,* Leakey believed that all the australopithecines simply died out. The earliest *Homo,* in his opinion, was yet to be discovered.

Father and son ponder a fossil monkey skull from Richard's camp at Koobi Fora, on Lake Rudolf, now Lake Turkana, in 1969. That same year, Richard discovered a nearly complete skull of *Australopithecus boisei,* the newer designation of *Zinjanthropus.*

Donald Johanson, "Lucy," and Beyond

YOUNG PALEOANTHROPOLOGISTS whom Louis Leakey had inspired were about to begin discovering older and older australopithecines in East Africa. As they did, they would bore in on the mystery of when and why these creatures developed a two-legged, or bipedal gait, and even more fundamentally, when and why they began to evolve away from the knuckle-walking, tree-dwelling apes. One member of this new generation was Donald Johanson, who as a schoolboy had read of *Zinjanthropus* in NATIONAL GEOGRAPHIC. Later, as a University of Illinois undergraduate, he had attended a seminar given by Louis Leakey. The experience made Johanson long single-mindedly to

join the East African bone rush.

He was about Richard Leakey's age and, just as Richard had done, he struck out for an area little known to paleoanthropologists: Hadar, Ethiopia, lay along the northern extension of the Rift Valley, in the deeply faulted Afar region. Like the Turkana fossil beds, Johanson's forbidding site was an ancient lake bed drowned in sediments that, along with volcanic ash, were excellent preservatives for ancient bones. Now, whenever seasonal flash floods scour those sediments, they can expose lodes of fossils.

During his fourth field season at Hadar, in 1974, Johanson and graduate student Tom

Studying the day's catch, Don Johanson, at center, and colleagues Yoel Rak, left, and Bill Kimbel of the Institute of Human Origins compare a partial *Australopithecus afarensis* jaw to chimp skulls and casts of other fossils from the vast hominid quarry of Ethiopia's Hadar.

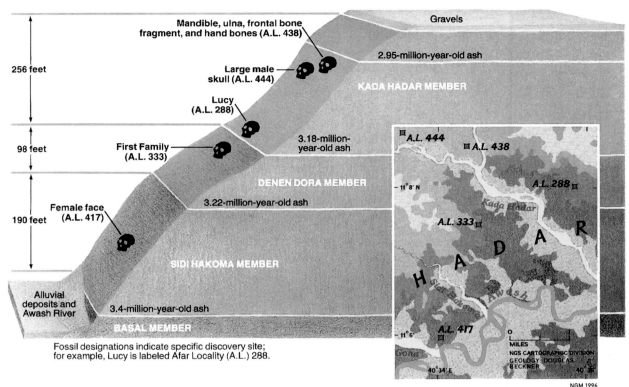

Mandible, ulna, frontal bone fragment, and hand bones (A.L. 438)

Large male skull (A.L. 444)

Lucy (A.L. 288)

First Family (A.L. 333)

Female face (A.L. 417)

256 feet

98 feet

190 feet

Gravels

2.95-million-year-old ash

KADA HADAR MEMBER

3.18-million-year-old ash

DENEN DORA MEMBER

3.22-million-year-old ash

SIDI HAKOMA MEMBER

Alluvial deposits and Awash River

3.4-million-year-old ash

BASAL MEMBER

Ancient ashfalls bestowed precisely measurable dates on Hadar's volcanic strata and the *afarensis* fossils they hold (right). Numbers identify sites: in 1974, Afar Locality 288 surrendered Lucy, the skeleton of a delicately built hominid (below) who walked upright 3.18 million years ago.

Fossil designations indicate specific discovery site; for example, Lucy is labeled Afar Locality (A.L.) 288.

A.L. 444 A.L. 438

11° 8' N Kada Hadar

A.L. 288

A.L. 333

H A D A R

Sidi Hakoma Awash

11° 6'

A.L. 417

Gona

MILES

NGS CARTOGRAPHIC DIVISION
GEOLOGY: DOUGLAS BECKNER

40° 34' E 40° 38'

NGM 1996

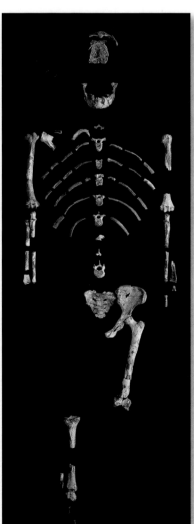

Gray found nearly half the bones of an individual who had lived more than three million years earlier. It was the first time that enough of one ancient hominid had been discovered to be called a skeleton. And it was at least a million years older than any other hominid fossils yet found. Inspired by the Beatles song, "Lucy in the Sky with Diamonds," which blared incessantly into the Ethiopian night from their camp, the researchers called the skeleton Lucy. The Afar tribesmen at Hadar had their own name for Lucy—Denkenesh, meaning "You are wonderful."

By any name, Lucy was strikingly different from fossils found up to that time. A delicately built little adult, only about three-and-a-half feet tall, this primitive australopithecine had a softball-size brain and long apelike arms, but the pelvic and leg bones proved the individual could stand upright. The environment had been far lusher than today's, with olive and evergreen conifer groves and open grasslands that provided lakeshore foraging. Beyond that, though, Lucy's portrait lost focus, and the scientists began to part company—disagreeing even on the question of gender.

Armed with a Society grant, Johanson returned to Hadar the following year. His results did not disappoint a world mesmerized by Lucy. Only a few weeks after his team arrived, Johanson had "the unnerving experience of picking up, almost side by side, two fibulas…. Another Lucy? No, these were both right legs, indicating the presence of more than one individual." Almost simultaneously, other team members began shouting about hominid fossils they were finding all over the same hillside. These also seemed to represent more than one individual.

Almost 200 hominid fossils, a little older than Lucy, came to light from the single slope known as Afar Locality 333 during the 1975 season. They had belonged to 13 individuals, including old and young adults and children. The media instantly dubbed the fossil find the First Family.

Although they provided scientists with important new clues about early hominids, the First Family also raised some baffling questions, because the adults varied dramatically in size. Some were tiny and fine-boned like Lucy; others much larger. Were the larger ones male? Or were they members of an entirely different species?

Though not a family in a modern sense, the First Family was, Johanson thought, a cohesive unit of adults and youngsters. They lacked fire to protect themselves from carnivores; perhaps cooperative behavior had given these hominids their survival edge. It also might have helped nudge their kind toward humanness. If so, it happened at least half a million years before they learned to make tools. The following year, 1976, Johanson's Hadar expedition found tools that, at that time, were the world's oldest known, hewn two-and-a-half million years ago.

MARY LEAKEY AND THE LAETOLI PRINTS

THEN, IN 1978, Mary Leakey's team discovered parallel trails of fossil hominid footprints at Laetoli, near Olduvai. About 3.6 million years ago, at least two hominids walked north across this volcano-fringed plateau, leaving their footprints in fresh ashfall that had been moistened by light rain. The ash dried and hardened, preserving the impressions like prints in a Hollywood sidewalk; later dustings of ash from other eruptions coated and preserved them.

Bared millions of years later by erosion, the footprints looked modern enough to have been made only yesterday. Raised arch, rounded heel, well-defined ball, forward-pointing big toe—all were clearly visible. So were pressure patterns that bespoke a striding gait. One set of prints was larger than the other, belonging to a hominid that stood perhaps four feet eight inches; the smaller hominid, about four feet tall, may have walked slightly ahead. At least one other hominid might have followed along behind.

"Was the larger one a male, the smaller a female?" Mary Leakey wondered. "Or was one mature, the other young? It is unlikely that we will ever know with certainty."

But in one fossilized gesture Mary perceived "a moment of doubt." At one point the smaller hominid had stopped, paused, and momentarily turned to the left, "to glance at some possible threat or irregularity," Mary suggested. "This motion, so intensely human, transcends time."

Whatever we might imagine about these creatures crossing the savanna, their footprints made one thing perfectly clear: They stood erect and comfortably negotiated their world on two feet. The prints also put to rest a chicken-and-egg debate that had dragged on since Darwin's day: Which developed first in hominids, larger brains or two-footed locomotion? These chimpanzee-brained beings that strode along 3.6 million years ago proved that bipedalism emerged first. This bolstered the theory that bipedalism had freed the hands to develop; only later had the brain grown larger. Fashioning tools, carrying infants, and performing other manual tasks may have further enhanced the brain's circuitry.

Might Lucy's kind have created the Laetoli footsteps? Hadar and Laetoli are a thousand miles apart, and the footprints dated to 400,000 years earlier than the Hadar hominids. Yet many similarities exist between the Hadar fossils and hominid fossils from Laetoli that are the same age as the footprints. There were so many similarities, in fact, that in 1978, Don Johanson and a colleague, Tim White (whose site was also in the Afar, 45 miles south of Hadar), christened a new species, *Australopithecus afarensis,* that included all the fossils from both Hadar and Laetoli. *A. afarensis,* they announced, was the common ancestor of *Homo* and the younger australopithecines such as *A. africanus* and *A. boisei.* On the family tree, Lucy's crowd would occupy the trunk.

Some scientists disagreed with this interpretation, none more sharply than Mary and Richard Leakey. A very early *Homo,* they believed, was also represented in at least some of the fossils from both sites. Other scientists, as well, wondered—and continue to wonder—about the dramatic variety in the size of the Hadar hominids. Some also doubted whether the long, curving toes of Lucy's kin could have left the modern-looking footprints in Laetoli's 3.6 million-year-old sediments. The search for the perfect fit continues.

Unlike a fairy tale, though, the quest for our earliest ancestor is unlikely to have a neat ending. The chance that any hominid fossil will survive for millions of years is minuscule. If it somehow does, the likelihood that even the best fossil hunter will spot it is even more remote. Not Cinderella, but Tolstoy's epic novel *War and Peace,* one scientist suggested, offers a good analogy: Charting the course of human evolution from a smattering of bones is like trying to follow the novel's story from a few pages torn from the book at random.

At best, just gathering the story's pieces is a process that proceeds fitfully. There are abundant field seasons and lean ones. Productive careers, such as Mary Leakey's, wind down with advancing age. Or they become diverted by other passions—in Richard Leakey's case, the plight of African wildlife. During the 1980s, the *afarensis* trail went cold, as political unrest kept Don Johanson and other scientists out of Ethiopia. At times, feuding scientists whacked away at theoretical evolutionary trees when new hominid fossils turned up.

Tectonic turbulence marks the Afar Triangle, where three plates meet at the head of the Great Rift Valley (above). From Afar's Hadar, in the north, to Laetoli in the south, the valley contains important hominid sites in East Africa shown here as of March 1996.

BACK TO ETHIOPIA AND KENYA

THE 1980s BROUGHT major technological advances, such as laser dating, to bear on the age of fossil bones; ecologists, physicists, climatologists, and researchers from other

Playthings of time, prehistoric elephant bones and other fossils of varied animals found at Hadar offer paleoanthropologist Don Johanson hints about species that may have shared an ancient stage with our own early ancestors.

fields tried to understand what the world had been like as apelike creatures became more like us. But chance still played a major role.

Often, scientists searching for one thing would find something quite unexpected and altogether different. Serendipity of this sort guided Alan Walker's discovery of the mysterious "Black Skull" during a National Geographic-sponsored expedition to the western shores of Lake Turkana in 1985.

Walker, an anatomist and paleoanthropologist, was still searching for the missing bones of Turkana Boy, the remarkably complete *Homo erectus* skeleton found by Kamoya Kimeu the previous year. Though he lived 1.6 million years ago, in appearance and size (five feet four inches) Turkana Boy was thoroughly modern.

But instead of finding more Turkana Boy fossils, Walker stumbled upon a strange, dark australopithecine skull some 2.5 million years old. It was so primitive that to many scientists the Black Skull suggested a kind of creature that had lived at the same time as Lucy's kin, rather than evolving from them.

Maybe our ancestors' early evolution resembled a bush more than a tree, some scientists suggested.

When Don Johanson's team began returning to Ethiopia in the early 1990s, new finds convinced many other scientists that *A. afarensis* did in fact deserve its place of

honor as the stem that gave rise to later hominids. Until then, the team had never found a complete skull. It was crucial, for, as Johanson said, "the differences between hominid species show up distinctly there."

In 1992, the prize turned up. It was a three-million-year-old male skull that was much larger than little Lucy but appeared to belong to her species. Here seemed to be evidence that *afarensis* individuals varied markedly by size.

The skull also belonged to the most recent known member of *afarensis*. When it was later compared to *afarensis* fossil fragments possibly 3.9 million-years-old, the two were very similar, even though they belonged to hominids that roamed the Afar close to a million years apart. Whatever its other characteristics, *afarensis* as a species was a phenomenal success.

But what species—if any—had walked the land before *afarensis?* Once again, a crackling radio telephone hookup brought the outside world exciting news from the remote Turkana Basin.

There in 1994 Meave Leakey and her Kenyan Hominid Gang, working with Society support, began finding fossils of a previously unknown creature in 4.1 million-year-old sediments. Was it an ape or a hominid?

Slowly, the pieces began to fit together. Wrist bones suggested powerful, tree-climbing hands. A mandible sported a relatively weak chin, more like a chimp's than Lucy's. But the upper jaw anchored vertical teeth roots, a hallmark of hominids. Even more revealing, the tibia, the large lower leg bone, enlarged near the ankle to bear the weight of an upright stance.

More primitive than *afarensis,* this creature nevertheless belonged in the australopithecine camp. Meave Leakey named it *A. anamensis,* which means "of the lake" in the Turkana language. Perhaps this was Lucy's ancestor. And in the way of family trees, the Leakeys' own fossil-hunting pedigree was growing longer.

By the mid-1990s Richard and Maeve's daughter, Louise—now a doctoral student and the third generation of Leakeys to take up paleoanthropology—was heading up field teams on her own at Turkana.

The Continuing Search for "Missing Links"

IN 1994 A WASHINGTON *POST* headline announced, "Fossils Reveal Oldest Known Ancestor of Human Beings." The accompanying story told of a spectacular find—not at Turkana, but at an Ethiopian site called Aramis. There, an international team was led by the anthropologist and former National Geographic grantee Tim White, whose earlier Society-supported work had yielded important insights into australopithecenes.

At Aramis, White was gathering the remains of a species that had lived 4.4 million years ago, roughly 300,000 years before *A. anamensis*. So different was it from anything found until then that White and his colleagues placed it in an entirely new genus, *Ardipithecus*, meaning "ground ape." Its species name, *ramidus*, means "root"—which is right where White's team placed it in the hominid lineage.

Although genetic studies of living species suggest that hominids and apes began going their separate evolutionary ways between four and six million years ago, the fossil record for that period is nearly blank.

Clearly, *Ardipithecus ramidus* was closer to chimpanzees than *afarensis*, or even *anamensis*. Still, details of its cranium, teeth, and elbows have convinced researchers that this species had already branched away from apes—and started on the long road toward humanity.

The fact that Aramis was forested more than four million years ago suggests that our earliest ancestors began moving toward bipedalism while they were still apelike tree-dwellers.

That scenario, in turn, challenges the leading theory that bipedalism came about in response to a cooler, drier environment as the global climate changed. In East Africa, the resulting shift from woodland to savanna would have favored bipeds, who could forage over great distances more easily than arboreal creatures could.

Or perhaps, as paleoanthropologist and current Society grantee Lee Berger proposes, different species took their first steps in different places. In particular, Berger

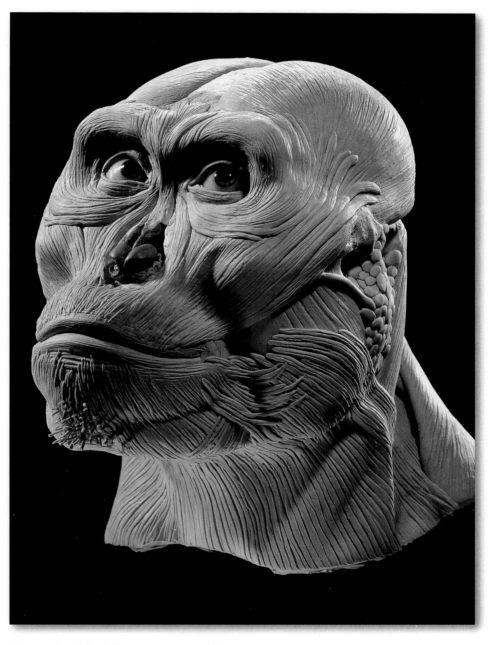

believes that bipedalism also emerged in South Africa, where he has been studying fossils of *A. africanus*. This lightly built australopithecine, which disappeared 2.3 million years ago, has long been some scientists' leading contender for the title of *Homo*'s true ancestor.

With Berger, an American, joining highly respected Johannesburg scientists to renew the search in post-apartheid South Africa, the story of human origins—or at least a subplot—swings back to the place where the first australopithecine fossil was found in 1925.

Computerized mirror imaging and stereolithography produced a three-dimensional model of a large male *afarensis* head from what began as about 60 fragments of a single skull found at Hadar in 1992. Plasticine muscles were added to the model.

Seeking relics of the human past, Ethiopian fossil hunters struggle for footing along Hadar's slippery, knife-pleated ridgetops (left). Seasonal rains scour the region's slopes and gullies, at times baring treasures for the keen of eye. Rains on a floodplain brought half a hominid jaw (above) to the light of day for the first time in untold millennia.

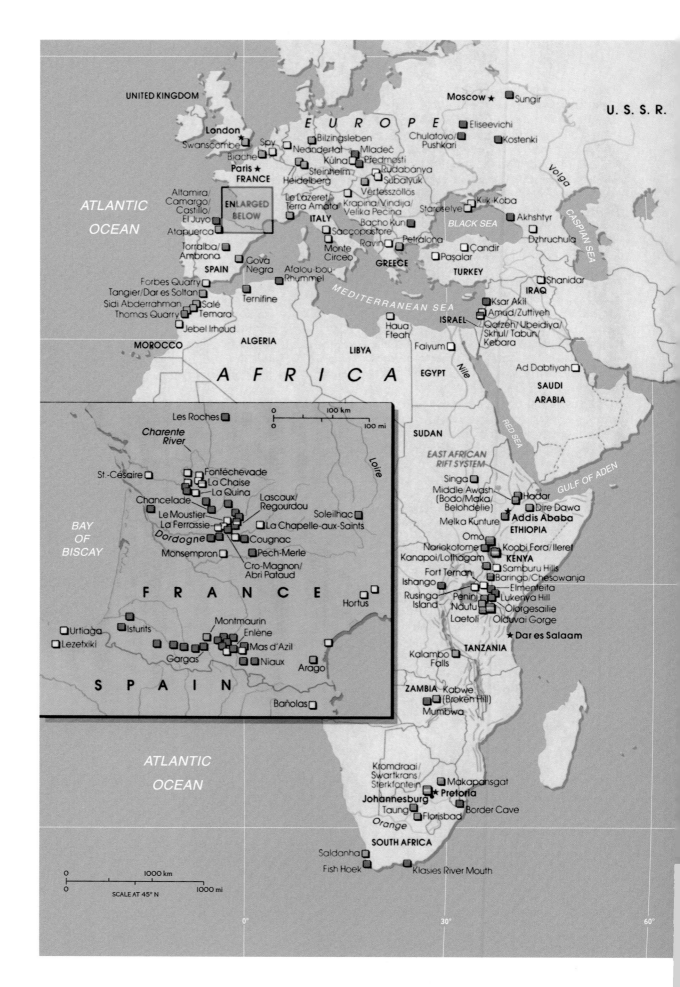

UNITED KINGDOM

Moscow ★ ■ Sungir

U. S. S. R.

London ★
Swanscombe
Spy
Biache
Bilzingsleben
Neandertal ■ Mladeč
Kúlna ■ Předmostí
Eliseevichi
Chulatovo/
Pushkari
Kostenki

E U R O P E

Paris ★
FRANCE
Steinheim
Heidelberg
Rudabanya
Subalyuk

volga

ATLANTIC
OCEAN

Altamira/
Camargo/
Castillo/
El Juyo
Atapuerca

ENLARGED
BELOW

Le Lazeret/
Terra Amata
ITALY
Krapina/Vindija/
Velika Pecina
Vértesszöllös

Staroselye
Kiik-Koba
Akhshtyr

CASPIAN SEA

BLACK SEA

Dzhruchula

Torralba/
Ambrona

SPAIN

Gova
Negra

Bacho Kiro
Saccopastore
Monte
Circeo
Ravin
Petralona

GREECE

Çandir
Paşalar

TURKEY

IRAQ

Shanidar

Forbes Quarry
Tangier/Dar es Soltan
Sidi Abderrahman
Thomas Quarry
Salé
Temara
Jebel Irhoud

Afalou-bou-
Rhummel
Ternifine

Haua
Fteah
Faiyum

MEDITERRANEAN SEA

Ksar Akil
Amud/Zuttiyeh
Qafzeh/Ubeidiya/
Skhul/ Tabun/
Kebara
ISRAEL

MOROCCO

ALGERIA

LIBYA

EGYPT

Nile

SAUDI
ARABIA

A F R I C A

Ad Dabtiyah

SUDAN

RED SEA

GULF OF ADEN

Les Roches

Charente
River

100 km
100 mi

Loire

EAST AFRICAN
RIFT SYSTEM

Singa
Middle Awash
(Bodo/Maka/
Belohdelie)
Melka Kunture

Hadar
Dire Dawa
Addis Ababa
ETHIOPIA

St.-Césaire
Fontéchevade
La Chaise
La Quina
Chancelade
Le Moustier
La Ferrassie
Lascaux/
Regourdou
Soleilhac
La Chapelle-aux-Saints

BAY
OF
BISCAY

Dordogne
Cougnac

Omo
Nariokotome
Kanapoi/Lothagam
Koobi Fora/Ileret
KENYA

Monsempron
Pech-Merle

F R A N C E

Cro-Magnon/
Abri Pataud

Fort Ternan
Ishango
Rusinga
Island
Samburu Hills
Baringo/Chesowanja
Elmenteita
Peninj
Ndutu
Lukenya Hill
Olorgesailie
Laetoli
Olduvai Gorge

Hortus

Urtiaga
Lezetxiki
Isturitz
Montmaurin
Enlène

★ Dar es Salaam

Gargas
Mas d'Azil
Niaux
Arago

S P A I N

Bañolas

TANZANIA

Kalambo
Falls

ZAMBIA
Kabwe
(Broken Hill)
Mumbwa

ATLANTIC
OCEAN

Kromdraai/
Swartkrans/
Sterkfontein
Johannesburg
Taung
Makapansgat
★ Pretoria

1000 km

Florisbad
Border Cave

Orange

1000 mi
SCALE AT 45° N

Saldanha
Fish Hoek

SOUTH AFRICA

Klasies River Mouth

0°
30°
60°

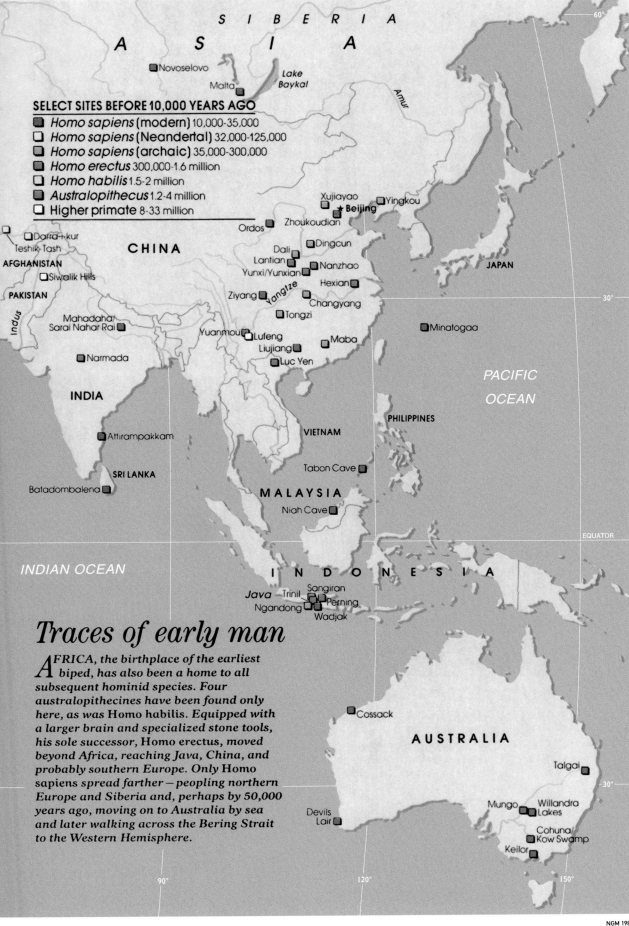

SELECT SITES BEFORE 10,000 YEARS AGO

- ■ *Homo sapiens* (modern) 10,000-35,000
- ☐ *Homo sapiens* (Neandertal) 32,000-125,000
- ▨ *Homo sapiens* (archaic) 35,000-300,000
- ■ *Homo erectus* 300,000-1.6 million
- ☐ *Homo habilis* 1.5-2 million
- ■ *Australopithecus* 1.2-4 million
- ☐ Higher primate 8-33 million

Out of Africa: Keeping to the world's second-largest continent for millions of years, human ancestors finally gave rise to a world-class wanderer: *Homo erectus. Erectus* dispersed rather rapidly throughout Europe and Asia, eventually giving rise to our own species within several hundreds of thousands of years— a short time, evolutionarily speaking.

Traces of early man

*A*FRICA, the birthplace of the earliest biped, has also been a home to all subsequent hominid species. Four australopithecines have been found only here, as was Homo habilis. Equipped with a larger brain and specialized stone tools, his sole successor, Homo erectus, moved beyond Africa, reaching Java, China, and probably southern Europe. Only Homo sapiens spread farther — peopling northern Europe and Siberia and, perhaps by 50,000 years ago, moving on to Australia by sea and later walking across the Bering Strait to the Western Hemisphere.

NGM 1985

JANE GOODALL: THE STUDENT BECOMES THE TEACHER

BIPEDALISM WAS NOT ALWAYS considered the defining characteristic that separated ancient apes from ancient humans. Into the 1960s, many scientists considered the making and using of tools as an ability that only the hominid lineage possessed. Then came the news that chimpanzees in the wild were also doing just that.

"The piece of straw…was held in the left hand, poked into the mound, and then removed coated with termites. The straw was raised to the mouth and the insects picked off with the lips along the length of the straw, starting in the middle."

When Jane Goodall recorded this diary entry in November 1960, she had been observing chimpanzees only for a few months. Straw, vines, twigs, leaves, sticks small and large, stones—all these and more, Goodall would report from her site in present-day Tanzania, chimps fashioned into fishing poles, prods, sponges, hammers, toys, or missiles.

This information, so unexpected, was significant enough to strike toolmaking from the standing definition of the human genus. For Goodall, it was only the beginning. Over the next quarter-century, with continuing Society support, she would amass a vast body of knowledge about the animals that most closely share our own evolutionary heritage.

At the outset, her mentor, Louis Leakey, was particularly curious about a group of chimps living by the wooded shores of Lake Tanganyika. He thought they might offer clues to the behavior of human ancestors, since hominid fossils were often found by ancient lakeshores. But Leakey's young secretary, just out from England, seemed to some observers an unlikely candidate for field researcher. Goodall, they said, looked too fragile for the remote bush, too inexperienced, too uneducated (though she would eventually earn a

Touching moment draws the venturesome 11-month-old baby chimp, Flint, to researcher Goodall. The last-born son of Flo soon returned to his mother's reassuring embrace.

doctorate from Cambridge, Leakey's alma mater). Her mentor saw only her affinity for animals and her sense of purpose. Moreover, he believed that women had more of the essential ingredient for successful field biology: patience.

Jane Goodall's abundant patience served her well, especially during the early years of her work at the Gombe Stream Game Reserve, now a national park. When she arrived, she endured malaria, strength-sapping humidity, loneliness, and frustration.

At first, the chimpanzees fled from her in fear. After eight months, she wrote, "almost all my information had been gleaned at distances of 100 meters or more." But after a year and a half, "I was able to approach within 50 meters of many of the chimpanzees without disrupting their activities."

Over time, the chimps' fear gave way to wary curiosity, then to glares of defiance, even to aggression fed by curiosity. After aggression yielded to nonchalance, one unusual chimp was the first to go a step further. It was the gentle, handsome David Greybeard, as she called him, who would be the first chimpanzee Goodall saw using a tool.

David was also the first chimp she saw eating meat (a baby bushpig), thus disproving the common belief of the time that chimpanzees were primarily vegetarian. He was the first to visit Goodall's camp, and kept returning for palm nuts and the bananas she put out for him, to the amazement of his chimp companions. But soon David was leading them into camp: the clownish William and the excitable alpha male Goliath—David's foil—who would receive reassuring pats from David whenever he became nervous in Goodall's presence.

Years later, beside a trickling stream, David would offer Goodall herself a reassuring gesture, gently holding her hand as she offered him a ripe red palm nut. It was a once-in-a-lifetime occurrence, Goodall wrote, and "the barrier of untold centuries which has grown up during the separate evolution of man and chimpanzee was, for those few seconds, broken down."

Unafraid to be labeled unscientific, Goodall believed that giving chimpanzees names distinguished them as the individuals she observed them to be. In magazine article

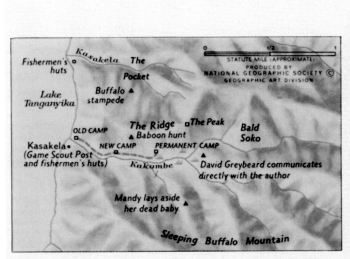

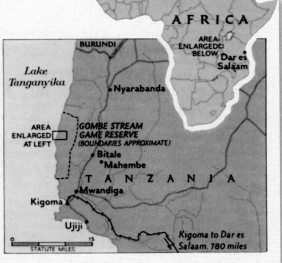

NGM 1965

Major milestones mark Goodall's early research, up to 1965, at Gombe (left). Her desire for conservation eventually helped secure national park status for the Gombe Stream Game Reserve.

after book after television special for the National Geographic Society, she presented them to a captivated world. There was feisty little Mike, canny enough to bluff his way up the power ladder by banging empty kerosene cans, intimidating larger males with his noisy displays. Goblin, another smaller-than-average male, rose to the position of alpha male by expertly playing a game of divide-and-conquer through shifting alliances.

Ragged-eared Flo, a high-ranking matriarch, and her many offspring provided Goodall with a wealth of information on family relationships, maternal behavior, infant development, and social structures. Late in life, Flo gave birth to Flint, whose glowing eyes and tiny pink fingers reached out to Goodall in the photographs of a 1965 NATIONAL GEOGRAPHIC article. But a few years later, other pictures told a different story: Flint lay disconsolate as his sister tried to comfort him. Their mother had never managed to enforce Flint's independence, and he soon lay down and died on the spot where she had expired.

Before she went to Gombe, Goodall was amazed when Louis Leakey told her that her research might take as long as ten years. By pushing on beyond that, she discovered a previously unknown dark side to chimpanzee society. It began after several chimps broke away from the main group in 1970 and became a separate community in the southern part of the home range.

The two groups kept their distance from each other until 1974, when members of the original group began brutally attacking the southerners. By 1977, they had killed the last male of the splinter group, dooming the group and reclaiming the southern range for themselves.

Even more shocking, in 1975 a female named Passion seized an infant chimp from its mother and killed it, sharing its flesh with her own adolescent daughter, Pom, and infant son, Prof. The killing and cannibalism continued: Pom, evidently taught and helped by Passion, later killed two more infants.

Seven other tiny babies that disappeared over a four-year period were probably their victims also; only after Passion and Pom both became pregnant did the horrifying spree end.

What caused it in the first place? Goodall still considers it a mystery but now reads meaning into the fact that Passion was a callous mother when Pom was born. Having observed several generations of chimp families, Goodall says that the single most important insight of her entire career is the lasting impact of an infant's early care on its later development.

As intertwined as some human and chimp evolutionary traits may be, the humans now wield unlimited power over their closest relatives. In recent years, Goodall has turned over day-to-day work at Gombe to others so she can crusade against man's continued inhumanity to ape. Traveling tirelessly, she fights the mistreatment of chimpanzees in medical laboratories, circuses, and other captive environments; the illegal exportation of chimp babies; and the loss of chimpanzee habitat to Africa's exploding human population.

Hair-pulling, although discouraged by the chimps' most accepted human companion, sometimes occurred. Many chimpanzee social gestures—hugs, kisses, reassuring pats, submissive bows—mirror similar human behaviors.

Nightfall, in this photograph published in August 1963, finds the peripatetic chimp researcher at a temporary campsite high above Lake Tanganyika. Prior to Goodall's work, naysayers claimed close-up observation of any of the great apes was impossible. But she began bridging gaps early on, shadowing small groups of chimpanzees through rugged terrain as they searched for food. Day's end, she reported, often found her subjects "sleeping like true nomads where dusk finds them"—and she relentlessly followed their lead.

Loyal member of the Gombe "Banana Club," a chimp named Fifi awaits a handout (opposite), taking a cue from the remarkably intelligent David Greybeard, first to venture into Goodall's camp and accept a banana. Though Goodall eventually expressed misgivings about such techniques, her organized feeding system yielded a wealth of ongoing observations on individual chimps in the wild. Accumulated insights and compassion nurtured during 35 years at Gombe now guide Goodall's crusade for humane treatment of man's closest relatives—including La Vieille (below), an aged chimp relocated from a Congo zoo to a chimpanzee sanctuary in 1994.

DIAN FOSSEY AND THE MOUNTAIN GORILLAS OF VIRUNGA

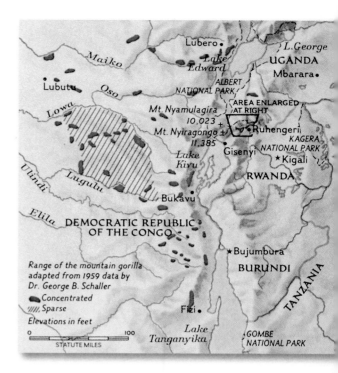

HUMAN INTRUSIONS also plagued mountain gorilla researcher Dian Fossey, a contemporary of Goodall who worked in central Africa's Virunga Mountains.

Like Goodall, Fossey—an occupational therapist who worked with children—had no prior field experience. Like Goodall, she longed to work with animals and was offered a job by Louis Leakey. Seeking to establish a long-term study on gorillas, the largest of primates, Leakey soon secured support for her work from the National Geographic Society and eventually arranged for Fossey to study for a Cambridge doctorate.

In 1967 Fossey made camp on a cold, mist-shrouded volcano in what was then, as it is now, the Democratic Republic of the Congo (although its name has also been Zaire). Only a few months later, political turmoil caused

Gleaned from forests surrounding her Rwanda cabin, fragments of gorilla skulls and other bones provide Dian Fossey with more than an evening's worth of anatomy lessons.

her to move just across the border into Rwanda and begin over again amid the lofty, stream-cut glades of Parc National des Volcans (Volcanoes National Park), her home for the next 18 years.

There, her Karisoke Research Centre took root; its rain-spattered tin huts would eventually draw students, scientists, and—as Fossey's fame grew—film crews and journalists from around the world.

Fossey's meticulously detailed long-term observations would yield much-needed knowledge, accurate and in-depth, about mountain gorillas, a species slightly larger and even more secretive than lowland gorillas.

She considered all gorillas "the most maligned creatures on earth," and struggled to show the world a gentle and intelligent vegetarian, totally at odds with its cartoonlike reputation as a brainless, chest-pounding King Kong. Gorillas' innate shyness partly accounted for the paucity of hard information about them prior to Fossey's work; at Karisoke that shyness was compounded by a well-justified fear of poachers.

To habituate the gorillas to her presence, Fossey threw out "textbook instructions...to sit and observe." Instead, her greatest breakthrough came after she began acting like a gorilla in their presence—grooming and scratching herself, munching wild celery, thumping her chest, belching deeply. She refined her vocalizing by learning from captive baby gorillas brought to her camp.

As the gorillas relaxed around Fossey, she drew their individual family trees and counted more than 200 individuals in almost three dozen shifting groups, each held together by a silverback male.

The groups were highly complex societies marked by unstable pecking orders, intergroup transfers, deep bonds of affection, and—on occasion—brutality and infanticide. Yet Fossey also observed adult males doting upon youngsters, grooming them, and in one instance, even tickling them with flowers.

Gorillas, Fossey learned tragically, will fight fiercely to protect the members of their group. A single attempt to capture an infant for a zoo or theme park may cause the deaths

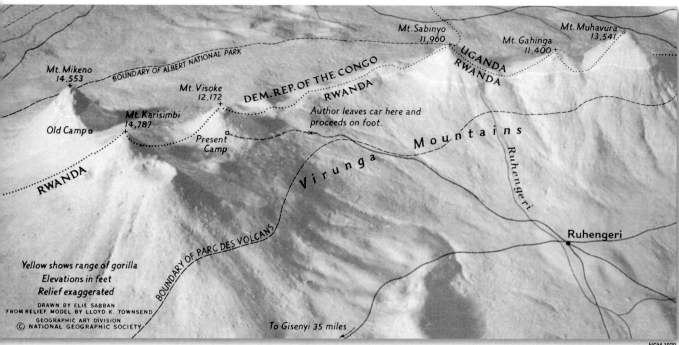

NGM 1970

Undulating line of volcanic peaks defines the remote but hotly contested realm of the endangered mountain gorilla. Political upheaval drove Fossey from the Democratic Republic of the Congo into Rwanda within months of her arrival in Africa. Her later years would be spent waging passionate war against poachers and herders. In between, her easy affinity for her subjects yielded playful moments (left) as well as a bounty of scientific observation.

of many others. On New Year's Eve, 1977, the silverback that Fossey called "my beloved Digit" held off six poachers and their dogs who unexpectedly encountered the gorillas while checking their antelope traplines. While 13 of his group members escaped, the enraged Digit took deadly spear wounds. In a final grisly scene, the killers hacked off Digit's head and hands, as prizes for curio hunters.

"From that moment on," Fossey wrote later, "I came to live within an insulated part of myself." Digit was only the first of many poachers' victims; still other gorillas died of gangrenous wounds caused by antelope snares. By 1981, the total Virunga population of mountain gorillas had slipped to a mere 239 individuals.

Increasingly, Fossey devoted her time to ridding Karisoke of antelope poachers and herdsmen, whose cattle mowed down the gorillas' shrinking rain forest habitat. Patrollers working for her cut upwards of 2,000 traps in one year—1984—alone, and released many gorillas from antelope snares.

By the end of the following year, just before her death, Fossey had the satisfaction of seeing the illegal traps almost completely eradicated. To be sure, poachers still hunted in the preserve, but now they hunted with bows, which spared the gorillas.

Fossey personally pursued poachers. Tactics mattered little to her; the survival of the mountain gorilla, poised on the very brink of extinction, was everything.

In December 1985, an enemy—the murder is still unsolved—slipped into Fossey's cabin and delivered six lethal blows to her

head with a panga knife. She was later buried amid the graves of slain gorillas. Some 60 people trekked up the volcano's slopes and through the forest for her funeral.

As of 1989, the most recent count, the number of Virunga mountain gorillas had risen to 310.

Mother's love envelops five-month-old Cantsbee during a family group's midday rest stop (right). Fossey's research showed that firm maternal attachments mark gorillas' early years; weaned at about age two, youngsters continue to share their mother's nest for another year or so. Adult males often dote upon the young as well, Fossey found, one of her many observations that helped dispel formerly prevalent perceptions about gorillas. A tireless bushwacker, Fossey (above) logged thousands of hours on often slippery, always challenging mountain trails—all to learn about these shy but very substantial primates.

Winning a temporary reprieve from life behind bars, gorillas Coco and Pucker Puss take off on a forest jaunt with Fossey in this photograph published by the GEOGRAPHIC in 1970. The researcher had nursed the stunned and sickly pair back to health after Rwandan park guards captured them for transfer to a European zoo. In the process, she learned much about gorillas' vocalization, feeding, and grooming habits. Though she deplored their fate and uncertain future, Fossey didn't fight park officials on this decision. But her attitude toward the capture of mountain gorillas—legal or otherwise—hardened into outright opposition.

Biruté Galdikas and Borneo's Orangutans

DIAN FOSSEY'S LEGACY includes, so far, a slight uptick in mountain gorilla numbers. But for those researchers who continue to study our closest animal relatives, the very survival of these species looms large. This has been particularly true for Society grantee Biruté Galdikas, a California graduate student until Louis Leakey dispatched her to study the third great ape on our planet, the endangered orangutan, in 1971.

From the beginning, her presence in Borneo's steamy rain forests reflected a dual purpose. One part was to learn more about the solitary, highly elusive, and poorly understood orangutan.

That knowledge, Galdikas said, would be not only about the orangutans themselves, "but also for the light their adaptations may throw on our own evolution."

The rest of the time, Galdikas and her then-husband, Rod Brindamour, spent rehabilitating formerly captive orangs and reintroducing them to the wild.

Over the years, Galdikas waded waist-deep through leech-infested swamps in search of the wild apes, which live 100 feet or more off the ground in the forest canopy. She confirmed the orangutan's essentially solitary nature—in marked contrast to that of other great apes—and sketched in the orangutan's social structure and mating patterns.

Raising her own baby, Binti, alongside an orphaned infant orang named Princess, she noted that "many of the traits associated with the emergence of humankind were already expressed in Bin's development before the age of 1: bipedal locomotion, food sharing, tool using, speech. These differentiated him sharply from an orangutan of equivalent age."

But later, when taught sign language,

Princess proved an apt pupil, learning 20 signs in less than a year. Bin, on the other hand, started dangling his arms orang-style and trying to follow Princess up the trees.

Speculating that the erratic fruiting cycles of rain forest trees may have contributed to the orangutan's evolution as a solitary creature, Galdikas and Brindamour monitored thousands of census trees each month, to record which were fruiting, flowering, leafing, or leafless. They eventually cataloged more than 300 different orangutan food types.

For Galdikas, studying orangutans has meant carefully studying their habitat. The same is true for anthropologist Cheryl Knott, an even more recent Society grantee. Knott's research has shown that the dramatic swings in food availability in the Borneo rain forest play a role in the orangutans' hormonal levels, which affect reproductive cycles.

This may explain why orangutans have the longest inter-birth intervals of any primate and why youngsters stay dependent on their mothers for such a long time. By investigating orangutan nutrition and reproduction, Knott aims to assess the orangutan's prospects for survival in its increasingly degraded rain forest home. Her work—and that of the National Geographic Society—continues.

The ongoing degradation of the orangutan's habitat parallels its own endangerment. As her years in Borneo passed, Galdikas—like Fossey, in a way—increasingly emphasized the need for genuine protection of the apes she was studying. Her rehabilitation camp began to overflow with ex-pets, orphans, and other once-captive orangs, many of them returned to Borneo after they had been smuggled abroad.

Orangutans can successfully be reintroduced to the wild, Galdikas found. But the sight of such reintroduced individuals returning to her camp to feed after long periods of time in the wild has been disheartening, because it hints that there may no longer be enough food in the forest for them.

And it begs a troubling question, echoed in the predicaments of the other great apes: How will they survive when their ever-shrinking forest habitat can no longer sustain them? The answer, when it comes, will be as much about our species as theirs.

Refugees from human captivity, former zoo orangutans find sanctuary with researcher Biruté Galdikas (opposite) in the Tanjung Puting Reserve on Indonesian Borneo. During the course of nearly three decades, dozens of animals arrived at the reserve. Many were rehabilitated and released to the wild by Galdikas, whose research focused on wild orangutans. Like Goodall and Fossey, she was greatly encouraged in her work by anthropologist Louis Leakey.

In training for forest freedom, an orphaned orang tentatively follows Galdikas through the Tanjung Puting Reserve. Logging remains the most immediate threat to the world's rarest ape, destroying habitat already shrunken to small areas in Borneo and Sumatra. In addition, loggers and poachers kill and injure the animals outright.

Partial List of National Geographic Grantees and Expeditions

1890   Israel Russell, Mount St. Elias Expedition
Carried out geologic and geographic studies in Alaska's Mount St. Elias region; redetermined height and attempted to climb the mountain; discovered Mount Logan. Second expedition undertaken in 1891

1898-99   Evelyn Briggs Baldwin, Wellman Polar Expedition
Mapped Franz Josef Land and discovered new Arctic islands; NGS's first involvement with polar exploration

1902   Robert Thomas Hill, Expedition to Mont Pelée
Investigated the eruptions of Martinique's Mont Pelée and St. Vincent's Soufrière volcanoes

1903-05   Anthony Fiala, Zeigler Polar Expeditions
Explored the Arctic archipelago of Franz Josef Land

1906-07   Henry B. Hersey, Wellman Polar Expedition
Attempted to take a dirigible to the North Pole

1908   Robert E. Peary, Peary North Polar Expedition
Peary's final attempt to reach the Pole

1909-11, 1913   Lawrence Martin, Expeditions to Alaska
Surveyed Yakutat Bay, Prince William Sound, Columbia Glacier, and the Malaspina Glacier

1912, 1914-15   Hiram Bingham, Yale-NGS Peruvian Expeditions
Explored the ruins of Machu Picchu and the Vilcabamba region of Peru

1912   George C. Martin, Investigation of the Eruption of Mount Katmai, Alaska
Surveyed area around Mount Katmai following its 1912 eruption

1915-1920, 1930   Robert F. Griggs, Revegetation of the Katmai District, Alaska
Began as a follow-up to the 1912 Mount Katmai investigation; discovered and studied the Valley of Ten Thousand Smokes

1920-27, 1929   Neil M. Judd, NGS-Smithsonian Pueblo Bonito Expedition
Archaeological investigation of Pueblo Bonito and other sites in Chaco Canyon, New Mexico; aided by tree-ring chronology research of A. E. Douglass, also funded by the Society

1921-25   Donald B. MacMillan

1921   MacMillan Baffin Expedition
Surveyed and studied the unexplored coastline of Baffin Island

1925   Macmillan Arctic Expedition
Investigated Norse ruins at Gadthaab, Greenland; U.S. Navy Lt. Cmdr. Richard E. Byrd, Jr., flew to the North Pole

1923-1930   Joseph F. Rock, NGS Expeditions to Western China

1923   Yunnan Province Expedition
Botanical exploration of China's northern Yunnan Province. Charted unmapped regions, discovered pre-Buddhist religions in practice, and introduced blight-resistant chestnut trees to America

1927   NGS Southwestern China Expedition
Surveyed Konkaling peaks, collected floral and faunal specimens

1923-24   Frederick R. Wulsin, Exploration of Kweichow, China
Collected plant and animal specimens from Inner Mongolia

1924   Willis T. Lee, Exploration of Carlsbad Caverns, New Mexico
Surveyed interior and exterior of caverns; Lee's work eventually led to the area's protection as a national park

1924-25   Georges-Marie Haardt, Citröen Central African Expedition
Journeyed by "caterpillar car" from Algeria through the Sahara and Equatorial jungles to Lake Victoria and the Indian Ocean

1928-1930, 1933-35   Richard E. Byrd, Jr., Byrd Antarctic Expeditions
Flew over the South Pole and surveyed 150,000 square miles by plane; determined that Antarctica is one continent; returned for more surveys in 1933-35

1930-35   Albert W. Stevens

1930   Aerial Survey of Latin America
Suveyed air-traffic lanes throughout the Caribbean and Central and South America; made aerial survey of Cerro Aconcagua and other Andean peaks

1932   Solar Eclipse Observation
Photographed the August 1932 solar eclipse and made aerial observations

1934   NGS-Army Air Corps Stratosphere Flight
Made scientific observations of the upper atmosphere from the balloon *Explorer*

1935   NGS-Army Air Corps Stratosphere Flight
Reached the stratosphere in the balloon *Explorer II*, setting an altitude record of 72,395 feet

1931   Georges-Marie Haardt, Citröen Haardt Central Asian Expedition
Collected scientific and educational data as the expedition motored 7,370 miles across Asia, from Beirut to Beijing

1933   Amos Burg, Voyage Southward Through the Straits of Magellan
Studied the islands and indigenous peoples of Tierra del Fuego and Cape Horn

1934   Lincoln Ellsworth
Mounted an aerial exploration of Antarctica

1934-1956   William Beebe

1934   NGS-New York Zoological Society Expedition
Observed sea creatures one-half mile beneath the surface of the Atlantic, off the coast of Bermuda in his bathysphere

1956   New York Zoological Society Study of Neotropical Butterflies
Expedition to Guyana to study ecology of butterflies and other invertebrates

1935-1999   Bradford Washburn

1935   NGS Yukon Expedition
Explored and mapped unknown portions of northern Canada; was first group to cross the St. Elias Range from Canada to Alaska

1936   Aerial Survey of Mount McKinley
Flew over Mount McKinley and took aerial photographs to accurately map the mountain

1938   Alaskan Glacier Study
Measured changes in glaciers since Tarr and Martin's expeditions of 1909-13; found many glaciers had receded five or six miles

1965   Mount Kennedy Expedition
Mapping survey of Mounts Hubbard, Alverstone, and Kennedy in Canada's Yukon Territory

1971-74, 1979   Mapping the Grand Canyon
Created the first precise large scale (1:4,800) map of the Grand Canyon

1984   Mount Everest Mapping Project
Made high-precision map of Mount Everest and the Khumbu/Rongbuk area

1997-99   Mount Everest GPS Expedition
Determined the mountain's rate of uplift; established that Everest was seven feet taller than previously thought and shifting north

1938-1967   Matthew W. Stirling, Archaeological Excavations in Central America

1938-1946   NGS-Smithsonian Archaeological Expedition to Veracruz
Discovered remains of the Olmec culture along the Gulf coast of Mexico

1947-53   Archaeological Projects in Panama
Investigated relationship between Olmec sites and those excavated in Panama; made an archaeological survey of central Panama

1956   Archaeological and Ethnological Expedition to Northwestern Ecuador

1964   NGS-Smithsonian Archaeological Expedition to Costa Rica
Excavated a site near Guacamo; investigated a site with enormous stone spheres

1967   Great Stone Spheres of Jalisco, Mexico
Investigated large spheres similar to those found in Costa Rica

1948-1954 Charles P. Mountford

1948 Arnhem Land Expedition
Ethnological investigation of the Aborigines of Australia's Northern Territory

1954 Study of the Aborigines of Melville Island
Visited the Aborigines of Australia's Melville Island, focusing on the Pukamuni burial ceremony

1947-48 Maurice Ewing, Survey of the Mid-Atlantic Ridge
Made the first study of the Mid-Atlantic Ridge

1949-1955 Ira S. Bowen, Mount Wilson-Palomar Observatory Sky Survey
Created a chart of all observable stars as a base for future comparison

1951 V. B. Meen, Investigation of the Origins of Chubb Crater, Quebec
Study of the Chubb Crater in northwestern Quebec, a crater many times larger than Arizona's Meteor Crater

1952 Gertrude S. Weeks, Weeks Africa Expedition
Expedition into French Equatorial Africa and the French Cameroons

1952-1967 Jacques-Yves Cousteau

1952-53 *Calypso* Oceanographic Expedition
Excavated 2,000-year-old Greek vessel off the coast of Marseilles, France

1954 *Calypso* Oceanographic Expedition
Made a geodetic survey of the Persian Gulf and the Indian Ocean,

1954 Construction of the *Turtle*
Developed a manned submersible known as a "diving saucer" or the *Turtle*

1956 NGS-*Calypso* Oceanographic Expedition
Photographed the Atlantic Ocean's Romanche Trench

1956 International Geophysical Year Studies
Took 7,500 marine samples in the Azores and Canary Islands

1958 NGS-*Calypso* Oceanographic Expedition
Used the *Turtle* to study animals and carbon levels at depths of 700-1,100 meters

1960 Project to Build an Experimental Boat
Developed a 60-foot boat that could carry 60 tons and be shipped by air

1960 Thousand-Meter Diving Saucer
Developed a faster, safer diving saucer that could dive as deep as as thousand meters

1961 NGS-*Calypso* Oceanographic Expedition
Studied currents at the Straits of Gibraltar

1961-62 Development of an Inflatable Boat
Developed an inflatable boat, *Amphitrite*, and tested it in the Arctic

1962 Construction of *Deep-Star*
Developed a three-person submarine to descend to 13,000 feet

1962-65 Conshelf One, Two, Three, and Four
Tested ways to allow people to live in underwater habitats

1964 NGS-*Calypso* Oceanographic Program
Explored the 16,650-foot-deep Mediterranean Trench, 40 miles west of Crete

1965-66 Construction of Submersibles
Designed two one-person submarines to work together as deep as 10,000 feet

1966-67 Videotape Recording System
Experimented with filming underwater using videotape
Note: Cousteau often worked with NGS grantee Harold E. Edgerton in observing and documenting the undersea world

1956-58 Carl F. Miller, NGS-Smithsonian Excavation of Russell Cave
Excavated an Alabama cave with records of human occupation from 7000 B.C. to A.D. 1650, now Russell Cave National Monument

1957-1970 E. Wyllys Andrews, IV

1957-1966 Tulane Dzibilchaltún Project
Archaeological investigation of an Early Classic Period Maya site including a cenote, or ceremonial well, and the Temple of the Seven Dolls

1968-1970 Archaeological Research in Campeche
Documented Maya chronology at Becan, in the Río Bec region of Yucatán

1958-1963 Douglas Osborne, Wetherill Mesa Archaeological Project
Made a complete archaeological survey of a site within Mesa Verde National Park

1959-1963 Edwin A. Link

1959-1960 Underwater Archaeological Expedition to Port Royal
Explored a site off the coast of Jamaica destroyed by an earthquake in 1692

1962 Sea Diver Expedition to Sicily
Searched for archaeological artifacts from a 5th-century B.C. naval battle in Syracuse harbor, Italy

1963 Man-in-Sea Project
Study of workers living 200 feet beneath the ocean's surface, tested diving equipment at greater depths

1959-1972 Louis S. B. Leakey, Investigations at Olduvai Gorge
Made various excavations, such as Olduvai Gorge, Tanzania, and elsewhere, seeking the remains of early hominids and other animals

1959-1976 Frank and John Craighead, Ecology of the Grizzly Bear
Monitored grizzly bears and other large mammals using radio and satellite technologies

1960-1983 Barry C. Bishop, Explorations in the Himalaya
Conducted glacial and meteorological tests in the Mount Everest region of Nepal; studied solar radiation; studied seasonal movement of people indigenous to Mount Everest region; studied cultural changes in Sichuan-Yunnan, China; made an ecological study of Bhutan

1961-69 Maynard Miller, Alaska Glacier Studies
Resurveyed the Juneau Icefield first surveyed by Tarr and Martin; surveyed other portions of the Coast Range

1961-1994 George F. Bass

1961-69, 1976 Excavation of a Byzantine-era Ship off the Coast of Turkey

1964-65, 1973 Search for Ancient Mediterranean Shipwrecks

1967-68 Excavation of a Roman-era Ship at Yassi Ada

1976 Excavation of an Archaic Shipwreck

1978-79 Excavation of a Medieval Islamic Shipwreck

1982 Excavation of an Ottoman Shipwreck circa 1571

1984-1994 Excavation of a Late Bronze Age ship at Ulu Burun, Turkey

1993 Multinational Search Throughout the Mediterranean for Ancient Shipwrecks

1999 Excavation of a 5th-Century B.C. Shipwreck South of Cesme, Turkey

1961-1971, 1977-78 Jane Goodall, Observations of Chimpanzee Behavior
Undertook long-term observations of chimpanzees at Gombe Stream Reserve on Lake Tanganyika, in hopes of revealing behavior of early Miocene primates; 1963 grant to Hugo Van Lawick for photographic record

1962-66 Kathleen Kenyon, Excavation of Jerusalem
Organized an archaeological investigation of Jerusalem's Old City

1962-63 Norman G. Dyhrenfurth, American Everest Expedition
Funding for equipment for the first successful American Everest Expedition; for Maynard Miller's glacier study; for Barry Bishop's mapping and solar radiation studies. Five Americans and one Tibetan summited Everest

1962-64 Henry B. Collins/Junius Bird/Helge Ingstad, L'anse aux Meadows Project
Archaeological excavation of a Viking settlement in northern Newfoundland, Canada

1963   Peter Gimbel/Brooks Baekeland, Exploration of Cordillera Vilcabamba
Parachuted into a remote region of Peru; searched for Inca presence and conducted scientific experiments

1963-69   Theresa B. Goell, Nemrud Dagh and Samosata Excavations
Directed archaeological excavations of ancient sites in eastern Turkey

1964   Bjorn Staib, Trans-Arctic North Pole Ski Expedition
Made first traverse of the Arctic Ocean by ski and foot via the North Pole; 11 men and 100 dogs participated

1965-1992   Richard Leakey

   1965   Excavation at Maralal, Kenya

   1967-68   Expedition to the Omo Valley, Ethiopia

   1968-1977, 1985   Excavations at Koobi Fora

   1969-1978, 1985   Excavations at Lake Turkana (Lake Rudolf), Kenya

1966-1984   Kenan T. Erim, Excavation of Aphrodisias
Made archaeological studies of the Greco-Roman city Aphrodisias, southwestern Turkey

1966   Arctic Institute of America, Icefield Ranges Research Project
Interdisciplinary study of the total environment of the St. Elias Range

1966   Nicholas Clinch, American Antarctic Mountaineering Expedition
Conducted scientific experiments in the mountains of Antarctica; climbed Vinson Massif and peaks in the Sentinel Range

1967-1983   Dian Fossey, Sustained Observations of Mountain Gorillas
Made intensive studies of territorial restrictions of gorillas in the Virunga Mountains, Rwanda

1968   Luis W. Alvarez, UAR-USA Pyramid Project
Searched for hidden rooms in the Pyramids at Giza, Egypt, using "super penetrating x-rays"

1970-1983   Mary Leakey, Paleontological Excavations at Olduvai Gorge and Laetoli
Continued previous Leakey research at Olduvai Gorge, Tanzania; uncovered faunal and hominid tracks at Laetoli, Tanzania

1970-1991   George B. Schaller, Wildlife Studies

   1970   Investigation of the Endangered Markhor Goat and Urial Sheep

   1971   Investigation of Large Ungulates in High-Elevation South America

   1972   Study of High-Altitude Mammals in Pakistans and Nepal

   1973   Study of Snow Leopards

   1976-1983   Study of Jaguars and Pumas in Brazil's Mato Grosso

1989-1991   Large-Mammal Study in the Tibetan Plateau of Xixang, China

1971-1998   Eugenie Clark, Undersea Studies

   1971   Ecology and Behavior of the Red Sea Garden Eel

   1973   Study of the Red Sea Sole as a Potential Shark Repellant

   1973-74   Sleeping Behavior of Sharks off the Coast of Mexico

   1975   Study of "Sleep" in Japanese Fish

   1980   Massive Swarming and Lek Behavior of Red Sea Blennoid Fish

   1986-87   Movement of Large Deep-Sea Fish off the Coast of Bermuda

   1988   Study of Deep-Sea Fish in Monterey Canyon, California

   1998   Study of Sand-Diving Fish off the Coast of Papua New Guinea

1971-1981   Biruté Galdikas, Orangutan Research
Carried out population and behavioral studies on the orangutans of Borneo and Sumatra

1973-74   John G. Newton, Search for the Wreck of the Monitor
Relocation, excavation, and preservation of the Civil War ironclad Monitor

1974-1999   George E. Stuart, Archaeology of Central America

   1974-78   Coba Archaeological Mapping Project
   Mapped and set up a chronology of the Maya cultural center of Coba

   1983-84   Maya Writing Project
   Initiated a comprehensive study of Maya writing

   1999   Center for Maya Research
   Broke ground in North Carolina for a building to house Maya research

1975-76   David Hurst Thomas, Excavation at Gatecliff Shelter
Excavation of remains over 7,500 years old at Gatecliff Shelter, Nevada

1976-77   Ray A. Williamson, Study of Pre-Columbian Towers in the Four Corners Area

1976, 1980, 1992-94   Donald C. Johanson, Paleoanthropological Studies in Hadar, Ethiopia
Search for early hominid and other remains, such as Australopithecus afarensis

1976-78   Ivor Noel Hume, Archaeological Investigation of 17th-Century Sites at Carter's Grove, Virginia

1978-1999   Robert D. Ballard, Deep-Sea Studies

   1978   Galápagos Rift Studies
   Investigation of hydrothermal vents in the Galápagos Rift

1983, 1986-87   Undersea Exploration of the Mid-Ocean Ridge
Used Argo and Jason to study the Mid-Ocean Ridge

1997   Deep-Water Excavation
Excavated a fourth-century shipwreck off the coast of Sicily in 850 meters of water

1998-99   Black Sea Project
Searched for ruins of ancient cities and ships along Turkish coast of the Black Sea

1999   Ashkelon Project
Used remote submarine NR-1 to locate Phoenician shipwrecks off the coast of Ashkelon, Israel

1981   Joseph B. MacInnis, Archaeological Dive to the H.M.S. Breadalbane in the Arctic Ocean

1981   John B. West, Biological Effects of Hypoxia and Extreme Elevations
Measured functions of the human lungs and heart at high altitudes during 1981 expedition to Everest

1983, 1995-99   Johan Reinhard, Ethno-archaeology of Andean Ruins

   1983   Study of Mountain Worship in the Andes

   1995-99   High Altitude Inca Burial Project
   Discovered Inca "Ice Maiden;" explored the summits of three Andean volcanoes for Inca burials and artifacts; excavated highest known archaeological site, atop 22,000-foot-high Llullaillaco

1983-1999   Paul Sereno, Dinosaur Studies

   1983   Phylogeny and Comparative Morphology of the Dinosaurian Family Psittacosauridae

   1990   Study of Early Bird-Like Vertebrates in China

   1992   Documentation of Fauna and Flora of Lower Cretaceous in West Africa

   1996   Study of Cretaceous Exposures in Northern Patagonia

   1997   Excavation of Several Sauropods in Niger

1983-86, 1993-94   Richard E. Adams, Río Azul Archaeological Project
Surveyed a classical Maya city, Río Azul, on the Belize-Guatemala border

1984-85, 1999   Thomas E. Miller, Survey of Chiquibul Caverns, Belize/Guatemala
Mapped 58 kilometers of passages of a cave system used by the Maya

1985-1995   Michael J. Novacek

   1985   Paleontology of Baja California
   Explored the Punta Prieta region of Baja California in search of Eocene fossil vertebrates

1988 Study of Tertiary Vertebrates in the Chilean Andes

1995 Exploration of Upper Cretaceous Fossil Beds in Mongolia
Studied regions visited decades earlier by Roy Chapman Andrews

1986-1999 Michael Fay

1986 Comparative Ecological Study of Lowland Gorillas

1999 African Forest Megatransect
Conducted a year-long walk across central Africa seeking correlations between large animal populations and human influences

1989-1991 David Oates, McDonald Institute Expedition to Northeastern Syria
Researched the Akkadian Empire (2334-2154 B.C.) and investigated ceremonial site at Tell Brak

1992-99 Peter S. Dunham, Maya Mountains Archaeological Project
Performed systematic archaeological and resource reconnaissance of the southern Maya Mountains

1992-96 Maurice Hornocker, Ecology and Conservation of the Siberian Tiger
Studied and worked for the protection of this isolated and threatened species

1992 Francis G. Carey, Migration of Blue Sharks
Tracked migratory patterns of 48,000 tagged blue sharks, via satellite

1992-99 Jeffrey S. Wilkerson, Cultural Ecology of El Pitál and the Nautla River Valley
Archaeological investigation of over 200 sites along Mexico's Gulf coast, encompassing 2,500 years of ruins

1993 Ihsan Al-Shehbaz, Botanical Exploration of Western Sichuan, China
Collected plant specimens from the mountains of western Sichuan

1994 Peter W. Glynn, Clipperton Expedition
Performed a zoogeographic analysis of reef-building corals and studied the biodiversity of the reefs of Clipperton Atoll

1994-98 Maeve G. Leakey, Paleontological Field Work at Kanapoi and Ekora, West Turkana, Kenya
Searched for Pliocene faunal remains at sites last investigated in 1967

1994-97 Cheryl D. Knott, Reproductive Ecology of Orangutans
Studied effects of nutritional intake and energy expenditure on ovarian function in orangutans in the rain forests of Borneo, Indonesia

1994 Catherine A. Forster, Dinosaur Studies at Los Rastros Formation, Argentina
Paleontological excavation of a highly stratified site in Argentina framing the period when dinosaurs are thought to have originated

1995 David Boufford, Botanical Exploration in Qinghai Province, China
Collected and studied floral samples in Qinghai province, an area little studied by botanists

1996 Albert J. Ammerman, Archaeological and Environmental Studies of Venice
Investigated the origins of Venice, two meters below sea level

1996 Kent R. Weeks, KV 5 and the Valley of the Kings
Excavated a 19th dynasty Egyptian tomb

1996 Thomas S. Parker, Economic Archaeology of Aila
Archaeological study of the economy of Aila, a Roman port on the Red Sea near present-day Aqaba, Jordan

1997 Will Steger, Expedition from the Pole
Attempted a solo trek from the North Pole to Canada

1997 David A. Yetman, Ethnobotany of the Guarijio (Markurawe)
Documented the use of plants by a tribe living in the forests of southeastern Sonora and Chihuahua, Mexico

1997-99 David Coulson, Sahara Rock Art Expedition
Made impressions of 7,000-year-old engraving of a giraffe in Saharan Niger

1998 Todd C. Feeley, Volcanology and Environmental Impact on St. Paul Island, Alaska
Made geochronological studies of volcanic effects on the human and fur seal populations of this island, one of the Pribilof group

1998 Wick Walker, Riddle of the Tsangpo Gorge
Attempted to kayak the entire course of the Tsangpo River, in the eastern Himalaya of Tibet

1998 Ian Baker, Secrets of the Tsangpo Gorge
Documented a legendary waterfall on the Tsangpo River

1998 Sylvia Earle, Sustainable Seas Project
A five-year, deep-water exploration of 12 U.S. Marine Sanctuaries

1998 Todd Skinner, Free Climb of Greenland's Ulamertorsuaq

1998 Galen Rowell, Bilafond Valley Climbs
Supported rock climbs in the high valleys of the Karakoram Himalaya of Pakistan

1998 Karin Muller, Royal Inca Highway Expedition
Traveled 3,200 miles along the spine of the Andes, retracing the Royal Inca Highway

1998 Kitty Calhoun, Latok III climb
Attempted to climb the West Face of Latok III in Pakistan's Karokoram Range

1998 Bill Stone, Wakulla II
Conducted the first three-dimensional mapping of the underwater cave systems of Wakulla Springs, Florida

1998 John Hare, Bactrian Camels of the Gashun Gobi
Conducted a survey of wild Bactrian camels living in a remote section of the Gobi

1999 Nevada Weir, Blue Nile Expedition
Traveled 500 miles of the Blue Nile from Lake Tana, Ethiopia, to the Sudanese border by raft and foot, documenting local peoples

1999 Ed Viesturs, Manaslu/Dhaulagiri Expedition
Reached the summits of Manaslu and Dhaulagiri without oxygen; hopes to become the first American to climb all 14 of the world's 8,000-meter peaks without supplemental oxygen

1999 Lee Berger, Hominid Paleontology in Free State Province, South Africa
Explored fossil deposits in western South Africa

1999 Karl M. Baipakov, Silk Road Studies
Excavated sites along the Silk Road in Kazakhstan that were destroyed by earthquakes

1999 Jim D. Darling, Study of Humpback Whales off the Coast of Gabon

1999 Greg Child, Arunachal Pradesh Frontier Expedition
Explored the headwaters and jungle of the Subansirei and Kurung rivers near the Tibet-India border

1999 Mark Synnott, Climbing Cameroon's Mandara Mountains
Organized an expedition to climb volcanic spires in northeast Cameroon

1999 Bruce Hayse, Chinko River Expedition
Planned to document the status of wildlife and extent of poaching along this little-known river in the rain forests of the Central African Republic

1999 Wesley Strong, Great White Sharks
Researched great white sharks off the coast of South Africa to determine if they associate geometric shapes with food

1999 Carsten Peter, Inside Vanuatu
Documented and ran tests inside the craters of highly active volcanoes on the South Pacific archipelago of Vanuatu

1999 Jon Bowermaster, Islands of the Four Mountains
Visited a group of remote Aleutian islands by sea kayak and explored on foot

1999 Heidi Howkins, Everest/K2 Expedition
Attempted to climb both Mount Everest and K2 in one season; K2 climb was postponed

1999 Jean Francois Pernette, Ultima Patagonia 2000
Explored caves and spectacular karstlands on the marble-and-limestone islands of southern Chile; discovered Chile's deepest known cave

Acknowledgments

The Book Division wishes to thank all the individuals, groups, and organizations mentioned in *National Geographic Expeditions Atlas* for their guidance and help. In addition, we are grateful to the following: Lyn Clement, John N. Hall, Anne Marie Houppert, Bonnie S. Lawrence, Rebecca Martin, and Julie Rushing.

Notes on Contributors

Peter H. Raven (Foreword) is chairman of the Society's Committee for Research and Exploration, on which he has served as a member since 1982. He is director of the Missouri Botanical Garden in St. Louis, one of the world's leading botanical research institutions, and is the Engelmann Professor of Botany at Washington University, also in St. Louis. Active in conservation and sustainable development around the world, he has been a leader in this field for more than 30 years.

A former Senior Assistant Editor at NATIONAL GEOGRAPHIC, **Bart McDowell** (Introduction) authored more than two dozen articles and five books during his 32-year sojourn with the Society. While many of his assignments focused on Latin American topics, he ranged the rest of the globe as well, writing on subjects as varied as Thailand, gypsies, the Revolutionary War, cowboys, and the Vatican. A Texan by birth, he still travels widely but hangs his hat mostly in Forest Heights, Maryland.

Cynthia Russ Ramsay (The Lay of the Land) learned about mountains, volcanoes, and glaciers first-hand on assignments during her 25 years with the Society's Book Division. During that time she hiked in the Alps, Rockies, and the Himalaya, explored ice fields in Alaska, and followed lava trails in Bali and Hawaii. Turning freelance in 1994, she recently completed a book about the conqueror of Everest, Sir Edmund Hillary, and his humanitarian efforts on behalf of the Sherpa people of Nepal.

Kim Heacox (To the Ends of the Earth) has written feature articles for a dozen national magazines and has authored three books for National Geographic, including *Shackleton: The Antarctic Challenge*, and *Antarctica: The Last Continent*. He lives with his wife among the moose and ravens of Southeast Alaska, in a small town reachable only by boat or plane.

William R. Newcott (Into Thin Air) is Senior Assistant Editor for Expeditions with NATIONAL GEOGRAPHIC magazine. His byline articles for the magazine include stories about the Hubble Space Telescope, Mars Pathfinder, and John Glenn's return to space, as well as down-to-earth pieces about the

Tower of London and Las Vegas. His article "Venus Revealed" won the 1993 Aviation/Space Writers Association award for excellence.

As a staff member for more than 20 years, **Toni Eugene** (Beyond the Horizon) wrote chapters for and edited numerous Book Division publications, including children's books and calendars. Since 1992 she has lived in Charlotte, North Carolina, where she is a freelance editor and writer. In those capacities she has contributed to more than 20 National Geographic books and has written a guide to the country music mecca of the United States entitled *Branson With Kids*.

Catherine Herbert Howell (The Deep), a former staff member of the National Geographic Society, is a freelance writer and editor. She has contributed to dozens of Society publications, including the *Field Guide to the Birds of North America*, and has authored volumes in the Nature Library and My First Pocket Guide series. She was also the editor of *Out of Ireland*, a companion volume to the PBS documentary of the same name. An anthropologist by training, she has conducted research in India and in New York City.

Retired after 38 years as staff archaeologist of the National Geographic Society, **George Stuart** (Searching for the Past) also served as the Society's vice president for Research and Exploration, and chaired its Committee for Research and Exploration. He is now president of the Center for Maya Research of Washington, D.C., and Barnardsville, North Carolina, and occasionally writes on archaeological subjects.

Author and journalist **Leslie Allen** (The Family of Man) is a former senior writer at the National Geographic Society. As a staffer, she wrote, among other things, *Liberty: The Statue and the American Dream*. As a freelance, her contributions to Society publications include chapters on early humans in *Unlocking Secrets of the Unknown* and *Wonders of the Ancient World*. She has written about natural history and the environment for the *New York Times*, *Audubon*, the Wilderness Society, and others; her work on social history has appeared in many national publications.

ILLUSTRATION CREDITS

Cover, Will Steger; 1, photographer unknown; 2-3, Georges-Marie Haardt; 4-5, Joseph F. Rock; 6-7, Loren McIntyre; 8-9, Luis Marden; 10-11, Gordon Wiltsie; 13, William J. Morden; 15, Submarine Film Corporation; 17, Library of Congress; 24-25, Medford Taylor; 26-27, 28-29, Barry C. Bishop; 30, James T. Lester; 31 (upper), Richard Emerson; 31 (lower), George F. Mobley; 32, 34-35, Courtesy U.S. Geological Survey; 38, B. B. Fulton; 38-39, Robert F. Griggs; 41, L. G. Folsom; 44, Ray V. Davis; 45, 46 (upper), Michael K. Nichols; 46 (lower), 47, 48-49 (all), Bradford Washburn; 51, 54, Royal Geographical Society; 55, MacGillivray Freeman Films; 56-57, Lawrence Martin; 58 (upper), John Roskelley; 58 (lower), Dianne Roberts; 59, John Roskelley; 60-1, Ned Gilllette; 62-3 (both), Carsten Peter; 64-65, Gordon Wiltsie; 66-67, Naomi Uemura; 68-69, 70-71 (all), Herbert G. Ponting; 75, Scott Polar Research Institute; 76-77, Frank Hurley Collection/ National Library of Australia; 77 (upper), Royal Geographic Society; 77 (lower), Image Library, State Library of New South Wales; 78, 80-81 (all), 82, Robert E. Peary Collection; 83, NYT Pictures; 84-85, United Press International; 85, Jacob Gayer; 86-87 (both), NYT Pictures; 90-91, James F. Calvert; 92, J. J. Krawczyk; 94-95, Ranulph Fiennes; 96-97 (both), Maynard Owen Williams; 98-99 (both), Gordon Wiltsie; 100-1, Will Steger; 102-103, Denis Balibouse, Agence de Press ARC; 104, L'Illustration Corbis Sygma; 105, U. S. Army Air Corps, Maj. H. Lee Wells, Jr., 106, Richard H. Stewart; 107 (upper), Edwin L. Wisherd; 107 (lower), Lieutenant Phillips & Master Sargeant Gilbert; 109, Volkmar Wentzel; 110, Marc Bulka/BLACK STAR; 110-111, Max & Kristian Anderson; 114-115, Pacific-Atlantic Photos; 116, Sir Ross Smith; 118-119, Captain Frank Hurley; 120-121 (both), James L. Stanfield; 122, West Indian Aërial Express; 124, National Air & Space Museum/Smithsonian Institution; 124-125, Pacific-Atlantic Photos; 126, The Ninety-Nines Inc.; 127, 128-9, Otis Imboden; 130-131 (both), Dean Conger; 134, NASA-Apollo 8; 135, Dean Conger; 136, 138-139, Bill Taub/NASA; 140-141, London *Times*; 141 (upper), AP/Wide World Photos; 141 (lower), photographer unknown; 142, Courtesy of Royal Italian Embassy by Institute of Aeronautic Construction; 143, AP/Wide World Photos; 144-145, Kevin Fleming; 146 (upper), Martin Luther King, Jr. Memorial Library; 146 (lower), Eliza Scidmore; 148-149, 150-151, 152, Hiram Bingham Collection/Yale University; 153, 154-155 (both), 156, Joseph F. Rock; 157, 158-159 (all), American Museum of Natural History; 160-161, Roy Chapman Andrews; 162, American Museum of Natural History; 163, Georges-Marie Haardt; 164-165, Maynard Owens Williams; 165, Felix Shay; 168, Charles Allmon; 169, Robin Lee Graham; 170, J. Holland; 171, 172-173 (both), Malcolm Kirk; 175, Richard Bradshaw; 176-177 (both), Loren McIntyre; 178 (all), Brooks Baekeland; 180, Jamie McEwan; 181, Ian Baker; 182-183, William J. Morden; 184-185, Volkmar Wentzel; 185, George Steinmetz; 186 (upper), Bruce Foster; 186 (lower), Seth Mortimer; 186-187, Richard Greenhill; 188-189, Michael K. Nichols; 190-191, David Doubilet; 192-193 (both), Dr. William Beebe; 194, Bates Littlehales; 196-197 (both), Thomas J. Abercrombie; 198, Luis Marden; 200-201, Thomas J. Abercrombie; 202, Robert Goodman; 203, Charles Nichols; 204 (both), Peter Throckmorton; 205, John Cochran; 206-207, Jonathan Blair; 208, Chuck Nicklin; 209, Al Giddings; 210, Chuck Nicklin; 211, Emory Kristof; 212, Robert Ballard; 213, 214-215, Emory Kristof; 215 (both), 216-217, Woods Hole Oceanographic Institution; 218-219, Robert Goodman; 220, Jeremiah S. Sullivan; 220-221, 222-223, David Doubilet; 224-225, Richard H. Stewart; 227, William W. Campbell; 228-229, 230, David Brill; 232, Neil M. Judd; 233, O. C. Havens; 234, Charles Martin; 235, 236-237, O. C. Havens; 237, photographer unknown; 238-239 (both), Richard H. Stewart; 240-241, British Library; 241 (upper), Dr. Sylvanus Morley/Carnegie Institution; 241 (lower) Edward H. Thompson; 242-243, British Museum; 244, Theresa Goell; 245, 246, Kenneth Garrett; 246-247, 248, AP/Wide World Photos; 249, Ledger Photo Service; 250-251 (both), 253, George F. Mobley; 254, Bill Ballenberg; 254-255, Martha Cooper; 256-257, Stephen L. Alvarez; 258-259 (both), Maria Stenzel; 261, George F. Mobley; 262, Theresa Goell; 262-263, Kenji Yamaguchi, NGS Staff; 264-265, Michael K. Nichols; 266, Robert F. Sisson; 267, Melville Bell Grosvenor; 268-269 Gilbert M. Grosvenor; 269 (both), Mrs. L. J. Beecher; 270-271 (both), David Brill; 272, Hugo Van Lawick; 273, Gordon Gahan; 274-275, Enrico Ferorelli; 276, David Brill; 278-279 (both), 280-281 (both), Enrico Ferorelli; 284, Hugo Van Lawick; 285, Derek Bryceson; 286-287, 288, Hugo Van Lawick; 288-289, Michael K. Nichols; 290-291 (both), 292, Bob Campbell; 292-293, Bill Weber & Amy Vedder; 294-295, Bob Campbell; 297, 298-299, Rod Brindamour.

ADDITIONAL READING

The reader may wish to consult the *National Geographic Index* for related articles and books, or *The Complete National Geographic* on CD-ROM. In addition, the Society has published:

The National Geographic Society: 100 Years of Adventure and Discovery

Great Adventures with National Geographic

The Adventure of Archaeology

Exploring the Deep Frontier

Shackleton: The Antarctic Challenge

Antarctica: The Last Continent

The reader may also find the following books helpful:

Robert D. Ballard, *The Discovery of the Titanic* (New York: Warner/Madison, 1987)

Pierre Berton, *The Arctic Grail* (New York: Viking, 1988)

Dian Fossey, *Gorillas in the Mist* (Boston: Houghton Mifflin, 1983)

Jane Goodall, *Through a Window: My Thirty Years with the Chimpanzees of Gombe* (Boston: Houghton Mifflin, 1990)

Roland Huntford, *Scott and Amundsen* (New York: Putnam, 1980)

Donald Johanson and Blake Edgar, *From Lucy to Language* (New York: Simon& Schuster, 1996)

Virginia Morell, *Ancestral Passions: The Leakey Family and the Quest for Humankind's Beginnings* (New York: Simon & Schuster, 1995)

Richard Munson, *Cousteau: The Captain and his World* (New York: William Morrow, 1989)

Bradford Washburn and David Roberts, *Mount McKinley: The Conquest of Denali* (New York: Harry N. Abrams, 1991)

INDEX

Boldface indicates illustrations.

Abruzzo, Ben 109, 110
Adams, Richard 249, 250, **251**, 252–253, **253**, 261
Adamson, Jameson Boyd 75, **75**
Aegean Sea: map 203; shipwrecks 202–203
Aerial photography 117; Alaskan mountains 46–47, 50; Mount Everest 15–16
Afar Triangle, Ethiopia: map 277
Africa: Citroën expeditions 2–3, 163, **163**, **165**, 166–167; early hominids 266–283; maps 163, 166, 171, 277, 282, 290–291; Weeks Expedition 185, **185–186**; see also countries by name
Airplanes: aerial photography and mapping 15–16, 46–47, 50; human-powered 126–127, **128–129**; London to Australia flight **116–122**; over Everest **140–141**; over polar regions **83–88**; see also Earhart, Amelia; Lindbergh, Charles; X-1; X-15
Alaska 17; aerial photography and mapping 46–47, 50–51; glaciers 33, **34–35**, 36, **56–57**, 57; Katmai **37–41**; maps 33, 37, 40, 50; Mount Crillon 46–47; Mount Hayes **46**, 48, **48**; Mount McKinley **47–51**, **60–61**, 93; St. Elias Mountains 14, **32–36**, 47, **47**
Alaskan Glacier Commemorative Project 36
Alaskan Glacier Studies (Tarr, Martin) 36, 57
Allen, Bryan 126–127, **127**, **128–129**
Altai Mountains, Asia **182–183**
Alva, Walter 260
Alvin (submersible) 212, 213, **214**, 216–217
Amadeo di Savoia, Luigi, Prince (Italy) 32–33
Amazon River, Brazil-Peru: Kamayura people **176**; map 175; source 146, 175, 179; waterfall **177**
American Mount Everest Expedition (1963) 15, **26–31**
American Museum of Natural History, New York 157, 160, 182, 185
Ampato, Nevado, Peru **256–257**, 260
Amphorae 203, **205**, 207
Amundsen, Roald 83; across the Northwest Passage 72–74; first to the South Pole 68, 69; North Pole via dirigible 142–143
Amundsen-Scott South Pole Station 93
Amun-Re (deity) 242
Anderson, Kristian **111**
Anderson, Maxie 109, 110, **110–111**
Anderson, Orvil A. 104, 105, 108–109
Anderson, William R. 88–89, 92, **92**
Andrews, E. Wyllys, IV 226–227, **227**, 301
Andrews, Roy Chapman 145; Gobi expedition 157, **157**, **158–159**, 162, **162**; with whale carcass **160–161**
ANGUS (undersea camera sled) 213, 216
Anker, Conrad **11**
Antarctica and Antarctic regions: climbing Rake-kniven **10–11**, **64–65**, 65; *Endurance* Expedition 89, 92; first flight over 83, **83**, **86–87**; first to the Pole 68, 69; maps 75, 89; *Nimrod* Expedition **74–75**, **75**, 78; Scott expedition 68, **68–69**, **70–71**, 71; Shackleton expeditions **74–78**, 89, 92; Steger expedition 100, **100–101**; transglobal expedition 93, **94–95**, 95; travel by vehicle 88, 89, 92, 93, **94–95**, 95
Antiochus I, King (Commagene) 244–245; law inscriptions **262**; sculptures of face **244**
Aphrodisias, Turkey **228–229**, 230–231; map locating 231
Aphrodite (deity) 230, 231; marble statue **230**

Apollo 8 (spacecraft) 134, **134**, 137
Apurimac River, Peru 176, 179
Aqua-Lung 194, **198**
Aramis, Ethiopia 279
Arctic regions: dirigible flight **143**; first flight over 83, **84**, 88; first to the Pole **78–82**; MacMillan Expedition 96, **96–97**; maps 72–73, 78–79; Northwest Passage exploration 68, 72–74; by snowmobile 95; solo to the Pole **66–67**, 68, 92–93; by submarine 88–89, **90–91**, 92; trans-Arctic expedition 98, **98–99**; transglobal expedition 93, **94–95**, 95; under-ice exploration 211
Ardipithecus ramidus 279
Argo (replica ship): retracing historical voyages **144–145**, 146, 186, **186**
Argo (submersible) 216
Arizona: Betatakin ruin 235; Grand Canyon 46, 51
Armstrong, Neil 132, 137
Army Air Corps, U.S. 107
Asmat people 174
Atlantic Ocean: Mid-Atlantic Ridge 212; North Atlantic map 123
Atlantis II (ship) 216
Australopithecus 266–267, 273; map 282–283
Australopithecus afarensis 274, 276–279; jaw 274, **275**; model of head **279**; skeleton **276**
Australopithecus africanus 267, 277, 279
Australopithecus anamensis 278
Automobile expeditions: Africa 163, **163**, **165**, 166–167; Gobi 157, **157**, 158, **158–159**, 162; Pueblo Bonito **235**

B-52 (aircraft) 127, **130–131**
Badlands, South Dakota 104; *Explorer* (balloon) expeditions 104, **105–109**
Baekeland, G. Brooks 175
Baker, Ian 180
Balchen, Bernt 83
Ballard, Robert D. 16, 212, **213**, 215, 216–217, 302
Balloon expeditions 16, **102–112**
Baluchitherium 162
Bandits **4–5**, 157, 182, 272
Barrow, John, Jr. 79
Barton, Otis 192, 192–193
Barya River, Africa **185–186**
Bass, Ann **204**
Bass, George F. 16, **202**, 202–203, **204**, 300
Bathyscaph 199, 200, **201**
Bathysphere 192, 192–193, **193**
Beebe, William 192, 192–193, **193**, 300
Bell, Alexander Graham 15, **15**, 16, 104, 116
Bends 194, 203
Bennett, Floyd 83, 85, 88
Bennett, J. M. 116–117, 122
Berger, Lee 279
Bermuda: bathysphere expeditions 192, 192–193; map 193
Berton, Pierre 68, 78, 79
Betatakin ruin, Arizona 235
Biami people **171**
Bingham, Hiram 16, **147–152**, 180, 231
Bipedalism 273, 277, 279
Bishop, Barry C. 15, **26–27**, **30**, 54, 301
Blackburn, Reid 15, 42
Bolivia: Tiwanacu 150, **150–151**
Borman, Frank 134, 137
Borneo (Kalimantan), Indonesia: Tanjung Puting Reserve 296, **297–299**

Bostelmann, Else 193
Bounty, H.M.S. 195, 198
Boyarsky, Victor **98**
Brahmaputra (river), Asia 179, 180
Brazil: Rio da Dúvida expedition 17, **17**
Breadalbane, H.M.S. 211
Breitling Orbiter 3 (balloon) **102–103**, 105
Brindamour, Rod 296
Bronze Age: shipwrecks 202–203, **204**
Buddhist lamaseries 153, 155, **155**
Bumstead, Albert H. 85
Buono, Giuseppe 200, **201**
Burg, Amos 167, 170
Byrd, Richard E. 14, **83–88**, 96, 122, 300

Cahill, Tim 46
Cairo Museum, Cairo, Egypt 245
Calypso (ship) 194–195, 198
Camels 157, **182–183**, 272
Canada: Mount Logan 14, 32, 33
Cannibalism: by chimpanzees 285; by humans 171, 174
Cape Horn, Horn Island, Chile 167, 170
Carlsbad Caverns, New Mexico 43, **44**, 46; map 43
Carter, Adams 47
Carter, Howard 245, 246, 248
Casts, latex **262–263**
Caving see Spelunking
Cenote (ceremonial well) **8–9**, 227, **227**
Central African Republic **188–189**, 189
Cerro Llullaillaco, Chile **258–259**
Cervantes, Miguel de 17
Chaco Canyon, New Mexico **232**, 234–235, **235**, **236–237**, 237; map locating 234
Chan Chan, Chimor, Peru 253
Chaulmoogra tree 153
Cherry-Garrard, Apsley 68, 69
Chichén Itzá, Yucatán, Mexico **240**, 241
Chile: Cape Horn 167, 170; Cerro Llullaillaco **258–259**
Chimpanzees 284–285, **285**, 287, **288–289**
China, People's Republic of: Lhotse (peak) **26–27**; map of Tibet border 153; Muli Kingdom 153, **154–155**, 155, 156; see also Everest, Mount, China-Nepal; K2 (mountain), China-Pakistan
Chocolate: from Maya tomb 253
Church, Donovan B. 40
Citroën expeditions 2–3, 163, **163**, **165**, 166–167
Clark, Eugenie **223**, 302
Colombia: volcanoes 15
Colorado: Mesa Verde National Park 234–235
Columbia (space shuttle): mapping Everest 52
Commagene, Turkey 244–245; maps 244, 245
Compasses 85
Conger, Dean 127, 130, 133
Conshelf Two (underwater habitat) **218–219**, 219
Cook, Frederick A. 61
Copper ingots **204**
Coropuna, Nevado, Peru 152
Coulson, David 262
Cousteau, Jacques-Yves 16, 192, **194**, 194–196, **197**, 198, 301; Conshelf Two 219
Cousteau, Simone 195, 219
Crampons **48**
Crillon, Mount, Alaska 46–47
Curtis, Tom 89
Curtsinger, William R. 211
Cygnet (kite) 116
Cyphers, Ann 260

David, Edgeworth 78
Davis, Ray V. 43
Deacon, Kev **190–191**
DeepWorker (submersible) 14, 217
Denali *see* McKinley, Mount, Alaska
Dendrochronology (tree-ring dating) 232, 234–235
Dinosaurs: fossil eggs 158, **159**, 162; *Protoceratops* fossils 158, **159**, 162; Titanothere fossils 162, **162**
Diocletian, Emperor (Rome) 230
Dirigibles 112–113, **114–115, 142, 143**
Disenchantment Bay, Alaska **56–57**
Diving saucer **196–197**, 198, 219
Dodge vehicles: Gobi expedition 157, **157**, 158, **158–159**, 162
Dogsleds **80–81**, 98, **100–101**
Dolomites (mountains), Italy **1**
Dorjun (boat) 167
Doubilet, David 138, **220–221**
Double Eagle II (balloon) **110**
Douglas, William K. **136**
Douglass, Andrew Ellicott 234–235
Dove (sloop) **168, 169,** 170
Dow Chemical Company 105
Dowmetal (material) 105, 106
Drucker, Philip 239
Dryden, Hugh L. 136
Dumas, Frédéric 194
Dúvida, Rio da, Brazil 17
Dzibilchaltún, Yucatán, Mexico **8–9**, 226–227, 261

Eagle, Alaska 74
Earhart, Amelia **124**, 126, **126**
Earle, Sylvia A. 191, **208–210**, 210–211
Edgerton, Harold E. 198
Egypt: maps 248, 249; Pyramids of Giza **120–121**; Valley of the Kings 245, **246**, 248–249
Elephant Island, Antarctica 77
Endurance (ship) **76–77**, 89, 92
English Channel: human-powered flight over 126–127, **128–129**
Erim, Kenan T. 230–231
Eskimos (Inuit) 72, 74, 80, 82, **82, 85, 96–97**
Espiritu Santo, Vanuatu: shipwreck **190–191**
Ethiopia: Aramis 279; Hadar 273, **274–276, 278, 280–281**; map of Afar Triangle 277
Everest, Mount, China-Nepal 15–16, **26–31**, 54–55, **140–141**; first ascent 51, **51**, 54, **54**; map 52–53
Explorer and *Explorer II* (balloons) 16, 104, **105–109**; flight map 105

Falco, Albert 194, 198
FAMOUS (French-American Mid-Ocean Undersea Study) 212
Fay, J. Michael **188–189**, 189
Field Museum of Natural History, Chicago, Illinois 158
Fiennes, Ginnie 93, 95
Fiennes, Ranulph 93, **93–94**, 95
Filippi, Fillipo de 32–33
Findley, Rowe 15, 42
Flaming Cliffs, Mongolia: dinosaur egg fossils 158, **159**, 162
Fletcher, John E. 134
Folsom, Lucius 40
Fossett, Steve 109, 112
Fossey, Dian 265, 290–291, **291–292**, 294, **295**, 296
Fossils: dating 267, 278
Franklin, John 68, 72, 73, 93

Friendship VII (spacecraft) **138–139**; flight map 136–137
Fuchs, Vivian 88, 92, 93; expedition map 89
Fumaroles **38–39**, 40

Gagnan, Émile 194
Galápagos Rift, Pacific Ocean 213
Galdikas, Biruté 296, **297**, 298, 299
Galeras (volcano), Colombia 15
Garner, William **24–25**
Geissler, Stefan **62–63**
Gelidonya, Cape, Turkey 202
General Mills 109
Geographos (asteroid) 132
Germany: ice caves **62–63**
Giddings, Al 210, **210**
Gillette, Ned 61
Gimbel, Peter R. 175
Giraffes: cast of rock carving 262, **263**
Glaciers: Alaska 33, **34–35**, 36, **56–57**, 57; Antarctica **100–101**; ice caves, Germany **62–63**; Pamirs **24–25**
Glenn, John 133, 136, 138, **138–139**; *Friendship VII* flight map 136–137
Gobi, China-Mongolia: Andrews expedition 157, **157, 158–159**, 162; map 157
Goell, Kermit 262
Goell, Theresa **244**, 244–245
Gombe Stream Game Reserve, Tanzania 284–285, **285–289**; map 285
Gombu, Nawang 31
Goodall, Jane 284–285, **285, 287–289**
Goodyear-Zeppelin Corporation 105
Gordon, Doug 17, 180, **180**
Gordon Bennett Cup International Balloon Race 104
Gorillas **264–265**, 290–291, **291–293**, 294, **295**; range map 290; skulls **290**
Gossamer Albatross (human-powered aircraft) 126–127, **128–129**
Gould, Laurence 83
Graham, Robin Lee: solo circumnavigation of globe **168–169**, 170, **170**
Grand Canyon, Arizona 46, 51
Gray, Tom 273, 276
Great Rift Valley, Africa: map of hominid sites 277; search for early man **266–281**
Greece: shipwreck **206–207**
Greenland 78, 82; Lindbergh flight 122
Griggs, Robert F. 17, 37, 38, **38**, 40–41, **41**
Grosvenor, Gilbert H. 47, 108–109, 147, 162, 171
Grosvenor, Melville Bell 83
Grouper (fish) 195
Guatemala: Quiriguá **242–243**; Río Azul 249, **250–251**, 252, **253**, 261

Haardt, Georges-Marie **164–165**, 166–167, 300
Habeler, Peter 55
Hadar, Ethiopia 273, 276; hominid fossils **274–276**; map 276
Hall, Grant 249, 252
Hardy, Osgood **150–151**
Hawaii: oceanic exploration **208**, 210
Hayes, Mount, Alaska 46, 48, **48**
Headhunters: New Guinea 171, 174
Heirtzler, J.R. 212
Heizer, Robert 239
Henson, Matthew **80**, 82

Herbert, Wally 82, 93
Hidden Falls of Dorje Phagmo, Tibet 17, 180, **181**
Hill, Robert T. 41
Hillary, Edmund 51, **51**, 54, **54**, 92
Hindenburg (dirigible) 113, 114
Hollis, Ralph 216–217
Homo erectus 266–267, **270–271**, 278, 283
Homo habilis 267, 272, 273
Horn, Cape, Horn Island, Chile 167, 170; map 167
Hornbein, Thomas 26, 54–55
Horses **225–226**
Hubbard, Gardiner Greene 27, 78
Hunt, John 51
Huntford, Roland 68
Hunza, India **164–165**
Hurley, Frank 77

Inca Empire, South America 16, **147–152**, 256, 260; map 260
India: Allahabad 117; Brahmaputra (river) 179, 180; Hunza **164–165**
Institut Français de Recherches pour l'Exploitation des Mers (IFREMER) 216
International Space Station 138
Intihuatana (sun observatory) 149
Inuit *see* Eskimos
In-you-gee-to (Eskimo mechanic) 85
Irian Jaya, Indonesia: Yali tribesmen 185, **185**, 186
Italy: Dolomites 1

Jagersky, Diana 58
Japan: hand-tinted photograph of child 146
Jarrat, Jim 210
Jason (remotely operated vehicle) 216, 217
Jason Jr. "J.J." (remotely operated vehicle) 215, 216, 217
Jehle, Daniel 63
Jerstad, Lute 26, 54
Jim (diving suit) **208**, 210, **210**
Johanson, Donald 273–274, **275**, 276–278, **278**
Johnston, David 42
Jones, Brian 16, **102–103**, 105, 112
Judd, Neil M. 232, **233**, 234, 235
June, Harold 83

K2 (mountain), China-Pakistan **58–59**
Kalahari Desert, Africa 171; map 171
Kamayura people **176**
Kamba tribesmen 267
Karisoke Research Centre, Rwanda **264–265**, 290–291
Katmai, Alaska 37, 38, **38–39**, 40–41; maps 37, 40
Kennedy, John F. 31
Kenya: Lake Turkana **270–271**, 272–273, 278
Kepner, William W. 105, 108–109
Kerr, Mark B. 32
Keyhoe, Donald E. 122
Kidby, Lang 119
Kimbel, Bill **274–275**
Kimeu, Kamoya 270, **271**, 278
Kingdon-Ward, Francis 179, 180
Kipfer, Paul **104**
Kirk, Malcom S. 171, 173, 174
Kittinger, Joseph W. 109, **109**; path of transatlantic balloon crossing 112–113
Kitty Hawk (balloon) **110–111**
Kivas (ritual chambers) **232–233**, 234
Knorr (ship) 213, 216
Knott, Cheryl 296
Kodiak Island, Alaska 37, 40

Koobi Fora, Kenya: hominid fossils 272
Krakauer, Jon 65
Kristof, Emory 216
KV 5, Valley of the Kings, Egypt 248–249

La Venta, Veracruz, Mexico 239, **239**
Laetoli (region), Tanzania 277; map 267
Lalor, William 89
Landsburg, Robert 42
Laser dating: fossils 267, 278
Latex casts 262, **262–263**
Lava flows: undersea 212
Leakey, Jonathan 267
Leakey, Louis S. B. 266–267, **268, 269,** 290, 296
Leakey, Mary D. 266–267, **267,** 272, 273, 277
Leakey, Meave 273, 278
Leakey, Richard E. **270–271,** 272, **272,** 273, 302
Lechuguilla Cave, New Mexico **45,** 46, **46**
Lee, Willis T. 43, 46
Leprosy 153
Lhotse (peak), China-Nepal **26–27**
Libbey Glacier, Alaska **34–35,** 35
Lindbergh, Anne Morrow 122, 123, 126
Lindbergh, Charles 16, 122, **122, 124–125;** map
    of North Atlantic flight 123
Little America, Antarctica 83, **86,** 88
Logan, Mount, Canada 14, 32, 33; map 33
Los Angeles (dirigible) **114–115**
Lost Falls of the Brahmaputra, Tibet 180
Lucy (australopithecine) 276, **276**

MacCready, Paul 126
Machiguenga Indians **6–7,** 175
Machu Picchu, Peru 16, 147, **148–149,** 152, 180, 231
MacInnis, Joseph E. 211
Mackay, Alistair 78
Mackey, Carol J. 253
MacMillan, Donald B.: Arctic expedition **96–97,** 300
Magnetic compasses 85
Magnetic poles 74, 78
Mallory, George Leigh 55
Marden, Ethel 198
Marden, Luis 16, 195, 198
Mariana Trench, Pacific Ocean: bathyscaph
    expedition 199, **200–201,** 202; map 199
Marshall, Eric 75, **75**
Martin, George C. 37
Martin, Lawrence: glacier studies 36, 37, **56–57,**
    57, 300
Martinique: Mont Pelée 15, 41
Masai people **268–269**
Maudslay, Alfred Percival 241, 242
Maudslay, Anne Cary 242, **243**
Mawson, Douglas 78
May, Manuel **227**
Maya 16; Dzibilchaltún **8–9,** 226–227, 261; map of
    archaeological sites 252; Palenque and Chichén
    Itzá **240–241;** Quiriguá **242–243;** Río Azul
    249–253, 261; similarities to Olmec 238, 239
McIntyre, Loren **6–7,** 146, 175, **175,** 176, 179
McKinley, Ashley 83, 86
McKinley, Mount, Alaska **47–51,** 93; ski trek **60–61**
McMillan, Peter 119
McNally, Joe 138
Mérida, Mexico 227
Messner, Reinhold 55, **55**
Mexico: Chichén Itzá **240–241;** Dzibilchaltún **8–9,**
    226–227, 261; La Venta, Veracruz **239;** map **239;**
    San Lorenzo (site) 239, 260

Michel, Jean Louis 216, 217
Mid-Atlantic Ridge, Atlantic Ocean 212; map 212
Miller, Maynard M. 33, 36, 301
Mintaka Pass, Pamirs, Tajikistan **13**
Mitzuga, Mount, China **154–155,** 155
Moche culture 253, **254–255,** 260
Mohammed Nazim Khan, Mir of Hunza **164–165**
Mongolia: Gobi expedition 157, **157, 158–159,**
    162; map 157
Monkeys: fossil skull **273**
Moon flights 136–138
Morden-Clark Asiatic Expedition **13,** 182, **182–183**
Moseley, Michael E. 253
Mount St. Elias Expedition (1890), Alaska 32, **32,**
    34–35; map 33
Muli Kingdom, Sichuan Province, China 153,
    154–155, 155, 156
Mummies **254–255,** 256, **258–259,** 260

Nansen, Fridtjof 72
Naranjo, Santiago **234**
National Aeronautics and Space Administration
    (NASA): space program **132–139**
National Air and Space Museum, Wash. D.C. 104
National Geographic Adventure (magazine) 179
NATIONAL GEOGRAPHIC magazine: bare-breasted
    women shown in 171; first color photographs
    146, **146**
National Geographic Society: Centennial Award
    217; Committee for Research and Exploration
    12, 14, 27, 179, 226, 266; Expeditions Council
    14, 179; expeditions history 12–17; Exploration
    Council 55; first archaeological grant 147; first
    expedition 14; first female Board member 146,
    146; flag 78, 109, 137; founding 14; Hubbard
    Medal 31, **31,** 51, 74, 82, 137, 162; membership
    37, 148, 152; Special Gold Medal 83, 198;
    website 189
National Geographic Television 198
National Geographic-Palomar Observatory Sky
    Survey 132
National Oceanic and Atmospheric Administra-
    tion (NOAA) 211, 217
National Park Service, U.S. 234–235
Nautilus, U.S.S. (submarine) 88–89, **92**
Navigation Foundation 82
Navy, U.S.: *Alvin* (submersible) 212
Naxi people 153
New Guinea: map 174; Yali tribesmen 185, **185**
New Mexico: Carlsbad Caverns 43, **44,** 46;
    Lechuguilla Cave **45,** 46, **46;** map 234; Pueblo
    Bonito **232–233,** 234–235, **236–237**
Newman, Larry 109, **110**
Nichols, Michael 46
Nimrod Expedition (1908-1909) 74–75, **75,** 78
Nitrogen narcosis 194
NOAA (National Oceanic and Atmospheric
    Administration) 211, 217
Nobile, Umberto 142
Norge (dirigible) **142, 143**
North Pole *see* Arctic regions
Northwest Passage 68, 72–74, 95; map 72–73
Norway: Spitsbergen **84–85, 143**
Nuytten, Phil **211**

Odeum (concert hall) **228–229,** 231
Olduvai Gorge, Tanzania 266–267
Olmec culture **238,** 238–239, **239,** 260
Orangutans 296, **297, 299**

Osborne, Douglas 234

Pacific Ocean: Galápagos Rift 213; *see also*
    Mariana Trench
Pakistan: K2 (mountain) **58–59**
Palenque, Chiapas, Mexico **240–241**
Palomar Observatory, California 132
Pamirs (mountains), Tajikistan **24–25;** Mintaka
    Pass **13**
Papua New Guinea **171–174**
Parachute jumps 109, **109,** 175
Peary, Josephine **80**
Peary, Marie **80**
Peary, Robert E. 74; North Pole expedition **78–82**
Pelée, Mont, Martinique 15, 41; eruption map 41
Pepper, Roy 170
Peru: Amazon River 175, **177,** 179; Machiguenga
    Indians **6–7,** 175; Machu Picchu 16, 147,
    148–149, 152; maps 147, 253; Moche culture
    253, **254–255,** 260; Nevado Ampato **256–257,**
    260; Nevado Coropuna 152; source of Amazon
    River 146
Phillips, Sam C. 137
Phipps, Susan **205**
Photography: underwater 198; *see also* Aerial
    photography
Piccard, Auguste 16, 104, **104,** 199
Piccard, Bertrand 16, **102–103,** 105, 112
Piccard, Jacques 16, 199–202
Pisa, Italy **121**
Plate tectonics 212
Poachers: gorillas 290, 291
Polar bear attack 92
Polar exploration *see* Antarctica and Antarctic
    regions; Arctic regions
Ponting, Herbert **71**
Potassium-argon dating: of fossils 267
Pottery **8–9, 227;** *see also* Amphorae
Power, Allan **190–191**
President Coolidge (shipwreck) **190–191,** 192
Prisoners: Muli, China 153
Project FAMOUS (French-American Mid-Ocean
    Undersea Study) 212
Protoceratops fossils 158, **159,** 162
Pueblo Bonito, New Mexico **232–233,** 234–235,
    236–237
Pumice **41**
Pygmies, Uganda 272
Pyramids: Egypt **120–121**

Quiriguá, Guatemala: stelae **242–243**

Radio signals: used to map the Gobi 158, **159**
Rak, Yoel **274–275**
Rakekniven, Queen Maud Land, Antarctica
    10–11, 64**–65**
Ramses II, Pharaoh (Egypt) 249; temple **246**
Ready (ship) 193
Reinhard, Johan 256, **257, 258–259,** 260, 302
Rhodes (island), Greece: shipwreck **206–207**
Ridgeway, Rick 58
Río Azul, Guatemala: Maya tombs 249, **250–251,**
    252, **253, 261**
Roberts, L. B. 162
Rock, Joseph F. **4–5,** 300; Asian expeditions **153–156**
Rome, Italy: view from dirigible **142**
Roosevelt, Theodore 17, **17,** 82, 192
Roosevelt (ship) **82**
Rosenquist, Gary 42

Ross Island, Antarctica **70–71**
Ruaha River, Tanzania **163**
Ruiz, Nevado del, Colombia 15
Russell, Israel C. 14, 32, **32**, **34–35**, 41, 146, 300
Rwanda: Karisoke Research Centre **264–265**, 290–291; map 290–291

Sabancaya (volcano), Peru **256**
Sacrifices **258–259**, 260
Sahara, Africa: Citroën expedition 166–167
St. Elias Mountains, Alaska **32–36**, 47, **47**; maps 33, 50
St. Helens, Mount, Washington 15, 41–42; eruption map 42
St. Pierre, Martinique 41
St. Thomas, Virgin Islands: Lindbergh flight **122**
San (Bushmen) 171
San Lorenzo (site), Mexico 239, 260
Schumaker, Lawrence 200, **201**
Scidmore, Eliza Ruhamah 146, **146**
Scott, David R. 137–138
Scott, Robert Falcon: South Pole expedition 68, **68–69**, **70–71**, 71, 93
Scuba 194
Sealskin boots 71
Selfridge, Thomas 116
Severin, Tim: nautical expeditions 186, **186–187**
Shackleton, Ernest 67, **74–78**, 89, 92
Sharks 220, **221**, **222–223**
Shay, Felix 163
Shay, Porter 163, **165**
Shenandoah (dirigible) 112–113, **114–115**; map of flight path across U.S. 113
Shepard, Alan B. 133, 134, **135**, 136
Shiers, W.H. 116–117, 122
Shipwrecks 16, **190–191**, 202–203, **204**, **206–207**, 211, 213, **215–217**; map locating in the Aegean 203
Sindbad the Sailor: Oman to Canton voyage retraced 186, **186–187**
Singora (Songkhla) 117
Sipán, Peru 253, **254–255**, 260
Siple, Paul 14–15
Skate, U.S.S. (submarine) **90–91**
Ski trek: Mount McKinley **60–61**
Skingle, Derek 171, **172–173**, 174
Slocum, Joshua 170
Smart, Maxwell 171, 173, 174
Smith, Keith 116–117, 122
Smith, Ross 116–117, 122
Smith, R.R.R. 230
Smithsonian Institution: National Air and Space Museum, Washington D.C. 104
Snakes: pit vipers 162, 180
Sohar (ship) **186–187**
Solar alignments: pueblos 235
Solo Spirit 3 (balloon) 109, 112
Soucoupe plongeante (diving saucer) **196–197**
South America: maps 175, 260; *see also* countries *by name*
South Dakota: balloon expeditions 104, **105–109**; map of 1935 balloon flight 105
South Georgia (island), South Atlantic Ocean 77, 89
South Pole *see* Antarctica and Antarctic regions
Space flights **132–149**
Space shuttles 52, 138
Spelunking 43, **44–45**, 46, 46
Sperm whale: carcass **160–161**
Spirit of St. Louis (airplane) 16, 122, **122**, **124–125**
Spitsbergen, Norway **84–85**, **143**

Star II (submersible) 210
Starrett, Randy **24–25**
Steger, Will 69, **98–101**
Steinmetz, George **185**
Stelae: Quiriguá, Guatemala **242–243**
Stevens, Albert W. 16, 104, 105, 108–109, 300
Stirling, Marion **225**, 226, **238–239**
Stirling, Matthew W. **225**, 226, **238–239**, 300
Storm, Ken 180, **181**
Strato-Lab (balloon) 109
Stuart, David 253
Stuart, George E. **261**, 302; Dzibilchaltún site 226–227; Río Azul tombs 249, 252–253
Sub-Igloo (submersible) 211
Submersibles 211; diving saucer 198; *see also Alvin; Argo; DeepWorker; Star II; Sub-Igloo;* WASP
Sun compasses 85
Sun observatory *(intihuatana)* **149**
Sustainable Seas Expeditions 211, 217

Taft, William Howard 82
Taillez, Philippe 194
Tanganyika *see* Tanzania
Tanjung Puting Reserve, Indonesia 296, **298–299**, 299; map locating 296
Tanzania: Gombe Stream Game Reserve 284–285, **285–289**; Laetoli 267, 277; Olduvai Gorge 266–267; Ruaha River **163**
Tarr, Ralph S.: glacier studies 36, 37, **56–57**, 57
Tatum, Robert 51
Taylor, Ron 220
Taylor, Valerie **220**
Tektite II (underwater habitat) 210
Temple of the Jaguars, Chichén Itzá, Mexico **241**
Temple of the Seven Dolls, Dzibilchaltún, Mexico 226–227
Tenzing Norgay 51, **51**, 54
Thermal springs (ocean floor vents) 213, 216
Thomas, Elizabeth Marshall 171
Tibet: maps 153, 179; Tsangpo Gorge 17, 179–180, **181**; Yunnan Province expeditions 153, 156, **156**
Timbuktu (Tombouctou), Mali 166
Time (magazine): hero for the planet award 211
Titanic, R.M.S. 213, **215–217**
Titanothere: fossils 162, **162**
Tiwanacu, Bolivia 150, **150–151**
Tomb robbing 245, 249
Tool making 284
Tree-ring dating (dendrochronology) 232, **234–235**
Tres Zapotes, Veracruz, Mexico 238, **238**
Trieste (bathyscaph) 199–200, **201**, 202
Truk Lagoon, Truk Islands: shipwrecks **208**, **209**
Tsangpo River, Tibet 17, 179–180, **181**
Tuareg people 166, 167
Turkana, Lake, Kenya **270–271**, **272–273**, 278
Turkana Boy (hominid skeleton) 270, 278
Turkey: Aphrodisias **228–229**, 230–231; Cape Gelidonya 202; Commagene 244–245; map 203; Nemrud Dagh **244**, 244–245, 262; Ulu Burun 203, **204**; Yassi Island 202, 203
Turquoise necklace: Pueblo Bonito **237**
Tutankhamun, Pharaoh (Egypt) 245; gold coffin **245**; portrait statue 248; tomb **246–247**

Uemura, Naomi **66–67**, **92–93**
Ulu Burun, Turkey: shipwreck 203, **204**
The Undersea World of Jacques Cousteau (television series) 198
Underwater photography 198

University of Hawaii: research sub *Star II* 210
Unsoeld, Willi 26, **31**, **54–55**
Urtyn Obo, Mongolia **162**
Urubamba River, Peru 6, 152, 175

Valley of Ten Thousand Smokes, Alaska 37, **38–39**, **40–41**
Valley of the Kings, Egypt **120–121**, 245, **246**, 248–249; map 245
Vents, ocean floor 213, 216
Vickers-Vimy (biplane): 1919 Expedition **116**, 116–117, **118–119**, 119, 122; 1994 replica flight 119, **120–121**, 121
Viesturs, Edmund 55
Vilcabamba Range, Andes, Peru 175; map 178
Virunga Mountains, Rwanda 290; map 291
Volcanoes 15, **37–42**, **256–257**; ashfall maps 40, 41, 42
Vosburgh, Frederick G. 127
Voyager (unmanned spacecraft) 138

Walker, Allen 278
Walker, Joseph 127, 132
Walker, Wick 180
Walsh, Don 199, 202
Washburn, Barbara 16, **46**, 50, 51
Washburn, Bradford **46**, 46–47, 48, 50–51, 52, 300; Everest map 15–16, 51, **52–53**
Washington *see* St. Helens, Mount, Washington
WASP (submersible) 211, **211**
Watkins, Casimir **152**
Watson, Bill 126
Weeks, Kent R. 248–249
Weeks Expedition 185, **185–186**, 301
Wentzel, Volkmar 109
Wetherill Mesa, Colorado **234–235**
Weyerhauser Glacier, Antarctica **100–101**
Whale shark **222–223**
Whales: sperm whale carcass **160–161**
White, James Larkin 43
White, Robert 132
White, Tim 277, 279
Whittaker, Jim 58
Wickwire, Jim 58
Wild, Frank 75, **75**, 78
Williams, Stanley 15
Williamson, Ray 235
Wolper, David 198
Wood, Junius B. 112–113
Woods Hole Oceanographic Institution (WHOI), Cape Cod, Mass. 212, 215
World maps 18-20, 168, 169, 282–283; hominid sites 282–283; maps 168, 169, 282–283

X-1 (aircraft) 127
X-15 (aircraft) 127, **130–131**; flight path diagram 132–133

Yali tribesmen 185, **185**
Yassi Island, Turkey 202, 203; map locating shipwrecks 203
Yeager, Chuck 127
Yucatán Peninsula, Mexico 226–227, **240–241**, 261; cenote **8–9**; map 226
Yukon Territory, Canada: map 50

Zinjanthropus boisei 266–267
Zoilos, C. Julius 230

The world's largest nonprofit scientific and educational organization, the National Geographic Society was founded in 1888 "for the increase and diffusion of geographic knowledge." Since then it has supported scientific exploration and spread information to its more than nine million members worldwide.

The National Geographic Society educates and inspires millions every day through magazines, books, television programs, videos, maps and atlases, research grants, the National Geography Bee, teacher workshops, and innovative classroom materials.

The Society is supported through membership dues and income from the sale of its educational products. Members receive NATIONAL GEOGRAPHIC magazine—the Society's official journal—discounts on Society products, and other benefits.

For more information about the National Geographic Society and its educational programs and publications, please call 1-800-NGS-LINE (647-5463), or write to the following address:

National Geographic Society
1145 17th Street N.W.
Washington, D.C. 20036-4688 U.S.A.

Visit the Society's website at
www.nationalgeographic.com.

Composition by the National Geographic Society Book Division. Printed and bound by R.R. Donnelley & Sons, Willard, Ohio. Color separations by NEC, Nashville, Tenn. Dust jacket printed by Miken Inc., Cheektowaga, N.Y.

Library of Congress Cataloging-in-Publication Data

National Geographic expeditions atlas / foreword by Peter H. Raven.
    p. cm
      ISBN 0-7922-7616-7 -- ISBN 0-7922-7617-5
      1. Voyages and travels. I. National Geographic Society (U.S.)
    G465 .N36 2000
    910.4--dc21
                  99-086883
                  CIP

NATIONAL GEOGRAPHIC

EXPEDITIONS ATLAS

Published by the National Geographic Society

John M. Fahey, Jr., *President and Chief Executive Officer*

Gilbert M. Grosvenor, *Chairman of the Board*

Nina D. Hoffman, *Senior Vice President*

Prepared by the Book Division

William R. Gray, *Vice President and Director*

Charles Kogod, *Assistant Director*

Barbara A. Payne, *Editorial Director and Managing Editor*

David Griffin, *Design Director*

Staff for This Book

Tom Melham, *Editor*

Martha C. Christian, *Text Editor*

Annie Griffiths Belt, *Illustrations Editor*

Lyle Rosbotham, *Art Director*

Carl Mehler, *Director of Maps*

Sallie M. Greenwood, *Researcher*

Alexander L. Cohn, *Assistant Researcher*

National Geographic Maps, Clayton Burneston, Alexander L. Cohn, Stephen Goldman, Bruce Avera Hunter, Joseph F. Ochlak, Michelle H. Picard, Nicholas P. Rosenbach, Gregory Ugiansky, XNR Productions, *Map Research and Production*

R. Gary Colbert, *Production Director*

Richard S. Wain, *Production Project Manager*

Janet Dustin, *Illustrations Assistant*

Peggy Candore, *Assistant to the Director*

Kathleen Barber, *Indexer*

Bill Bonner, *Archivist, NGS Image Collection*

Manufacturing and Quality Control

George V. White, *Director*

John T. Dunn, *Associate Director*

Vincent P. Ryan, *Manager*

Phillip L. Schlosser, *Financial Analyst*